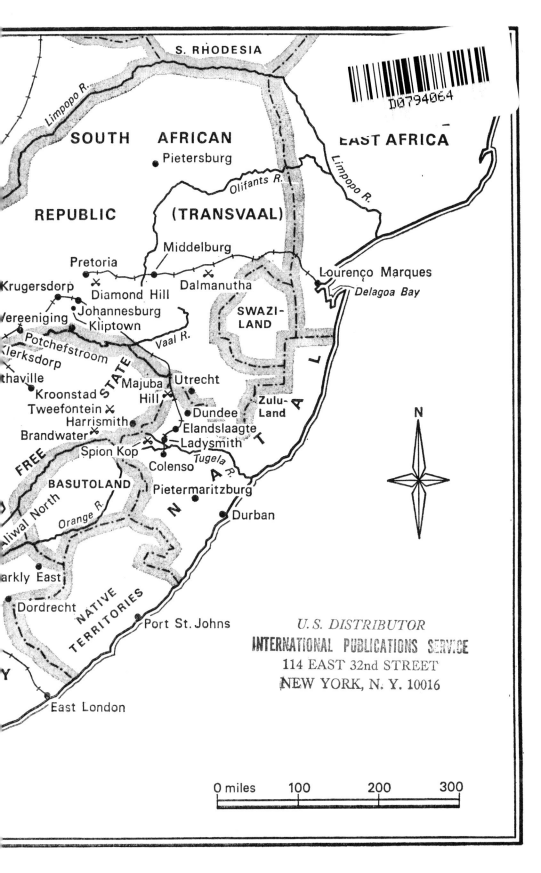

S. RHODESIA

SOUTH AFRICAN

Limpopo R.

EAST AFRICA

Pietersburg

Limpopo R.

REPUBLIC (TRANSVAAL)

Olifants R.

Middelburg

Pretoria

Dalmanutha

Lourenço Marques

Diamond Hill

Delagoa Bay

Krugersdorp

Johannesburg

SWAZI-LAND

Vereeniging

Kliptown

Vaal R.

Potchefstroom

Klerksdorp

STATE

thaville

Majuba Hill

Utrecht

Kroonstad

Zulu-Land

Tweefontein

Dundee

Harrismith

Elandslaagte

Brandwater

Ladysmith

FREE

Spion Kop

Colenso

Tugela R.

BASUTOLAND

Pietermaritzburg

Aliwal North

Orange R.

Durban

N A T A L

arkly East

Dordrecht

NATIVE TERRITORIES

Port St. Johns

N

East London

0 miles   100   200   300

PAUL KRUGER
His Life and Times

John Fisher was born in 1909
in Stoke d'Abernon, Surrey,
the son of Arthur O. Fisher, a
successful author and writer
of sketches on Exmoor and
Irish life. He won a history
scholarship to Balliol College,
Oxford, and took a history
honours degree there.
Afterwards he studied in
Berlin. For fifteen years he
was diplomatic correspondent
for a group of English
newspapers, and has covered
assignments in twenty
countries. He is married with
a son and a daughter, and his
favourite hobby is sailing.

ALSO BY JOHN FISHER:

The Afrikaners
Eighteen Fifteen
The Elysian Fields
Eye Witness
That Miss Hobhouse

PAUL KRUGER
His Life and Times

John Fisher

SECKER & WARBURG
LONDON

First published in England 1974 by
Martin Secker & Warburg Limited
14 Carlisle Street, London W1V 6NN

SBN: 436 15703 9

Maps by Cartographic Enterprises

Printed in Great Britain by
Richard Clay (The Chaucer Press) Ltd
Bungay, Suffolk

*To my wife, with whom I traversed
much of Kruger's Republic*

Contents

List of Illustrations

Acknowledgements

The author wishes to express his thanks for the gracious permission given by Her Majesty Queen Elizabeth II to him to make use of material from the Royal Archives in Windsor Castle. This material includes a private letter written by Sir Evelyn Wood to Queen Victoria on 24 March 1881, a letter from Queen Victoria to Kaiser Wilhelm II following the Jameson Raid of 1895, and a letter written on 12 October 1900 to Queen Victoria by Lord Kitchener.

Through the kindness of Professor Johann Barnard of the University of South Africa, I have been able to examine Frederik Rompel's *Uit den Tweeden Vryheidsoorlog, Schetsen en Portretten*, published in Amsterdam in 1900, which gave some interesting details connected with the Bloemfontein negotiations between Kruger and Lord Milner.

The author and publishers would also like to thank the following for permission to reprint copyright material: Constable & Company Limited (*Lord de Villiers and His Times* by Eric Walker, 1925; *The Pace of the Ox* by Marjorie Juta, 1937); George G. Harrap & Company Ltd (*The Story of Melina Rorke* by Melina Rorke, 1939); Maskew Miller Limited, Cape Town (*Memoirs and Reminiscences* by Sir John Gilbert Kotze, 1929); John Murray (Publishers) Ltd (*Rifleman and Hussar* by Colonel Sir Percival Marling, 1931).

Other works to which any student of the period must remain particularly indebted include Dr Denys Rhoodie's *Conspirators in Conflict*, a scholarly and almost indispensable work on the sequence of events in the Jameson Raid, S. J. Marais' *The Fall of Kruger's Republic*, a masterly study of the workings of Kruger's Government, and C. T. Gordon's *The Growth of Boer Opposition to Kruger*.

Manfred Nathan, in his work *Paul Kruger*, has assembled an impressive collection of vintage Kruger anecdotes.

I am also grateful to Miss Ann Hoffmann for her successful researches in the Public Record Office and elsewhere for additional material on Kruger's life and times.

The author and publishers thank the following for permission to reproduce illustrations: Radio Times Hulton Picture Library (1, 12); Africana Museum, Johannesburg (2, 3, 4, 5, 6, 7, 8, 9); Cape Archives, Cape Town (10); Mansell Collection (11, 13, 14); Mary Evans Picture Library (15); *Illustrated London News* (16).

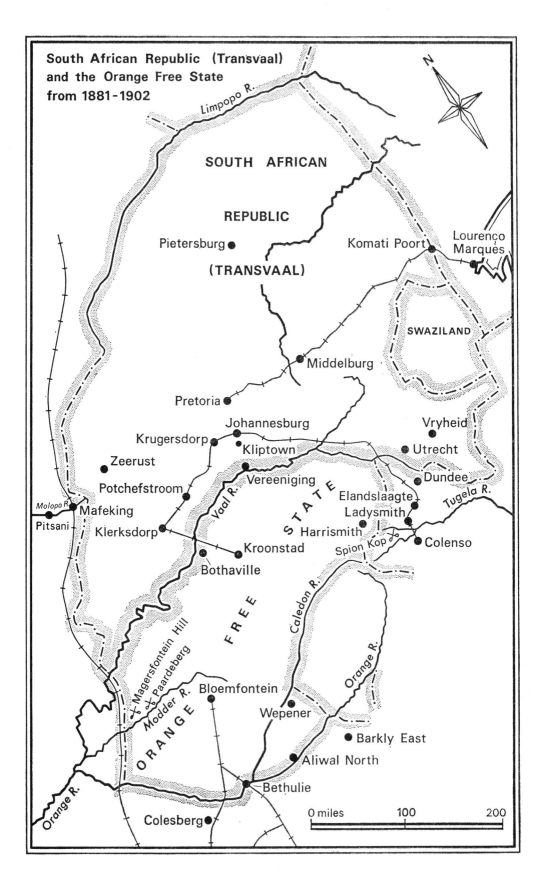

Chapter 1

Two Weddings and a Trek

As a boy he herded cows. His schooldays were over in three months.

He became a cattle-farmer, a commando leader (in his day the two were often linked) and, finally, near-dictator and President of the 19th-century gold-mine Republic of the Transvaal. Once a British official, later a rebel, he called Queen Victoria a "difficult" woman, and defied her prime ministers and generals in succession for nearly a quarter of a century.

To some he was a coarse-mannered bigoted old peasant who dragged his people into a war with Britain that they were certain to lose, and then ran away to Europe when defeat ensued. Joseph Chamberlain, the statesman with the eyeglass and the perpetual orchid in his buttonhole, called him "an ignorant, dirty and obstinate man who has known how to feather his own nest and enrich all his family and dependants". But perhaps Chamberlain was prejudiced. To others, Kruger was a brilliant negotiator who perceived, sooner than anyone else, that the days of British imperialist expansion were over. They saw him as the man who turned the tide in the first modern guerrilla war of independence. The man, moreover, who realised that world opinion, properly organised, could slow up and eventually exhaust the martial spirit of a great power.

And when at last he was forced into exile, the Dutch Queen despatched a warship to carry him safely to Europe, and the French President sent a special train to bring him from Marseilles to Paris.

Myths gathered round his Presidential top-hat like clouds about the summit of some lofty peak. Many fables, if not literally true of him, were highly plausible. His disapproval of the sleeveless, low-necked evening gowns which women of mid-Victorian times wore on formal occasions was proverbial, and yielded many an anecdote. Arriving at a concert at Durban for the opening of the Natal railway to the Transvaal, he told his hosts: "I fear we have come too early. The ladies in the audience have not yet finished dressing." During one of his visits to London Kruger felt obliged to attend a banquet at which some of "society's" most fashionable women were on show. The next morning one of his friends, feeling in the mood for some Presidential fireworks, asked: "President, did the ladies wear beautiful dresses last night?" "I don't know. I never looked under the table."

Other, less endearing myths were superimposed. One was that Paul Kruger believed the world was flat (this was probably untrue, though he accepted almost every word of the Bible literally). According to another widely circulated "true story" he drank out of the Kaiser's finger-bowl at a State Banquet (this, too, was unconfirmed, but Kruger's table-manners – he was a hearty, high-speed eater – were not beyond reproach). It was said, moreover, that all he could write was his signature, but many official documents in his handwriting prove the contrary.

There has also been uncertainty as to where and when he was born. Kruger in his memoirs said, "My recollections go back to the time when, as a boy of nine, I left the land of my birth with my parents and my uncles Gert and Theunis Kruger. Till then we had lived at Vaal-bank Farm which is now in the Colesberg district in Cape Colony where I was born on 10th October 1825 as the third child of Caspar Jan Hendrik Kruger and Elisa Steijn his wife of Bulhoek Farm behind the Zuurberg [mountain] in Cape Colony."

Strictly interpreted, this sentence could mean that Kruger re-membered nothing before he was nine but had always understood that he was born at Vaalbank Farm and spent the first years of his life there. But it could also mean merely that he was born somewhere in the Colesberg district of the Cape Colony or even in a part of the Cape Colony which was not in the Colesberg district.

Kruger was baptised by the Revd J. Taylor on 19 March 1826 in the Dutch Reformed Church at Cradock about 100 miles south of Colesberg. Entry number 1665 in the Baptismal Register there records that Stephanus Johannes Paulus Kruger was born in the Ward of Field Cornet Abraham Pretorius (which covers the Braak river area) without however mentioning the residence of the parents. There are indeed records of a Bulhoek Farm in the Braak river ward near Steynsburg, and a Kruger museum has been established there.

According to this theory, then, Kruger lived for most of his boy-hood at Vaalbank, but his mother went to her parents' farm – Bulhoek Farm – for the birth of her third child.

But here we encounter another uncertainty. The Steynsburg near which Bulhoek Farm is located is not ordinarily regarded as lying "behind the Zuurberg" since it is situated to the south of it and nearer to the coastal plains. We could imagine that Kruger was describing the position of Bulhoek Farm from the point of view of someone living on the north side of the Zuurberg; but this would still be almost like saying that Brighton lies "behind the South Downs".

However, not even this rationalisation has been accepted without question, for, according to Professor C. J. Uys of the University of the Orange Free State, quoted in South Africa's *Dictionary of National Biography*, Kruger's birth took place at an entirely different farm called Soutpansdrif near Venterstad to the east of Colesberg and not "behind the Zuurberg". The Soutpansdrif farm was owned by Kruger's grandfather Stephanus Johannes Kruger.

Nor has the date of Kruger's birth been established beyond doubt. For the baptismal register at Cradock shows the date of birth as 1 October and not 10 October. The entry recording the birth appears to have been written at the same time as the baptism entry, i.e. on 19 March 1826 and not at the time of the birth. So there could have been a copying error, particularly since the Recorder first entered the family name on the register as "Steenkamp" instead of "Kruger".

Possibly it is unwise in every case to accept the wording of the Kruger memoirs. They were dictated by Kruger when he was in exile and more than 75 years old, in the form of disconnected notes, to his private secretary, Mr Bredell, and to Piet Grobler, former Under-Secretary of State in Kruger's republic. These notes were then handed to an editor, the Revd Dr A. Schowalter, who found them far from clear and thought it necessary to draw up a list of "some 150 to 200 questions" which he put to the President. The results were then pieced together with the help of official documents into a coherent narrative which was translated from Kruger's Afrikaans first into German, and from a revised version of this, into English.

What is clear is that Paul Kruger was born about ten years after the battle of Waterloo in a remote frontier area of Cape Colony where record-keeping was none too reliable and that, because of the distance to the nearest church, the birth might well not have been officially recorded until many weeks after it had taken place.

The Boers of those days lived like Old Testament patriarchs, sleeping beneath the canvas "sails" of their wagons, driving their flocks into a kraal, or enclosure, each night and hearing nothing of the great wide world for months at a time.

Colesberg, which even today is a small country town, did not exist when Kruger was born. The sole trace of officialdom in the area was a stone "beacon" erected in 1778 by Governor van Plettenberg of the Dutch East India Company to mark the boundary of the Company's domains beyond which it was hoped that neither the Boers nor their cattle would stray. The journey to Cape Town and back took a month by ox-cart, and no Boer in his right mind considered leaving his farm at the mercy of bushmen and Hottentots to go there. Indeed it was to escape from the "civilisation" of Capetown that the Boers had wandered further and further north.

The Kruger family originally came from the village of Sadenbeck 80 miles north of Berlin, and if the family name was anything to go by they had at some time been jug- and perhaps tankard-makers, possibly in pewter or silver. Jacob Kruger had arrived in South Africa some time between 1710 and 1720 as a soldier in the service of the Dutch East India Company at the Cape, where the Company kept a garrison, a vegetable-garden and a maritime "pull-in" for their ships. The family soon began to multiply. Jacob had 63 grandchildren, and Paul's great-great-grandfather, Henrik Kruger, could claim 136 descendants by the end of the 18th century.

But, like many early settlers, the Krugers found that prosperity and freedom were more easily attained in the hinterland than in the Cape under the stern eye of the Company. They accepted the live-stock the Company offered to suitable burghers, but eventually moved further and further away from the seat of authority north-wards and eastwards. Their path, like that of many other trek-farmers, lay along the borders of one of the world's most ancient and picturesque deserts: the Karroo. Here their sheep and oxen trekked across a blanket of cinnamon-coloured dust and cracked mud strewn with boulders and dotted with strangely formed squat plants and shrubs that scorn to attract, some ridged and spiny, some golden and wiry, others glaucous like the swell of the sea. Here and there the landscape was peppered with clumps of prickly pears with warty green ping-pong bats for leaves, and aloes like flowering telegraph poles: this was Karroo with its candlebushes, its fire lilies, its ink plants, its scorpions and lizards and hunting spiders, its vultures. Overhead, an azure vault trimmed sometimes with white wool clouds, the unful-filled promises of rain to come; on the horizon hill-tops, a wreath of royal purple haze that vanishes only with the evening's fiery sunset. By day, the windless silence of the lonely uplands. At night, the moon riding high, an owl on a thorn tree, a buck at the salt-pan, a hare frightened of its shadow. A strange upbringing for a boy, as isolated in the wilderness as John the Baptist.

Chief Justice Kotze once asked Kruger: "Tell me, President, if you had the chance, would you like to live your life over again?"

"No. I had too hard a time in my young days," Kruger averred.

Most old men tend to make capital out of the hardships of growing up, but one doubts if Kruger exaggerated. His was not the style of life that encourages romanticism.

Today the Karroo, dotted with dams and water-wheels that turn in the breeze, is a tourist's desert. A century and a half ago there were no roads and often no tracks. Lions slept in the shade of the witgat trees, the eagles waited for the lambing season. By day the air was furnace-hot, but it could freeze at night and sometimes the dew fell heavily enough to soak through the thickest canvas.

The fare was tough meat, some milk and the Boer's stand-by, coffee – perhaps genuine or perhaps made from burnt barley. Kruger, to his dying day, never asked for more.

Kruger's mother died in 1831 when he was six – leaving a family of six children, and, three years later, Caspar married again. Paul's stepmother, a du Plessis, bore Caspar several more children, and though Paul spoke kindly of her he could not, from the nature of things, have been fussed-over much. Young Paul's first task was to look after the lambs. Soon he was promoted to caring for the sheep. He was not yet trusted with a gun but was relied upon to give the alarm if jackals, wild dogs or birds of prey were seen to be taking an undue interest in the stock. As a boy of eight he used a jack-knife to save his own life and that of a young girl when the two were attacked by an unidentified wild beast. There were no doctors, flying or otherwise.

There were no luxuries, some disappointments and many risks. But the Krugers, and others like them, willingly endured the hardships of their life because of the freedom and independence which they brought. Already, 30 years before Paul was born, the Boers of South Africa had defied the tyranny of the Dutch East India Company by setting up their own miniature republics at Graaff Reinet and Swellendam in which they could elect their own officials and decide what taxes they wished to pay. Then at the turn of the century the English had seized power from the Dutch at the Cape and the Boers moved further away still from the seat of authority. They prospered too. As each son grew up he was given first a few sheep and cattle, and later, if he wished to settle, a farm, the size of which was frequently determined by a man riding for half an hour in a straight line to each of the four points of the compass. And so, as the Boer population grew, more and more land was needed to be bought, bartered or battled for.

In time the Boers reached the Orange river, the natural boundary of the Cape Colony. Some, even after fording the river into territory where in practice no writ ran, continued to pay taxes to the British from outside the colony. But a combination of circumstances encouraged the Boers to take the decision that was to alter their whole history. They resolved to separate themselves not only from British authority but also from all other influences than their own. "We leave the Colony," in the words of the manifesto published by Piet Retief, one of the early trekkers, or voortrekkers as they were called, "under the firm assurance that the English Government has nothing more to require of us and will allow us in the future to govern ourselves without further hindrance." And so a third of the colony made its exodus.

What put the Boers in this frame of mind? One reason, but not the most important, was the decision taken in 1833 to free all slaves throughout the British Empire. The compensation offered to the Boers for their slaves was inadequate and not realisable in cash.

There were many other inducements to quit British territory. The Boers were no more anxious to swear the oath of loyalty to good King William IV of England than they had previously been to acknowledge the overlordship of the Dutch East India Company. They did not find that allegiance to His Majesty afforded them the protection that they felt entitled to claim. For example, they were forbidden to reclaim cattle stolen by the natives unless the animals could be picked out individually from the native herd, and, if they accepted the help of British soldiers for the purpose, the beasts that were recovered were often retained by the British to pay for the costs of the expedition. And on top of this the British had recently surrendered an enormous area of frontier territory to the Xhosas, who in the war of 1834 had burnt some 400 Boer farms.

And then it also appeared to the Boers that the British had for many years nursed prejudices against them and in favour of the natives. For example, in 1812 the British, to please the London Missionary Society, had sent judges on circuit to hear cases brought by the Hottentots against their masters with the help and encouragement of the missionaries. Though few convictions were obtained, it became clear during the trials that the British were prepared to attach as much weight to the evidence of a Hottentot as to that of a Boer or his wife – which was an intolerable state of affairs. The British made things worse by trying to replace the Ministers of the Dutch Reformed Church by Ministers from Scotland who would teach English in the schools. Then, in 1832, it had been decided that Crown lands would no longer be granted to the Boers but would have to be bought at auction. But the Boers knew where they could find more living room.

The Krugers themselves had not suffered directly from the hardships of British rule; they had moved too far away from it. But they were caught up in the trek movement. Already in 1834 a number of scouting expeditions had been sent out to seek the promised lands that the Afrikaners believed that the Lord had in store for them.

Some time during the same year Paul's grandfather, aged 57, his three surviving sons and their children, a party of about 20 in all, sold their homes for horses, cattle and sheep (nearly 30,000 of them) and trekked to the banks of the Orange river. There Paul's father sold 3,000 of his sheep to a local butcher, and the Krugers then left

British territory, as they thought, for good. They moved on north and camped on the banks of the Caledon river, a tributary of the Orange river. They were soon joined there by other families from the settled districts further south who had suffered even more acutely than they from the heavy-handed British. Hendrik Potgieter, who left Tarka, some distance to the south-east of Colesberg, early in 1836 with 40 armed men and about the same number of wagons, was among the new arrivals. So was Sarel Cilliers, a former Elder who was to become the Boers' spiritual leader, and Gerrit Maritz, a prosperous wagon-builder from Graaff-Reinet who brought 700 people with him and provided the only law-books that the pioneers possessed.

And so, not long before Queen Victoria ascended the throne, the Great Trek – the most important event in South Africa's history – got under way. No single Moses led these 19th-century Israelites. It was an epidemic – a fever which spread from one farm to the next. Families clung to each other for safety, chose their own leaders and travelled into the unknown together. Nothing, perhaps, was more remarkable than the primitive covered wagons in which these voor-trekkers, their wives and children travelled out of the land of the Pharaohs. They were built narrow enough to pass easily between the rocks, short enough to turn easily, and carried enormous wheels as high as a man's shoulder to help them to pass smoothly over the ridges and craters of rough country. With the wheels removed the wagon became a shallow-draught raft. It could be jacked up for repairs with the help of a support rod hinged beneath it.

A voorkis, or case, containing the family valuables made a handy front seat; the beds, wooden-framed with leather thongs stretched across, were slung by day under the floor, and the canvas hood could be peeled off at night to form a tent. The wagon was drawn by a team of oxen, the hindmost pair being harnessed to the single short shaft. This shaft in turn was fixed to the front pair of wheels and pivoted with them to make the wagon easily manoeuvrable. It could be braked when going downhill by locking the wheels, with skids wedged in front of the main wheels and held there with chains.

Once on the move, the routine was the same. At dawn the flocks, which had been kraaled for safety overnight within an enclosure of thorn bushes, were let out to feed. Breakfast consisted of coffee brewed up in a pot hung over the fire and some so-called "cakes" made of meal and water and baked in the ashes. Before eating, there were family prayers and a psalm. Then, while the day was still cool, the oxen were in-spanned, or harnessed, and the leisurely procession moved off at a speed of about three miles an hour, the men in their broad hats of felt or plaited mealie-stalks, moleskin jackets, open-neck shirts, leather trousers and rawhide shoes, the women in their print dresses and sun-bonnets designed to protect their delicate skins from the sun. Paul Kruger's job was to keep the herds of sheep and cattle together and to protect them during the trek. A "voorloper" went ahead to point out the easiest path over the rough ground ahead. Sometimes Kruger himself acted as voorloper.

If a suitable camping site for the night was discovered, even if it were only five or six miles further on, the oxen were halted and out-spanned, more coffee was brewed, the next meal roasted and the washing hung out on a thorn bush to dry. The men, if opportunity offered, shot buck for the pot, looked to their firearms, the wagon and its tack and, as the day drew on, settled down to their pipes of tobacco. Before supper the sheep, cattle and oxen were once more kraaled, the grey speckled hens shut up, and the day closed as it had begun with prayers and a psalm.

The children found their own amusements, making their own dolls, or oxen fashioned out of clay with a pair of sharp thorns for the horns.

Regular school was out of the question but the Boer parents did their best not to let the rising generation lapse into ignorance. Said Kruger in his memoirs:

Every Boer taught his children to read and write, and, above all, instructed them in God's word. At dinner and supper, as the children sat round the table, they had to read part of the Sacred Scriptures and to repeat from memory or write down now this and now that text; and this was done day by day unless circum-stances made it impossible. That is how my father taught me the Bible, and instructed me in its teaching during the evenings. My other course of instructions was covered altogether by a period of about three months, with frequent interruptions. My master's name was Tielman Roos, who found much difficulty in carrying out his mission. Whenever the trek came to a resting-place and we out-spanned, a small hut was built of grass and reeds, and this became the schoolroom for the trekkers' children.

The voortrekkers had arranged to rally together at the Blesberg, near the present site of Bloemfontein and not far from Thaba Nchu, a mountain landmark rising 2,000 feet above the surrounding plain. There they would set up a government of their own, with a council to make laws, a magistrate to settle disputes and a commander to lead their forces.

In the meantime, Potgieter, whom the Krugers had joined, showed more enterprise than any other of the potential leaders. He was a tall, lean, dark-haired man with a scrubby beard, uncompromising, a good man in a tight corner, intolerant, unforgiving, deeply religious and disdainful of popularity. Potgieter reached the Blesberg and pushed on still further north into the High Veld, where the nights are cold and the hailstorms deadly, and on across the Vaal river into what we know as the Transvaal, before he turned back and won a famous battle against the Matabele at Vechtkop.

Paul Kruger described the battle in his memoirs and recounted how women and children took part in it, loading and reloading the guns and, though he does not say so in his memoirs, he probably took part in it himself. At any rate he recalled how the wagons of the voortrekkers were formed into a square or laager, each shaft beneath the next wagon and lashed to it with leather straps; how the wheels were packed between the spokes with thorn bushes so that the attackers could not force their way in; how the women helped to load the guns; how the muzzles grew hot as the tribesmen got nearer and nearer; how the spears fell in the centre of the laager where there was no one to be hit; and how the enemy was forced at last to withdraw, taking with them, however, all the Boers' sheep, oxen and cattle so that Potgieter was stuck fast for 15 days and had to send south for help in order to make his way back to the Blesberg.

When he got there he was elected Commandant of the Great Trek and Chairman of the Council of War. Potgieter was one of the "Doppers" – a religious sect which adhered to the decrees of the Synod of Dordrecht of 1619. The Doppers wore distinctive coats buttoned up to the throat, abhorred hymns in church (because the verses were not part of Holy Writ), worried about whether or not the altar cloth used for the Communion service should be the same as for other services, and distrusted anything else which might be thought to challenge the intended workings of the Divine Providence. Both Caspar Kruger and Paul were strongly influenced by Dopper beliefs.

Eventually Potgieter quarrelled with his followers and lost his post to Piet Retief who set up the "Community of the Free Province of New Holland in South East Africa" at Winburg in what is now the Orange Free State, about 100 miles north-east of the Blesberg.

But this was not the end of the story. Retief and his men found a pass through the crags of the Drakensberg mountains into the "garden province" of Natal and down to the Indian Ocean, and Potgieter, not wishing to miss a good thing, followed reluctantly, still convinced that the High Veld, which had been largely cleared of the Matabele, was the promised land, rather than the green paradise of Natal which was dominated by the Zulus.

In the end Potgieter was proved right. Retief was treacherously murdered by the Zulu Chief Dingaan, and Potgieter's party, with young Kruger inside the laager, was surrounded and attacked. Finally the Boers were pushed back, not, it is true, by the Zulus but by the British, who had caught up with the trekkers by travelling along the sea coast to what is now the port of Durban. So Natal, like the Cape Province became a British colony, and Potgieter, who had prudently held aloof from fighting the British, recrossed the Drakensberg in 1838, the year of Queen Victoria's accession, and set up his capital at Potchefstroom in the Transvaal.

At first, after their return from Natal, the Krugers camped at Liebenberg Vlei, in what is now the Orange Free State. But in 1839, when he was only 14, young Paul took part in a further expedition with Potgieter against the Matabele to the north in the Magaliesberg Hills – and again in the following year. Thus he became a Transvaler and never settled south of the Vaal river.

In between these two expeditions, the commando, in Kruger's words "returned to the women's camp on the Rhenoster and Vaal rivers" – a journey which, as we shall see, could have been significant for Paul's future. Potgieter, in order to escape from the jurisdiction which the British claimed up to the 25th parallel south of the Equator, now set himself up in a new capital, Schoemansdal, in what is now the Northern Transvaal; but Paul's father stayed in the Magaliesberg country further south and settled there. Paul, when he reached the age of 16, became entitled according to Boer custom to choose two farms for himself, one for grazing and one for growing crops. He, too, selected land in the Magaliesberg area near the site of Rustenburg. One farm where he lived was called Waterkloof, and the other Boekenhoutfontein. There he settled into a double-storeyed white house with its own stoep (verandah) and a fine wooden staircase with a spiral rail inside. The farm had its own dam and produced tobacco, oranges, mealies, bamboo, barley, apricots – in fact almost anything.

In the meantime Paul had been courting Miss Maria du Plessis, a member of the du Plessis clan. These du Plessis had trekked with Potgieter from Tarka and probably Paul renewed his acquaintanceship on that visit to the women's camp. Her family, like his own, came from the Cape and had afterwards farmed in the Kroonstad region of the Free State.

Paul Kruger was a traditionalist in most matters and he probably followed the custom of "opsitting", according to which the suitor and his intended bride are permitted by the girl's family to stay up talking after supper for so long as a tallow candle provided for them is still alight – doubtless the length of the candle varied somewhat according to the eligibility of the suitor. But of course he was not a man to tarry unduly over any enterprise, and on one of his visits to Maria, finding that the ferry over the Vaal river had been closed because of flooding, with the ferryman immovable on the far bank, he drove his horses and cart into the stream and swam with them to the other side.

Teenage weddings were heartily approved of in Boer society as an aid to the birthrate and as a safeguard against immorality. (There is a legend that already, before his marriage, Kruger was tempted to sin with an attractive native girl whom he saw bathing naked in a pool; he resisted of course.) Certainly Boer girls scattered over the promised land provided a civilising influence in the home and prevented many a Boer from forgetting his religion and sinking to the level of the Hottentots around him. Often the women of the family provided the willpower needed to cling to a homestead that might otherwise have been abandoned.

In 1842 Paul brought Maria north with him and they were married by the magistrate in Potchefstroom which was then still too small to have a church.

Soon however the Krugers were on the move again. Kruger's father was a member of a Commission appointed to define the frontier between Boer territory and Portuguese Mozambique to the east, and Paul went with the expedition as Deputy Field Cornet, taking his wife with him. Having settled the frontier question, the Krugers went as far north as Ohrigstad but found that it was fever country and unsuited to livestock. So Paul and his wife returned to the Magaliesberg area where he acquired several more farms by barter, including one near Pilaansberg for winter grazing.

Then, in January 1846, in the heat of the summer, Paul suffered a tragedy. His young wife and her baby died of fever, leaving him alone in the world. From this point his thoughts, it is said, turned more and more to religion as the source of consolation for worldly misfortune.

But evidently married life still possessed attractions, and in the following year he married Maria's cousin, Gezina Suzanna Frederika Wilhelmina du Plessis. Gezina, who was five years younger than Paul, eventually bore him nine sons and seven daughters. Kruger was already rich. Surrounded by a happy home and a large family he could still have remained obscure.

Chapter 2

Exit, Firing

The Victorians knew Kruger for what he had become on the drawing-boards of British cartoonists: a coarse old peasant with fists like hams, a sullen expression, swollen eyelids (the lashes grew inwards and caused Kruger intense discomfort), a scrubby beard, a barrel chest over which his frock-coat could scarcely be buttoned, a theatrical sash of office, baggy trousers, a reeking pipe and an incongruous top-hat.

The Afrikaner citizens ("my burghers") who supported him knew him on the other hand for what he had once been: a hunter and a mighty warrior, and although today neither of these roles would win votes, in those times it was different. Not many men could fire from the saddle at full gallop to hit a pursuing buffalo, and when Kruger did so it was not to perfect a circus trick but to save his life. He shot lions not in order to provide hearth-rugs but to protect cattle, and hunted buck for meat, as well as sport. Powder was scarce and every shot had to count.

The natives, too, played a different role a century ago. The tribesmen of those times did not live in "locations". They did not line up in the boulevards or the squares of the cities wearing white men's clothes in order to make demonstrations, before being dispersed with tear-gas or rifle fire. They were as formidable as the game they hunted. It was "the Kaffirs" who ambushed by day or kidnapped by night, spiriting away cattle and burning homesteads. There was no frontier, no treaties that endured, and when one Chief sought the protection of the white men, his enemies became theirs. When a commando was called out to recover cattle or to drive off infiltrators, women and children had to be left behind in laagers virtually unprotected. And 300 Afrikaner men, women and children, were once massacred in a single night near the Blaaukrans river in Natal because they slept in open tents instead of in a laager. The campaigns were fought on Old Testament lines with an eye for an eye and a tooth for a tooth. Nor was victory assured, as the British found when they took on the Zulus. Marksmanship, local knowledge and the ability to make use of it, psychology, the art of concealment – all were needed for survival, whether against man or beast, and an Afrikaner who performed exploits on horseback, on foot, who could lead, who could improvise, who could endure, who could survive in the field was not merely a hero to be admired – he was a saviour to be followed.

Kruger shot his first lion when he was 14 – one that had killed several head of cattle near the banks of the Rhenoster river, in what is now the Orange Free State. He had not really been invited as one of the shooting party of six. His job would be to hold the horses for them when they got near enough to dismount and close in on the lion. The party split into two groups with a fair distance between them, and Kruger went with his father, his uncle and his brother. The lion sighted the Krugers before they got level with it, broke cover some distance away, and moved towards them.

No horse could be expected to face a charging lion and the Krugers quickly dismounted and tethered the horses together with their heads away from the lion so that they would be less likely to bolt. Kruger wrote:

My relatives placed us. I was told to sit behind – or, from the lion's point of view, in front of – the horses, with my rifle covering him. His last bound brought him close to me; then he crouched with the intention it seemed to me, of jumping right over me onto the horses. As he rose, I fired, and was fortunate enough to kill him outright, so that he nearly fell on top of me. My companions ran to my assistance; but I needed no help for the lion was dead.

When the Krugers had recovered their breath they began to examine the trophy.

He was obviously a strong beast with remarkably fine teeth and one of the party, referred to as "Hugo", knelt down to measure them. Paul, without malice aforethought, jumped on the dead beast's stomach:

. . . As I did so, the air shook with a tremendous roar, which so frightened Hugo that he forgot his tooth-measurements and fell down flat on his back.

The others shook with laughter, for every hunter knows that, if you tread upon a lion's body within a short time after his death, he will give a final roar, as though he were still alive. Hugo of course knew this, but he had forgotten it, and was greatly ashamed of his fright. In fact he was so angry that he turned on me to give me a good hiding.

But the others stepped in and kept the peace.

Kruger's second encounter with a lion was almost as remarkable:

My uncle, Theunis Kruger, and I were after a herd of antelope when, my horse being done up, I was left behind, alone. Riding at a walking-pace, I came upon a pride of lions. Escape on a tired horse was out of the question. Suddenly one of the lions left the group and made a dash for me. I allowed him to come up to within twenty paces and then shot him through the head. The charge passed through the head and into the body. The lion fell with his head turned away from me, but jumped up again immediately and returned to his companions, while I reloaded. The moment he reached the herd, he fell down dead.

Then there was the time that Kruger was rhinoceros-hunting with his brother-in-law "and faithful hunting companion", N. Theunissen, and they had each agreed that if either behaved recklessly or, through cowardice, failed to find and finish off a wounded animal, he should receive a sound thrashing. They came across three white rhinoceroses, a bull and two cows. Kruger went ahead of the bull, jumped off his horse and shot him dead as he charged. Meanwhile Theunissen had been following the two cows through the thick undergrowth, firing from time to time to show where he was. When Kruger came up with him he saw that one of the cows had been wounded and was making off through the bush. "Don't jump off in front of her," Theunissen shouted. "She is savage and very fast." Kruger continues:

I did not pay much attention to the warning, knowing Theunissen to be over-cautious, but jumped off my horse and ran obliquely past the rhinoceros. She had scarcely caught sight of me before she was in hot pursuit. I let her come to within three or four yards. Then at the critical moment the percussion cap failed to explode, and there was no time for a second shot. The animal was close upon me, and there was nothing to be done but to turn round and run for dear life . . . But while I was trying to get away my foot got caught in the root of a thorn tree and I came down flat on my face. The beast caught up with me; her horn just missed my back; she pinned me to the ground with her nose, intending to trample me to death. But at that moment, I turned under her and let her have the contents of the second barrel full under the shoulder-blade, right into her heart. I owed my life to not letting go my hold on the gun during this dangerous adventure. The rhinoceros sprang away from me, but fell down a few yards away.

My brother-in-law hurried up as fast as he could, for he thought that I had mortally wounded myself with my own gun. When he saw, however, that I was standing up safe and sound, he took his sjambok and, "according to contract", commenced to belabour me soundly because I had, he said, acted recklessly in disregarding his warning.

Theunissen brushed aside Kruger's plea that he had been bruised enough already, and Paul had to take refuge in the cover of some thorn bushes where no sjambok could reach him. It was the first and last time that he earned a hiding from Theunissen.

Buffaloes were also a cause of anxiety to Kruger as he discovered when he plunged into a jungle of thorn trees, five to six feet high, in search of some. Unfortunately he passed by one herd without seeing it:

Before long, however, I came right up to a second herd. A big buffalo at once turned his attention to me, but, fortunately, his horns were so wide apart that when he butted, trees and bushes got caught up between them, which not only broke the force of his attack, but hid me very effectively, if only for a few moments, from his sight. Trying to get out of the wood, I found myself suddenly amongst the herd which I had passed a little while before, without noticing them at the time. Even now, I did not realise what had happened until when I ran right up against a buffalo that was just getting up from the ground. Angered at being disturbed the beast tore my clothes from my back with his hoof. My comrades, as they stood outside the wood, took the buffalo's hoof for his horns, so high did he raise it in attacking me. Fortunately I escaped with a fright.

Later, a wounded buffalo gave Kruger an even closer call when, once again with his brother-in-law, N. Theunissen, he was hunting near Vleeschkraal, in the Waterburg district:

I had hit a buffalo cow and she had escaped into a covert of dense thorn bushes. As it was impossible to follow on horseback, I gave my horse to my brother Nicholas, and went after the buffalo on foot. The great thing was not to lose sight of her in the thick under-growth. Believing that I was still the pursuer, I was unpleasantly surprised to find her suddenly facing me and on the attack. I got ready to shoot, but my flint-lock missed fire so that I had to run for it. The rains had been heavy, and just behind me was a big swamp into which I fell as I jumped out of the enraged animal's way. The buffalo fell in after me, and was already standing over me in a threatening attitude before I had time to get up.

My rifle was in the water and therefore useless; but fortunately for me, as the buffalo butted at me, she rammed one of her horns fast into the ground of the swamp, where it stuck. I got hold of the other and tried with all my strength to force the animal's head under water and so suffocate her. It was a difficult thing to do, for the horn was very slippery on account of the slimy water, and I needed both hands and every atom of strength I had, to keep her head under. When I felt it going, I removed one hand to get at the hunting knife I carried on my hip, in order to rid myself of my antagonist. But, having failed to hold the brute with two hands, I certainly could not hold her with one, and she freed herself with a final effort. She was in a sad plight, however, nearly suffocated, and her eyes so full of slime that she could not see me. My appearance was no less disreputable than the buffalo's, for I was covered from head to foot with slime. Theunissen, hearing the row we made, knew that something was amiss, but he could not come to my assistance. It was impossible to get through the undergrowth of thorns on horseback.

When I had cleaned myself down a little, I got on the track of the rest of the herd, and succeeded in shooting two.

Not surprisingly Kruger, with his bull-like torso and powerful lungs, was a fine swimmer. During one of his hunting expeditions the party noticed that a number of hides, which they had been counting on, presumably, to use for making shoes or breeches, had disappeared. The same thing happened several nights running. Kruger, while walking, noticed what looked like one of the skins in a rocky cavern below the surface of the water on the opposite side of the river near to which they were encamped. He stripped and dived into the water and discovered the remains of most of the missing skins in the cavern. But he also surprised the culprits – a group of half a dozen crocodiles who were so panic-stricken that they rushed out of the cave and into the water.

In his younger days he was not too heavily built to be something of an athlete. He could outdistance a horse – over rough ground, one supposes – for at least half a mile. He vaulted into the saddle without using stirrups and when he was thrown he more often than not landed on his feet. When wanting to get from one side of an ox team to the other, he was known to use the stock of his long whip to make a pole for vaulting over – just to save walking round.

Stories of this kind, not all of them provided by Kruger himself, soon began to circulate on a thousand stoeps and in front parlours throughout Boerland in a kind of self-perpetuating election campaign for the man who performed them.

When Kruger was still 20 he lost the thumb of his left hand in another hunting accident. In fact he had to cut some of it off himself.

He had gone off alone to hunt near the Steenpoort river in the northern Transvaal, carrying his favourite heavy old four-pounder elephant-gun:

After about an hour's ride, I came across a rhinoceros and shot at it. But I succeeded only in wounding the animal and it fled into the wood. I dismounted quickly, ready to shoot again, but moved only a few steps away from my horse, lest the rhinoceros should turn to attack me, in which case I would have to remount at once. I succeeded in getting a second shot; but at that very moment, my gun exploded just where I held it with my left hand, and I saw my left thumb, the lock and the ramrod lying on the ground in front of me and the barrel of the gun behind me. I had no time to think, for the furious animal was almost upon me; so I jumped on my horse and galloped away as fast as I could, with the rhinoceros in hot pursuit, until we came to the ford of a little spruit, when my pursuer came to the ground and so allowed me to ride quietly in the direction of our wagons.

During the next day, our people, guided by the track of my horse, went to the spot, and there they found the rhinoceros still alive, and, following the trail of blood, discovered the remains of the rifle and my thumb.

My hand was in a horrible state. The great veins were torn asunder and the muscles lay exposed. The flesh was hanging in strips. I bled like a slaughtered calf. I had succeeded in tying a large pocket handkerchief round the wound while riding to save the horse from being splashed with blood. When I got to the wagons, my wife and sister-in-law were sitting by the fire, and I went up to them laughing so as not to frighten them. My sister-in-law pointed to my hand which looked like a great piece of raw meat, the handkerchief being soaked with blood: "Look what fat game Brother Paul has been shooting," she said.

I called out to my wife to go to the wagon and fetch some turpentine, as I had hurt my hand. Then I asked my sister-in-law to take off my bandolier, and she saw that my hand was torn and noticed how white I was, for I had hardly any blood left in my body.

I kept on renewing the turpentine bandages, for turpentine is a good remedy to "burn the veins up" as the Boers say, and thus to stop the bleeding. I sent my youngest brother – he was still really young at the time – to borrow as much turpentine as he could get from the nearest farm, which was about half an hour's ride away. Herman Potgieter, who was afterwards so cruelly murdered by the

Kaffirs, came over with his brother. The former got into the wagon, and when he saw the wound cried out: "That hand will never heal; it is an awful wound!"

He had to get down again as quickly as possible, for he was near to fainting. But his brother said, possibly to comfort me: "Nonsense; I have seen worse wounds than that. Get plenty of turpentine."

We inspanned and drove to the farm. Everyone there advised me to send for a doctor and have the hand amputated; but I positively refused to allow myself to be mutilated still further of my own free will. The two joints of what was once my thumb had gone, but it appeared that it would still be necessary to take out a piece of bone. I took my knife, intending to perform the operation, but they took it away from me. I got hold of another a little later and cut across the ball of the thumb, removing as much as was necessary. The worst bleeding was over, but the operation was a very painful one. I had no means by me of deadening the pain, so I tried to persuade myself that the hand on which I was performing this surgical operation belonged to somebody else.

The wound healed very slowly. The women sprinkled finely powdered sugar on it, and from time to time, I had to remove the dead flesh with my pocket knife; but gangrene set in after all. Different remedies were tried; but all seemed useless, for the black marks spread up as far as the shoulder. Then they killed a goat, took out the stomach and cut it open. I put my hand into it while it was still warm. This Boer remedy succeeded, for when it came to the turn of the second goat, my hand was already easier and the danger less. The wound took over six months to heal, and, before it was quite cured, I was out hunting again.

In the 30 years which followed his second marriage, Kruger, who had hitherto prospered as a farmer and a hunter, established himself as a negotiator and politician. His raw materials were his fellow Boers and "the Kaffirs". If only he had kept a diary! But he was far too busy.

We had left him settled in Rustenburg, newly married for the second time and about to produce a numerous family. But isolation in the country was impossible in those times of unrest, for each Afrikaner depended for safety on his neighbours and Kruger was accordingly fated to become the leader around which the Afrikaners, as if attracted by the gravitational pull of some immensely powerful stellar-mass, became satellites.

When the Boers, disconsolate, rode back inland from Natal over the Drakensberg, they had split after their usual fashion into several different groups, each of which fancied itself as a budding Republic. Potgieter and his followers had, as we have seen, moved north to Ohrigstad (1845) and then further north still to Soutpansberg at the very edge of beyond; and a second group from Natal set themselves up at Lydenburg in the eastern Transvaal. There were others yet again who had moved into the Potchefstroom–Winburg area to the south-west and became followers of Andries Pretorius, who had recrossed the Drakensberg in 1847 nine years after his final victory over Dingaan. Rustenburg, where Paul Kruger had settled, considered itself independent, but in practice accepted the authority of Potchefstroom, and thus of Pretorius.

And so it was as an ally of Pretorius that Paul Kruger first came on a direct collision course towards the British.

The seeds of trouble started to spread when the redcoats, having driven the Afrikaners out of Natal and annexed it as a colony, began pushing forward not only along the eastern coast between the Cape and Natal but also along the route which the Afrikaners themselves had followed during the Great Trek.

In 1843 Sir George Napier, British Governor at the Cape, signed treaties with two of the most important Chiefs ruling in the area between the Cape and the new Boer settlements to the north. Five years later Napier's successor at the Cape, Sir Harry Smith, proclaimed British sovereignty over all the Boer settlements in what is now called the Orange Free State. All protests were in vain.

It was Pretorius who organised such resistance as there was to the British advance. He drove the British officials out of Bloemfontein, prepared – and lost – a skirmish at Boomplaats and was forced to flee with a price of £2,000 on his head.

The Krugers are believed to have fought at Boomplaats, and one uncharitable story relates that it was Paul's father who fired the first shot in the battle – the shot that prematurely disclosed the Boer positions and thus saved the British from being ambushed.

But the defeat was not fatal, for, soon afterwards, Whitehall decided to make one of its celebrated right-about turns. Queen Victoria's ministers did not feel that they could go so far as to give back the Orange River Colony its freedom so soon after Sir Harry Smith had taken it away – but they were willing to make an arrangement with Pretorius the outlaw, and his followers further north beyond the Vaal river, in order to prevent them from interfering further south.

And so in 1852 at Venter's Farm, Britain signed the Sand River Convention giving independence to the "emigrant farmers north of the Vaal river". The British agreed amongst other things not to conclude any treaties with the Bantu north of the Vaal (i.e. not to combine with the natives against the Afrikaners), and each side also undertook not to supply arms or ammunition to the Bantu, and to extradite each other's criminals. The Transvaal, with Kruger in it, had officially become free. Two years later a similar convention freed the Orange River Colony immediately south of the Vaal, which then became the Republic of the Orange Free State.

The events of the next ten years brought little or no profit (or credit) to any of those who took part in them, and amounted, in short, to a series of unsuccessful attempts by Pretorious to annex the Orange Free State by means of coups organised by his supporters of the Free State.

But having obtained independence, the Boers decided to quarrel amongst themselves about who was to stay independent.

It was a Wild West story transported from America to Africa. The two republics – the South African Republic (as Pretorius' young republic came to be called), and the even younger Orange Free State Republic to the south – began bickering in 1853 when Andries Pretorius died and was succeeded in the Transvaal by his son, Marthinus Wessel Pretorius. The new man was a distinguished-looking figure, with a high domed forehead and a candid and serene expression, who could perhaps have been a university don. He was, however, a political expansionist.

Some of the Free Staters, moved partly by their fear of attack by the surrounding tribes, urged that the new Pretorius should be chosen also as their own President, and Pretorius, even if he had not inspired their views, was prepared to fall in with them. He advanced on Bloemfontein at the head of a commando. Other Free Staters were, however, less enthusiastic about the idea of being taken over, and President Boshoff organised a counter-commando. In May 1857 two opposing commandos, one pro-Pretorius and one anti-Pretorius, confronted each other across the Rhenoster river. Unfortunately Pretorius was somewhat outnumbered. It was clear that the game was up, and Kruger, who had been promoted to Full Commandant, was sent across the river with a white flag as envoy to make the best terms he could for the Pretorius faction in the Free State.

He tried conciliation and bluster in turn and, when Koos Venter threatened to wring Pretorius' neck, he challenged him to single combat.

The challenge, however, was not accepted, and eventually the Transvaal, in a treaty between the two sides, promised not to intervene in the Free State in future.

But Kruger for all his bargaining was unable to secure an amnesty for the rebels of the Free State; in fact the treaty laid down that Free State supporters of Pretorius could be brought to trial and punished. In due course two of them were found guilty and sentenced to death.

Here Kruger again intervened. He argued that the peace terms did, indeed, allow the Free State Government to punish or chastise, that is to "correct", those rebels who had supported Pretorius, and, in this sense, the threat of death could legitimately be regarded as a punishment. But the act of execution itself was entirely distinct from punishment or chastisement as understood in the Bible, and Kruger was able to give examples to prove his case.

The sentences were commuted.

It was a technique he was often to use in the future. Find more quotations from the Bible than your opponent and, within a devout community, your arguments must prevail.

Kruger was also involved in a new bout of diplomatic activity in 1860 when the Free Staters, still unsure of their ability to defend themselves, tried once more to adopt Pretorius as their President as well as of the Transvaal. This time the coup succeeded. The Transvaal Volksraad, or Parliament, gave Pretorius six months' leave and he was installed soon after at Bloemfontein as President of the Free State. But then his Transvaal subjects, who had sent him away, changed their minds. They were afraid that Pretorius' connection with Bloemfontein might involve them in new wars, and resolved that no one man should be allowed to hold the two Presidencies. They were supported in this decision by the British who announced that they would regard a union between the two states as a breach of the Conventions which had established them.

So Pretorius had to resign his Transvaal office. But his hopes of a single united Boer Republic did not fade. He still wanted to retain his influence in the north. So, instead of allowing the oldest member of the Executive Council to be appointed as Acting President of the Transvaal as provided by the Constitution, he put forward one of his own supporters, Stephanus Schoeman, the man with the longest service, a thruster from Lydenburg, whom he hoped would "keep his seat warm". It was one of Pretorius' least sensible moves.

For here Paul Kruger came to the fore again. He had been a follower of Pretorius, but not of Schoeman, who, he was prepared to argue, had not been legally appointed. And so there was more fighting with each leader claiming that the other was a rebel.

Kruger first appealed for a special court to be set up to look into the matter. Schoeman retorted by swooping on Pretoria (now the capital) and seizing the official Government records (it was not so long since Pretorius had kept them all in the rafters of his three-room farm).

Kruger raced to Schoeman's house and gave notice that he did not recognise his authority. And in September 1862 he drove him out of Potchefstroom and into the Free State.

As long as Pretorius remained in the Transvaal, Kruger supported him, but during his absence he declined to be ruled by Pretorius' nominee Schoeman.

In the spring of 1864 Pretorius finally renounced the Free State and resigned himself to ruling only the Transvaal, or the South African Republic to give it its official title. He was re-elected President and Kruger was confirmed as Commandant-General – the highest military post in the South African Republic. But he had earned it as much by diplomacy as by military skill, for the Boers, when confronting one another in the field, showed a marked reluctance to open fire. Christians were too scarce in those parts and Christianity too well observed for shooting to be lightly enterprised. On several occasions honour was satisfied by both sides discharging volleys into the air.

When fighting the tribes, however, practices were less restrictive, and Kruger was able to show that in addition to a negotiating talent he possessed one more attribute of leadership, namely the ability to respond to unexpected events in such a way as to profit from them.

Sometimes the motive was expansion. Sometimes it was revenge, or the recovery of stolen cattle. One has only to read Whitehall records to realise that the prospect of native wars raised the most lively apprehensions among Her Majesty's minister. But it is not difficult to understand why a Boer whose hut had been burnt over his head was concerned to punish the men who had done it. He might have to do so to survive.

In 16 years – between the ages of 27 and 42 – Kruger took part in nine major campaigns against the "Kaffirs" each of which, however unedifying in modern eyes, was a fight to stay alive. The first of these campaigns was against the Bechuana Chief Secheli, the protector of another Chief, Moselele, who was "wanted for several murders in the Transvaal". Secheli was unmoved by the approach of the Boer commando. To them he sent a message: "Anyone who wants Moselele can come and fetch him out of my stomach."

Later he sent a postscript saying that he would leave the Boers alone on the following day because that was Sunday, and would settle his account with them the day after. In the meantime, would they send him some sugar and coffee on account. The Boers replied, according to their story, that they had no sugar or coffee to spare but they would give him pepper on Monday.

But as it turned out Kruger was lucky (once more) to escape with his life. One of the Boers' own cannon-balls bounced off a rock and knocked him out, and only sharp shooting by his brother's Hottentot servant saved him from being picked off. Later, while still half-dazed, with his head in a cloth, he was hit in the chest by a shot which tore his jacket in two.

It was enough to make most men cautious. But the following year Kruger was to the fore again in an expedition undertaken against two other Chiefs, Mapela and Makapaan, to avenge the murder of Herman Potgieter, the brother of Hendrik. Herman, while on an elephant hunt to which he had been invited by Mapela, had been flayed alive in the presence of his groom. At about the same time Makapaan had attacked a party of women and children who were on their way from Soutpansberg to Pretoria.

Two commandos were sent to take revenge, one from Pretoria with Kruger as second-in-command, and the other from Soutpansberg under Herman Potgieter's nephew, Piet. But the Kaffirs played safe and fled to some inaccessible caves from which only a prolonged siege could dislodge them.

Kruger however had other ideas. After dark he crept unseen into the largest cave and pretended to be one of the natives, talking to them in their own language. He suggested that it would be better to surrender than to die of starvation, and offered to negotiate with the Boers who, he was sure, would spare their lives.

Suddenly a native shouted "*Magoa! Magoa!*" (White man! White man!). But no one could find Kruger, for most of the natives had promptly run right to the back of the cave and he ran with them. They looked everywhere else for him. When they had given up the search, Kruger, still posing as a Kaffir, again urged the enemy to surrender. But although he was successful in getting about 180 women and children volunteers to leave the cave, the warriors stayed behind and the siege could not be raised.

Needless to say the old Pretorius – it was one of his last campaigns – was highly displeased at this "recklessness", but Kruger was able to make amends by recovering the dead body of Piet Potgieter, his close friend, who had been killed by a sniper. Under heavy fire Kruger climbed over the parapet of the Boer trench, picked up the body and, protected by the smoke of the firing, carried it back safely.

He was lucky again, soon after, in another expedition against Mapela. The Chief had entrenched himself on the summit of a rocky hill surrounded by sheer drops, except at one point where there was a steep gorge. Up this Kruger and 100 volunteers crept after dark in their bare feet, their shoes strung round their necks. Half-way up the mountain Kruger, who led the advance patrol, was detected. The sentry allowed him to approach quite close and then let fly. But the gun misfired, Kruger heard the trigger click, took aim and the sentry fell dead at his feet. The defenders replied with a hail of rifle fire. But Kruger ran back to the waiting party. "Forward. Shoes on! and let them have it," he cried. And so the pass was seized, and at first light the enemy was driven off the top of the hill. Mapela escaped, but it was a night to remember.

Next came a foray against Chief Montsioa, who lived on the High Veld in the western Transvaal. Montsioa had taken advantage of a fall of snow to rustle a considerable number of cattle. Here the Boers were in luck and were able to approach close to without being detected, for the natives mistook the dust they raised in their advance for a cloud of locusts of which there were many in the area, and took no precautions.

The cattle were recovered.

In 1858, shortly after Kruger had mediated in the dispute between the two Republics, he was able to put the Free State Government under a further obligation to him. Taking a commando of 50 men, he went with Marthinus Wessel Pretorius via Winburg to Bloemfontein, and offered to negotiate a peace with Moshesh, Chief of the Basuto, whose men had been rustling cattle from the Free State. The offer was accepted and the Free State Government gave him two escorts for company. When the three of them came to the foot of Thaba Bosigo, the mountain on which Moshesh lived, Kruger sent up a message saying that he had come to talk peace, not to fight the Basuto. Moshesh sent a reply that he would come down at once to talk with Mr Kruger.

In Kruger's own words:

I was not disposed to wait, however, and at once climbed the mountain so as to go straight to Moshesh' town. When we reached the top, Moshesh was just coming to meet us. Magato, the Kaffir captain from the Rustenburg neighbourhood, whom we knew, and who happened to be with Moshesh, introduced me to him, saying:

"This is Paul Kruger."

Moshesh gave me his hand and said:

"Is that Paul Kruger? How is it possible? I have heard tell of him for so many years, and now I am so old. How, then, can he still be so young?"

He took hold of my arm and led me to his house and into a room which no black dared enter, but which was always ready for the reception of white men.

After taking some refreshments, we at once proceeded to business. I began: "Why do you kill one another for such a trifle? Why not, rather, arrange the matter amicably? You must surely see that war does you damage and makes you block the high roads for other nations with whom you are living at peace."

After much argument on both sides, Moshesh said at last: "What you say is true, for everything I want in this house I have to buy from other nations. And when the roads are blocked by war, of course I can get nothing."

That same evening we made an agreement that the war was to stop at once. Moshesh agreed to call in his Kaffirs as soon as he received word that the Orange Free State had accepted the terms. A peace document was drawn up and signed the following morning.

Moshesh then invited me to stay with him a little longer as he wanted to pick me out a fine saddle-horse. I accepted the invitation, but my companions did not care to wait any longer and went back alone. Moshesh then brought me an excellent saddle-horse as a present.

So once again diplomacy paid.

But already, before quitting Moshesh, Kruger got a message from Pretorius asking him to go as Assistant-General on an expedition against Gasibone, a Chief in the Harts river area of the South-West Transvaal. During the next three days he spent 50 hours in the saddle on his new mount riding north. After one day at his farm he joined the commando that had been waiting for him at Klerksdorp. But the men had no cattle for food, and hardly any ammunition. In fact they were so short of powder that they had to drive the game into a bend of the Vaal river and club it to death in order to get food. Later they were joined by a commando from the Free State and, after a battle among the rocks and coves, they recovered the cattle that had been stolen, together with an old woman and a girl of 18 who had been kidnapped.

"Then the commando returned home again," wrote Kruger. "For me it had been a year of hard work."

And it was no way to make a decent living.

In the early sixties Kruger was, as we have seen, fully engaged in sorting out the Boers' troubles, but in 1865 when the so-called Great Basuto War broke out in the Free State he was again in the field, and in considerable danger because, on one occasion, under cover of darkness, rising mist and a continuous drizzle, the Basutos and their allies, the Zulus, succeeded in penetrating the Boer camp. In the end they were driven out, but the Transvaal commando turned for home when they heard that the Free State Government was not, after all, going to award them farms in any territory they helped to conquer.

One day the following year Kruger, through recklessness again though not in the field of battle, found himself in real trouble. He was driving home in a two-wheeled mule-cart from a session of the Volksraad at which he had delivered a report on the situation in the Rustenburg area. Near Schoonkloof Farm, just beyond Elephant's Pass and not so far from his own home, he had to cross a sluit or ditch. The ditch itself was dry, but the road leading to it was still a mud-pan and badly cracked. Rather than turn back on a long detour, Kruger, never the most patient of men, decided to take a chance. He would whip up the mules and get them to jump across the ditch on to firm ground on the other side, and they could then pull the cart after them. Unfortunately the cart turned over, and Kruger smashed his left leg at the knee. With only a Kaffir piccaninny to help him, he had to right the cart and drive along a dirt road in a jolting cart for an hour and a half, without having been able to bind up his leg. Kruger was more or less out of action for nine months afterwards, and his left leg became permanently a little shorter than the other.

He was out and about the following year in the northern Transvaal, but he and the Boers had to abandon the village of Schoemansdal to the natives for want of gunpowder. However, he returned to the area in 1868 with only one burgher for company, and succeeded in getting an undertaking from at least one Chief not to attack the settlers.

But then, as he might have put it himself, at the age of 45 he suddenly realised he had been fighting the wrong people. For unfortunately, further south, diamonds were being mined by his old enemy the British, and some of the fields appeared to lie in Transvaal territory.

Chapter 3

Kruger Obscured

The first spectacular diamond was noticed and picked up in 1866 on the De Kalk farm near Hopetown in Cape Colony by a small boy, Erasmus Stephanus Jacobs, who thought it was a pebble. But its appearance was unusual enough for it to have been passed on to a farmer, Schalk van Niekerk, and by him to John O'Reilly, a travelling trader, who was almost certain of it being a genuine diamond. Dr Atherton, the Cape Colony's official mineralogist at Grahamstown, confirmed the good news, and the stone was eventually sold for £500 to Sir Philip Wodehouse, the High Commissioner at the Cape.

Next year the prospectors found other diamonds at Hebron and Klipdrift on the north bank of the Vaal river near its junction with the Harts river, and also at Pniel, on the Orange Free State side of the Vaal. In 1870 even richer fields were discovered further south near the present site of Kimberley.

But what was most surprising of all was that there should have been any doubt as to which government owned the new diamond-fields. Hopetown, being south of the Orange river, was undoubtedly in Cape Colony; Pniel, being north of the Orange river but south of the Vaal, was obviously in the Orange Free State; and Hebron and Klipdrift, being north of the Vaal, were clearly in the Transvaal.

Or were they? For things in South Africa are rarely what they seem.

The first complication was that the region to the west of the Transvaal in which the diamond-fields lay was an area of low rainfall and for this reason sparsely inhabited. The frontier and ownership of the territory had never been clearly defined, and it was only in 1868 that Pretorius laid claim to the area between the Harts and the Vaal. In June 1870, however, he made up for his negligence at a single stroke. At the end of a session of the Volksraad, he rushed through a Bill granting a diamond monopoly in the Klipdrift–Hebron area for 21 years to three of his friends, and, shortly afterwards, he appointed a magistrate, de Villiers, to take charge of his new possession.

Immediate protests followed, however, not only from his own burghers but also from the diamond prospectors, who not only ran de Villiers out of town but set up their own private "Republic" with

Stafford Parker as President. Parker was one of those characters that only a 19th-century diamond rush could have produced. Born at Maldon in Essex he had served in both the Royal Navy and the US Navy, and having landed at the South African naval station at Simonstown made his way inland to Colesberg where he joined the Cape Mounted Rifles. Moving onwards to the diamond-fields, he became adviser to Barend Bloems, Chief of the Korana Hottentots, whose headquarters were at Hebron. As Bloems' Field Cornet he was intermediary between the diggers and the Koranas. He was impressively tall and wiry with magnificent whiskers and affected a white top-hat, dark glasses and adopted a theatrical yet rough and ready style of oratory which appealed to the diggers. He eventually became a well-known and respected figure on the Rand.

Pretorius and Kruger had both visited the Klipdrifters and offered them self-government in an attempt to win them over. But, to use Kruger's words, "I was very uncivilly received by the English miners who had gathered there," and it was clear that the diggers preferred to deal with the local Bantu Chiefs who had lived in the territory a good deal longer – and were a softer touch – than the Boers.

Whitehall manifested its sympathy with the diggers' view, and in September sent Pretorius a warning not to interfere with tribes which, he claimed, were in alliance with Her Majesty (although the terms of the Sand River Convention would appear to have precluded any such thing). Two months later Hay, the Acting High Commissioner, sent his own magistrate, John Campbell, to Klipdrift to provide respectability for the Diggers' Republic and to maintain law and order there under the ancient Cape Punishment Act, which, it will be remembered, had once theoretically extended British jurisdiction up to the 25th parallel south of the Equator.

Pretorius, meantime, had been trying to come to an arrangement with those Chiefs whose claims conflicted with his own. He had first approached Nicolaas Waterboer, the Griqua Chief, and had parted from him in disagreement. Waterboer, acting on the advice of David Arnot, a solicitor from the Cape, then turned to the British and canvassed the possibilities of receiving the protection of Queen Victoria.

Having failed with Waterboer, Pretorius negotiated with the Chiefs of the Batlapin and Korana tribes, who were claiming only non-diamond-producing land to the west of the Harts river, and with Montsioa, the Barolong Chief, who maintained that the diamond-fields lying between the Harts and the Vaal were his by virtue of a treaty signed by Potgieter back in 1837. One day, after several other inconclusive meetings had taken place, Pretorius, while talking with the Revd J. Ludorf, a Wesleyan Minister and supporter of the Griquas, was shown what appeared to be a treaty, dated 1851, which recognised the independence of Montsioa only on the western (non-diamond) side of the Harts, and which therefore confirmed the Transvaal's possession of the diamond-fields east of the river.

Kruger, as one of the few survivors with first-hand knowledge of the wanderings of the voortrekkers in the western Transvaal, was asked for his opinion on the treaty. He doubted whether such an agreement had been made. There were no supporting documents for it and the events from 1851 onwards were inconsistent with its supposed provisions. But he was not prepared to issue a categorical denial.

Pretorius on the other hand was delighted. For this treaty seemed to demolish both Montsioa's case and that of Waterboer. In this mood of over-confidence, he persuaded the Transvaal Volksraad to authorise him to submit the question to an arbitration to be arranged by the British High Commissioner. General Hay did not himself appoint the arbitrators because his successor, Sir Henry Barkly, was expected to arrive at the Cape at any moment, and Barkly, a veteran with 22 years' colonial experience in British Guiana, Jamaica, Australia and Mauritius, suggested that Pretorius and the other claimants should submit their case to a team of three arbitrators, one chosen for the Transvaal, a second for the claimants, with a third to give the casting vote if the other two arbitrators disagreed. The claimants agreed to John Campbell, the magistrate who had been sent to Klipdrift to take over from "President" Parker, as one arbitrator, the Transvalers were satisfied with Landdrost Anthony O'Reilly from Wakkerstroom, and Barkly put forward Robert Keate, the Lieutenant-Governor of Natal, to give the casting vote, a choice which was warmly welcomed by Pretorius in as much as Keate had not long before decided a frontier dispute with the Free State in favour of the Transvaal.

Notwithstanding these favourable omens, Kruger was opposed to any arbitration affecting the internal affairs of the Transvaal – and, even if he had agreed to go to court, he would probably have handled matters a great deal better than Pretorius contrived to do.

At Bloemhof on the Vaal river, where the arbitration took place, Pretorius, accompanied by his State Attorney, Frederick Kleyn, pleaded the Transvaal case in person. But he not only neglected to produce written evidence from the Transvaal archives to support his arguments, he failed to detect that the document which he claimed to be the original 1851 Treaty was made out on paper the watermark of which was dated 17 years after it was supposed to have been signed.

Arnot, on the other hand, presented the case of the other claimants in a highly convincing manner.

The hearings lasted for two months, and at the end of them the two arbitrators, as might have been expected, disagreed. Keate was called on to exercise the casting vote. On the basis of the evidence produced he felt compelled to decide against Pretorius. In a judgement announced on 17 October 1871 he awarded the Klipdrift–Hebron area, that is the southern, diamond-producing area, to Waterboer, and also gave a large area further north to the Koranas and Batlapins.

Then things began to happen.

Waterboer, whose territory known as Griqualand West had now been considerably enlarged, renewed his request for British protection and only ten days later his possessions were annexed to the British Crown. Afterwards the eastern boundary of the newly acquired territory was "delineated" in such a way as to detach Kimberley from the Free State and include it as the capital of Griqualand West.

The Afrikaners today agree that the Keate arbitration was fair in view of the facts submitted to him, but, even if other evidence had been produced and had been taken into consideration, the loss of the diamond-fields could well have followed just the same.

Already, Hay, before he left the Cape, had suggested to Whitehall that, in view of the numbers of British subjects and the capital involved in the diamond-fields, they should be taken over by the Cape Government. In May 1871 Barkly made the same suggestion to Lord Kimberley, Secretary of State for the Colonies, who was gracious enough to agree, some months ahead of the arbitration decision, that annexation would be permissible provided that Waterboer and the diggers acquiesced. In July 1871 the Cape Parliament, which had not yet been granted responsible party government, agreed by a single vote to do its part. But the manner in which arbitration stripped the Transvaal not only of the diamond-fields but also of a large slice of territory further north, sickened the Afrikaners in the Cape to such an extent that after achieving self-government they refused to take over the new, grossly enlarged Griqualand West – and for some time afterwards it remained a separate British colony.

When the Volksraad met to discuss the award, State Secretary Proes and State Attorney Kleyn resigned at once and Pretorius followed soon after. The loss of the diamond-fields and a part of the western Transvaal exerted a powerful influence on Paul Kruger's future career. Politically, Kruger had watched the imperial steam-roller in action and had noted the fact that an undertaking such as the Sand River Convention did not halt its onward drive. The annexation had brought the British in Griqualand West up to the banks of the

Vaal river and had given them a common frontier with the Transvaal. Thus the British had caught up with the Great Trek. And incidentally they were now not so very far from Kruger's own home in Rustenburg. Moreover, they had denied the claim of the Transvaal to the territory to the west of the Harts river through which the great trade routes ran north to central Africa.

In practice, the Transvaal "acted independent" and disregarded that part of the Keate award which lay outside the diamond-fields. (Matthew Smith, a British magistrate sent to enforce the award, had his house burnt over his head.) Kruger was chosen to be a member of the Commission appointed by his government to discuss the consequences of the award. With his support the South African Republic repudiated the Keate award on the technical ground that Pretorius had acted beyond his authority. He had not been given written authorisation to submit anything except the diamond-fields to arbitration. As a result Pretorius was compelled to hand over his Seals of Office in November 1871.

But Kruger had not yet become the heir-apparent to Pretorius and, when they came to choose a new President, the Transvalers, who had just been worsted by a smart Cape lawyer, were dazzled into voting for an equally sophisticated man from the Cape, the Reverend Thomas François Burgers.

Burgers, nine years younger than Kruger, was the youngest son of the third marriage of Barend Burgers, a cattle-farmer of Graaff Reinet. At school, his intelligence attracted the interest of the Scottish teachers introduced by an earlier Governor, Lord Charles Somerset, and some of his compatriots believed that he had been in danger of being "verengels", that is turned into an Englishman. In the end, however, he went to the Dutch University of Utrecht to take his degree in theology. Even as an undergraduate he showed a marked individuality which made it difficult for him to avoid various forms of controversy in later life. It was not hard to find grounds for dispute within the bosom of the Dutch Reformed Church, whose Minister in Hanover (Cape Province) he became on his return to South Africa. The Cape Synod of the Church attacked him for allegedly refusing to admit that the devil had a tail, and passed a resolution dismissing him from his post.

Burgers took the case first to the Appeal Court at the Cape and later, on appeal, to the Privy Council. He won both actions. He also obtained an injunction forbidding members of the Presbytery of Graaff Reinet to interfere with his work among his flock.

Two special considerations induced the Afrikaners of the Transvaal (or some of them) to adopt him as their candidate for the new

Presidency. The first was that President Brand of the Free State, whom many would have preferred as President of the Transvaal, had refused the honour. The other was the arrival of Burgers himself in 1871 on a preaching tour of the Transvaal. His distinguished appearance, the luxuriant wavy auburn hair, the eyes of a visionary, the friendly manner and intelligence, together with his wit and eloquence, deeply impressed his audiences. His wife, née Mary Bryson, was of Scottish descent, so that he spoke both English and Dutch. In his address of acceptance Burgers offered his hearers the prospect of a new and better life – wider roads, more bridges, a sound currency, a seaport on the east coast, better administration, development of the mines and industry, and a place among the nations of the world.

Kruger did not hesitate to oppose this upstart Burgers and published a "Toelichting" or explanation, arguing that since so many Transvalers would have preferred President Brand to rule them the new election should be regarded as provisional until something more permanent could be arranged. Kruger even went beyond his rights by making use of his office as Commandant-General to write on official paper to the Field Cornets urging his views on them – for which, incidentally, he was strongly criticised by the *Transvaal Advocate and Commercial Advertiser* the only newspaper in the area.

When it appeared likely that the election would nevertheless be held and the result fully recognised, Kruger began to organise an opposition. His own chances of election were slim. Not only was he comparatively inexperienced, but his reputation as a leader had suffered because of his failure to protect Schoemansdal, and the best opposition candidate he could produce was his old friend and hunting companion, William Robinson.

Robinson had been born in Kent, England, and like his more famous brother Sir Joseph Robinson, the mining magnate, he tended to cultivate the friendship of the Boers. He had indeed once been a schoolmaster. But his main accomplishment, apart from elephant-hunting, was a series of trips into unknown parts of Africa during one of which he reached Lake Ngami, almost immediately after Livingstone.

Appealing though these qualifications might seem to a rural community, they were not powerful enough to attract the votes and, on polling day, Burgers was given 2,964 votes and Robinson 388. The result, according to Sir Henry Barkly, was influenced by the "discovery" that Robinson wore a wig and the Boers were so horrified at the idea that he carried "a dead man's hair on his head" that they refused to vote for him.

It was a crushing defeat for Kruger. But he was not entirely abashed. Even at the inauguration on 1 July 1872 he declared publicly the line that he proposed to take. Kruger writes in his memoirs:

After the President had taken the oath of office, I rose and addressed him in the following words:

"Your Honour, I have done my best to prevent your election. Principally, because of your religious views, which appear to me to be mistaken. But, as you have now been elected by the majority, I submit as a good republican to the vote of the people, trusting that you are a more earnest believer than I thought, in which case I will congratulate you with all my heart."

To this the President answered: "Burgher, who voted against me for conscience sake, you are as dear to me as those who voted for me."

Many burghers now came up to me to express their gratification at my outspokenness; many had thought that I would keep my own counsel.

Kruger's declaration could have been a piece of political tactics, but no doubt he felt strongly about the heresies and moral weakness which he feared might be introduced by the new President to the Transvaal's Garden of Eden.

The first weeks of Burgers' administration promised well. He succeeded in raising a loan of £66,000 from the Cape Commercial Bank, though at a fairly high rate of interest, to redeem the liability on the Transvaal banknotes, then worth only about a quarter of their nominal value. He persuaded the Volksraad to agree to a new red and blue flag based on an earlier design of Potgieter's, and a revised coat of arms. He encouraged the Australian, Scottish and other prospectors who had rushed to the newly discovered alluvial gold deposits at Lydenburg; he appointed a Gold Commissioner – a status symbol for diggers – and gave them two seats in the Volksraad, one of which went to Herbert Rhodes, brother of the great Cecil. He had sovereigns struck with his own image and title engraved on them. All these innovations – especially the making of the graven image – displeased the more conservative Transvalers. And Kruger was particularly critical of Burgers' new education plan which did not sufficiently provide for religious teaching in schools.

Within a year there was an open clash. Burgers, with the idea of improving the administration of law and order, appointed a Cape advocate, James Buchanan, as State Attorney. Buchanan, an authority on Roman–Dutch law, was an extremely able barrister who was to rise in later years to be a judge in the Orange Free State and Judge-President of Griqualand West. Burgers, in order to induce him to come to the outback (and to provide him with the necessary authority for his position) had felt it necessary to promise him a seat on the Executive Council or Cabinet of the South African Republic. Unfortunately, under the Constitution of the Republic the number of seats was limited to five, and there was no vacancy. Hints were dropped that Kruger might like to make life easier for the President by giving up his seat to Buchanan, but Kruger remained unresponsive until March 1873 when he retired to the country "at his own request". Burgers, eager to rid himself of a trouble-maker, abolished the office of Commandant-General in peace-time.

It was enough to make any good Afrikaner believe that Burgers was thinking of handing the Transvaal over to the British (for how could a Republic defend itself without a Commandant-General?). In May 1875 Kruger seriously considered trekking with 300 other farmers and their dependants including, incidentally, his aged step-mother, who were off to make a new life for themselves in south-west Africa. But he was already 49, and suffering intermittently from malaria and enteric, and he had much more to lose now than in the days when he and his father crossed the Orange river more than 30 years back. So he decided that independence began at home, and built himself a new house at Boekenhoutfontein, near Rustenburg. He may perhaps also have been aware that Burgers had fallen ill through overwork. He had to retire for several months from public life, and at one time his life was despaired of.

When Burgers recovered, however, he was more active than ever. He aimed at providing the Transvaal with its own railway to the sea so that it should no longer have to depend on Cape Colony for its supplies. Burgers estimated, apparently off the cuff, that the work would cost £300,000, and he hoped to borrow the money from the Portuguese on the security of 500 State Farms each of about 6,000 acres. He would go to Europe, he would visit Belgium, Germany and Holland as well as Portugal. He would show bankers Transvaal gold, cobalt, coal and other minerals which would not only pay for the rails but provide the traffic after they had been laid. The Volks-raad reluctantly gave Burgers leave to visit Europe and, seeing that the office of Commandant-General had been abolished, Piet Joubert, the Volksraad President, was appointed to serve in Burgers' stead.

In Cape Town, Burgers engaged a surveyor, R. T. Hall, to plot the line that he was already pledged to build, and, in April 1875 the President was already at sea, writing back in a letter to Joubert of the days to come when the South African Republic would possess its own fleet of merchant ships under its own flag.

The European visit, although extended to include Switzerland and

Italy, failed to live up to the high hopes which Burgers had entertained. Less than one-third of the money that he had hoped to raise was forthcoming – and even this was loaned by the Dutch at a high rate of interest. In consequence most of the rails never got further than the quayside at Flushing where they gradually rusted away.

No doubt the British, fearing that the new Transvaal railway would rival the Cape line and encourage a spirit of independence in the Transvaal, did their best to discourage bankers who might otherwise have felt inclined to invest money in the Transvaal; but the short answer was that neither the resources nor the inclinations of the Transvalers warranted an enterprise on the scale which Burgers proposed.

The situation which the President found on his return to the Transvaal was even less promising. While he was still in Europe he heard that the Volksraad had demoted his new flag to the status of a Presidential emblem that would be flown alongside the National colours only when he was present in person. Such inconstancy was, as Burgers pointed out to Joubert, damaging to the credibility of the Transvaal Government and insulting to himself. Shortly before his departure the Dopper faction of the Volksraad had passed a resolution ousting Buchanan from the Executive Council on the grounds that he was a salaried official and not a burgher with voting rights and had substituted Paul Kruger in his place. And Kruger was now asking more and more awkward questions about the Hollanders which Burgers had brought back with him from the Netherlands in the hope of raising the standard of education. Kruger insisted, for example, that W. J. van Gorkom, who had been selected as Superintendent of Education, should make a declaration that he was a member of a Christian Protestant Church, and closely cross-questioned one of the other appointees, Dr E. J. P. Jorissen, on his religious beliefs.

The railway tax which Burgers had imposed to help pay the construction costs was not producing even sufficient to pay the first half-year's interest on the Dutch loan, still less the costs of construction, and a rival railway had begun to advance towards the Transvaal from Natal. In any case some of the burghers doubted whether they needed a railway. It might, they said, be displeasing in the sight of the Almighty and could even precipitate the last trump. The transport drivers, who would lose their jobs to the steam horse, agreed. The Government's credit fell disastrously again.

Then came another set-back: the campaign against the Bapedi Chief Sekukuni who had refused to pay hut tax or to allow prospectors to survey his country. At least one Government tenant in that farm area had had cattle seized. Kruger, as a member of the Executive Council, voted that an expedition be sent to subdue him.

Burgers, possibly to maintain prestige, decided to accompany the expedition himself, and Kruger was equally determined not to lead the commando unless he were to be in full charge of it.

"Burgers asked the reason for my refusal," Kruger said in his memoirs, "and I replied, 'I cannot lead the commando if you come; for, with your merry evenings in laager and your Sunday dances, the enemy will shoot me even through the wall; for God's blessing will not rest on our expedition.' Burgers answered that it was in my power as Commandant-General to forbid anything that I did not approve of. But I said, 'Do you think that the burghers would listen to anything I might say, once you, as President, have set them the example?' "

He might also have appreciated better than Burgers how low the morale of the Boers had sunk.

"Then he asked me," Kruger continued, "whom I advised him to take with him as fighting general. I recommended Nicholas Smit [afterwards Vice-President of the South African Republic] and ex-President Pretorius. Burgers accepted my recommendations and marched with a fairly strong force against Sekukuni. Before coming to close quarters with him, they attacked one of his subordinates called Magali, who lived in a very ugly rock fastness. The commando succeeded in driving the Kaffirs out of their caves and gorges, whereupon Burgers flew into such an ecstasy that he exclaimed: 'Now Gibraltar is mine!' "

Kruger's refusal to co-operate with Burgers was perhaps not unreasonable since Burgers had abolished the office of Commandant-General in peace-time, and one might also suppose – although Burgers may not have danced on Sunday – that his presence in the field might have had an adverse effect on discipline.

But Kruger's personal aversion to the President must have been considerably increased by Burgers' boast, for only an ungodly man would attribute the capture of "Gibraltar" to his own right hand rather than to the Almighty, as most Boers would have done.

Kruger was not surprised, nor, one must suppose, too upset, when the main attack on the Bapedi, mounted shortly afterwards, was less successful. The country was dangerous enough for in the warmer months it was fever country and there was "horse sickness"; and when a key position captured with great difficulty had to be given up for lack of reinforcements, the Boers and the Swazis who had been helping them cried "Enough". Despite all Burgers' eloquence they turned for home. Only a few volunteers under a German officer and an Irish commandant, on the promise of payment in looted cattle and farms, stayed to hold off the enraged Bapedi, who eventually seemed ready for peace. Burgers then had forts constructed as a permanent protection for the farmers.

But then all this had to be paid for, and the President levied a special tax of £5 on every burgher. There was no other way to raise the money. But most of the burghers refused to pay.

The Cape Commercial Bank now began to press for the repayment of its loan; the Post-Master-General had to accept his salary in stamps, the Surveyor-General in land, and the Transvaal's next-door neighbours had to pay the Transvaal mail contractor to deliver their letters to Pretoria.

The way was clear for the British to mount a take-over bid for Kruger's own country, the Transvaal.

Chapter 4

With Shepstone to Pretoria

Henry Howard Molyneux Herbert, fourth Earl of Carnarvon, was indeed a catch for any latter-day designing young woman from the pages of Jane Austen. Tutored at Eton and Christ Church College, Oxford, he succeeded to the title at the age of 18, and to a position which might have turned the head of many a young sprig. Henry, however, was of a studious nature. He left Oxford with a first class honours degree in Classics, and thereafter took a special interest in the affairs of the British Empire. He entered the House of Lords as a Conservative. As Colonial Secretary to Lord Derby, he helped to pilot the British North America Act, which fused the four principal Canadian self-governing colonies into one Dominion of Canada, through the British Parliament.

Carnarvon, together with Lord Cranborne, who as Marquis of Salisbury was later to become Prime Minister, resigned from the Government in opposition to the Reform Bill of 1867 – to the great annoyance of Queen Victoria, who believed that a French Revolution might be visited on her country if the Bill failed to pass.

On Disraeli's return to power in 1874 Carnarvon, known to his colleagues as "Twitters" because of his nervous style of address, was re-appointed to his post as Colonial Secretary, and it was not, perhaps, surprising that he considered repeating in South Africa the success that he had enjoyed in Canada with his scheme for a confederation.

The idea was not altogether new. In 1858 Sir George Grey, undoubtedly one of the most able High Commissioners that Britain had ever sent to the Cape, had proposed such a scheme to an earlier Colonial Secretary, the poet, novelist and statesman Edward Bulwer, Lord Lytton. Grey believed that it was absurd to separate the Cape Colonists from the republicans north of the Orange river, and because of the controversies which afterwards ensued it is worth quoting his views on the two groups at some length.

"They have," he wrote, "the same sympathies, the same prejudices, the same habits, and frequently the same feelings regarding the native races, although marked and rapid changes in public opinion, in relation to this subject, are taking place, as also in reference to the increasing use of English language and the adoption of English customs."

Grey pointed out that, at the moment, the only bond of union between the various states, both native and European, was the High Commissioner himself. There was nothing to prevent any one of them from declaring war against the tribes, thus prejudicing the position of the others: "For if a state is successful in the war it is waging, a native race will be broken up, and none can tell what territories its dispersed hordes may fall upon. Nor can the other states be assured that the coloured tribes generally will not sympathise in the war, and that a general rising may not take place."

Large areas of South Africa had, in consequence, remained in a constant state of anxiety and apprehension about the future, Grey said, and the small size and weakness of the states, and the knowledge that they stood alone, had encouraged the natives to resist them and, in the absence of guarantees by Britain, to combine with one another "and thus to acquire a sense of strength and boldness such as they had not hitherto shown."

Grey added that small ("white") states of the kind which existed in South Africa were bound to be subject to intrigue, internal unrest, revolution and wars with one another:

The affairs which occupy their legislatures are so small that they can raise no class of statesmen to take enlarged and liberal views. They cannot adequately provide for the education or religious instruction of their people. They can possess no able Bar, no learned Judges, can have no efficient administration of justice. Trade and commerce must therefore necessarily languish. Their revenues will be so small that they cannot efficiently provide for their protection. Hence a new incentive is given to the surrounding native races to attack them.

His conclusion was that South Africa appeared to be drifting, by not very slow degrees, into disorder and barbarism.

But Lord Lytton was not, apparently, inclined to address himself to this particular problem. What he had envisaged was a report from Grey describing the methods by which the three British colonies of the Cape, Natal, and Griqualand West, could be merged so that they would need only one force for their defence; a transformation which would enable Whitehall to save money and devote more troops to India, which only two years before had endured its most sensational mutiny.

Grey was recalled from his post, an action which, despite his popularity, met with the approval of the Afrikaners who saw his proposals in a very different light. In their eyes the British wished to link up two South African republics which had won their freedom with some British colonies which had failed to do so. And the Union Jack would be flying over the lot. It was to avoid this very situation that the Afrikaners had undertaken the Great Trek.

These misgivings, however, found no echo in the mind of Carnarvon, who was described by one of his contemporaries as "crochety, nervous of being found fault with, and obstinate to a degree when he has once got an idea into his mind."

He did, however, realise from the beginning that the ground must first be well prepared. For example, if future wars were to be avoided there must be only one uniform policy towards the natives throughout the territories of the proposed confederation, and he therefore decided that closer control must be exercised over native affairs in Natal where the large numbers of Bantu made the situation precarious.

Sir Garnet Wolseley, the immaculate military man with his twirled moustache and discreet goatee beard, had already distinguished himself on military service in Burma, the Crimea, as well as in the Indian Mutiny, and in April 1875 he was sent to Natal as "Administrator", an appointment which proved highly popular both with the Natal sugar planters and with their wives and daughters. Wolseley and his staff entertained lavishly, and Sir Garnet dropped hints that, with his support, the colony would be granted loans to encourage immigration and would be allotted a larger garrison for its protection. Fortified by liberal potions of sherry and champagne, the Colony's Legislative Council which, until then, had included 15 elected members and five officials, was persuaded to vote away its own freedom by agreeing to receive eight government officials and five tame nominees among its number.

So the reforms which Sir Garnet considered necessary were duly passed, and Natal rested safely in the British Government's pocket.

As for the Cape, those living in the west and the middle parts of Cape Colony welcomed the idea of confederation, because closer linkage between Cape and the republics in the north would mean more traffic for the Cape railways. The colonists living in the eastern areas of the colony were also favourable to confederation which offered them their best chance of breaking away from the domination of Cape politicians.

Others nearer to Cape Town were less enthusiastic. For three years now they had enjoyed the luxury of "responsible government" with a Prime Minister of their own, and they were proud of the fact.

Confederation would mean surrendering this special privilege, and with it the superiority they already possessed.

Also, confederation might involve the Cape in heavy expenditure on the frontier wars of the north and – despite Wolseley's reforms – in the risk of a Zulu war in Natal.

As for the two republics in the north, the Free State was still smarting from the injustice of the diamond-fields' award but Carnarvon hoped that President Brand could be mollified by compensation for the loss of the diamond-fields (although only £90,000 finally changed hands).

And the Transvaal might be placated with the assurance that in a federation their frontiers would be protected by the resources of a much larger community, and which would share with them the customs revenue levied at Durban and Cape Town.

Furthermore, although the Cape, with which the Republics were being asked to join up, was only a colony, it had greater influence with London, and possessed the best port in southern Africa.

These, then, were the circumstances in which Carnarvon proposed in May 1875 to the High Commissioner at the Cape, Sir Henry Barkly, that a round-table conference should be held to discuss a comprehensive native policy, as well as measures to prevent the tribes from receiving arms, and if in this connection the question of confederation were to arise, Britain would be delighted to discuss it.

Carnarvon suggested that James Anthony Froude, the historian and supporter of confederation, a personal friend who had recently visited South Africa, should represent Britain at the conference, that Sir John Molteno, the Cape Colony Prime Minister, should speak for the western province of Cape Colony, and Mr John Paterson for the eastern province.

But Carnarvon's proposal, put in this form, at once raised fears in the minds of the Cape politicians that their colony was about to be split into two provinces, and Molteno persuaded the Cape Lower House to pass a motion declaring that the time was not ripe for such a conference. John Gordon Sprigg, Leader of the Opposition, supported him by arguing that confederation must be a voluntary movement from within South Africa and must not be imposed from without.

Froude, who was still in South Africa at the time, was not, however, dismayed. Wolseley had by now completed his reforms in Natal. The colony of Griqualand West was in favour of the conference, and Piet Joubert, Acting President of the South African Republic in Burgers' absence in Europe, was prepared to recommend to his Executive Council that the South African Republic should take part provided that its special interests were safeguarded. Clearly nothing could be done as long as Molteno was in office, and Froude set to work to make as much trouble as possible for him in the eastern province of Cape Colony, which, as we have seen, was in favour of breaking away on its own, confederation or no confederation.

In this he was successful to the extent that the Cape Upper House ultimately voted in favour of a conference and the Lower House disowned Molteno's condemnation of Froude's campaign. Molteno, however, might still have won a general election if one had been held.

In the Transvaal moreover, the tide, in spite of Joubert's co-operative attitude, was running against confederation and towards separatism. The South African Republic had begun to expand again under its own self-generated pressure. It was claiming parts of Zululand, and had signed a treaty turning the kingdom of Swaziland into a kind of Transvaal dependency.

And then, in 1875, the MacMahon Award settling a dispute between Britain and Portugal was announced. It confirmed that the Portuguese were entitled to hold both Delagoa Bay and the port of Lourenço Marques. The Transvalers thereupon quickly perceived that if a railway could be built from their territory across Mozambique to Lourenço Marques, the Transvaal need no longer be permanently dependent on a British-owned port for vital supplies. In fact the Transvaal could have a future of its own without joining a con-federation.

At this point Carnarvon intervened, and suggested that, since the issues that he had wished to raise at his proposed conference had now been fully aired in public, the time had come for further discussions in London.

The London Conference was duly held in August 1876, but with deeply disappointing results. Carnarvon himself was in the chair with Wolseley as Vice-Chairman; Natal sent two elected members – and Froude represented Griqualand West. But President Brand of the Orange Free State had been empowered by his Executive Council to talk only on subjects not connected with confederation, for traffic to and from the diamond-fields was bringing prosperity to the Free State too – making confederation less attractive than before – and Molteno, although he was already in London, refused to take part.

Burgers, irked by Britain's opposition to his railway loan plans and with the enthusiastic support of his Executive Council, sent no one.

Once more, however, Carnarvon remained undaunted. He pre-pared what was called a Permissive Federation Bill which would allow colonies and republics in South Africa to federate if they wished.

But later another, more practical, scheme occurred to him. This was simply to annex the South African Republic. At a single stroke this would ensure the Transvaal's acceptance of confederation, and put pressure on the Free State, which would then be completely isolated, to do the same. Furthermore, Carnarvon could claim that annexation was needed if war between the Boers and the Zulus was to be avoided. And any such war would be a disaster. If the Boers won, then, as Grey had predicted, more Zulus would flee for refuge into Natal; and if the Boers lost, other native tribes might feel encouraged to rise.

The man chosen by Carnarvon to carry out this remarkable enterprise was Sir Theophilus Shepstone, the Agent for Native Affairs in the Colony of Natal, who had been called back to London for the Confederation Conference.

Sir Theophilus was undoubtedly one of the most remarkable of Queen Victoria's empire-builders. Sir Bartle Frere described him as an Afrikander Talleyrand. To one of his political opponents he was "a crafty-looking, silent man who never used an unnecessary word or gesture".

On Sir John, later Chief Justice, Kotze, who saw him towards the end of April 1877, Shepstone made a more favourable impact:

> As he rose from his chair he turned towards me, and with a pleasant shake of the hand asked me to be seated. My first impression of him was of a clean-shaven man about 5 ft 9 inches who had turned 60. His face indicated strength and kindness, with quick and observant eye, well-shaped head, easy manner and pleasant address. In time I discerned that he was all this and much more . . . I was rather struck by the apparent frankness with which he spoke.

He was indeed already 60 at the time he comes into our story. His parents, who were missionaries, came to South Africa with the British settlers of 1820 under a scheme sponsored by the Government to combat the hardships which followed the Napoleonic wars. Shepstone was three years old when his parents landed. He soon proved to be a brilliant linguist with a special interest in native affairs and a flare for dealing with the Chiefs. At 18 he was an interpreter between the two sides in the war against the Xhosas. At 22 he was British Resident in Kaffraria, the area on the coast round East London which afterwards became a part of Cape Colony.

In 1845 tribes in the Algoa Bay region killed a missionary whom they had mistaken for Shepstone. By 1846 he had risen to be a Diplomatic Agent to Natal and a member of the Land Commission which was given the task of separating the ever-increasing number of Bantu in Natal from the white farmers. For this purpose eight reserves totalling more than 1,000,000 acres were set up and Shepstone succeeded in inducing some 80,000 Bantu to enter them. After a struggle with the authorities he got permission for justice in the reserves to be administered by the Chiefs under Bantu law, with appeal to European native magistrates and ultimately to Shepstone himself.

Of course he could speak Zulu fluently and had earned the respect of these formidable warriors; and, when their King Panda died in 1873, it was Shepstone who at the request of the Zulu Chiefs had crowned his successor Cetewayo.

Dealing with the natives had taught Shepstone how to keep his own counsel and to conceal his true motives behind a bland and impenetrable mask.

Carnarvon's plans were revealed to Shepstone at the Colonial Office on 31 July 1876, and shortly afterwards he learnt that in view of his services in the past and to come, Her Majesty Queen Victoria would be pleased to confer on him the honour of a Knighthood.

Two weeks later Carnarvon had obtained the approval of the Cabinet for his project to annex the Transvaal, and revealed them in a letter to the Queen:

If only the war [between the Boers and Sekukuni] can now be brought to an end, there is, Lord Carnarvon hopes [it was the custom to write to the monarch in the third person] a very reasonable prospect of bringing back the Transvaal under your Majesty's rule [it had never been under it] and of carrying out the policy for which he has laboured during the last two years. For when only [he meant "if only"] the Transvaal Republic becomes British, the Orange Free State cannot maintain its independence.

A week later, presumably after the Queen's approval had been secured, Shepstone sailed for the Cape. The Royal Commission was signed at Balmoral and forwarded to him on 5 October. He was appointed a Special Commissioner for Her Majesty and was given wide powers of discretion to act if he was forced to do so even without consulting Sir Henry Barkly, the High Commissioner at the Cape, whose task was to exercise a general supervision over events throughout southern Africa. Queen Victoria wrote:

If the emergency should seem to you to be such as to render it necessary, in order to secure the peace and safety of our said colonies and of our subjects elsewhere, that the said territories or any portion or portions of the same, should provisionally be administered in our name and on our behalf, then in such case only we do further authorise you by proclamation to annex such territories aforesaid, as to you shall seem fit after due consideration; provided that no such proclamation shall be issued unless you shall be satisfied that the inhabitants of such territory or portion thereof, or a sufficient number of them, or the legislature thereof, desire to become our subjects.

These instructions were, however, considerably watered down by orders which Carnarvon in a "Twitters" mood gave personally to Shepstone. In these Carnarvon made it clear that no proclamation was to be issued until it had been approved by Sir Henry Barkly in his three-fold capacity as Governor and Commander-in-Chief of Cape Colony and as High Commissioner, and on 4 October Carnarvon added a further warning following a talk which he had had with Molteno:

If they [the Dutch population] think they have it in their power to say that they have been coerced into Union, much of the good of the annexation will be lost; for they will remain a discontented element in the body politic, allying themselves with everything that is factious troublesome and anti-English.

In the same note Carnarvon stressed the importance of getting the consent of the Volksraad unless the circumstances were "so grave as to justify us on the ground of unquestionable general safety. I hope that you may secure this even if on your arrival you find that the vote is not what is desired."

But in the event Carnarvon's warnings had to be disregarded. The mailboat on which Shepstone was travelling was wrecked on Dassen Island near Cape Town, and Sir Henry Barkly, with whom he was supposed to co-operate, had left before he landed; moreover, the departure of the troops which it had been thought necessary to send in support of the operation had been delayed.

Nevertheless Shepstone accomplished his mission. The annexation was carried out without a shot being fired, before even the new High Commissioner, Sir Bartle Frere, who had arrived at his post on 31 March, knew anything about it.

Put like this, the whole performance takes one's breath away. Yet Carnarvon had received considerable encouragement before he took action. In 1875 Colonel Colley who, as General Sir George Colley was later to fight at Majuba, had been sent to the Transvaal in the guise of a tourist; he reported that many of the Boers, as well as the

English-speaking population, favoured a "take-over". There had also been reports from Sir Henry Barkly of the Transvaal's economic bankruptcy and political instability.

In August 1876, after Burgers' unsuccessful campaign, Sir Henry, shortly before leaving for home, had sent a hair-raising message to Carnarvon: "Army of the President totally routed," it said. "Deserters pouring into Pretoria. Sekukuni pursuing in force. Meeting at Landdrost office in Lydenburg agreed to ask the British Government to take over Transvaal."

Burgers, during his trip to Europe, had called on Carnarvon and had seemed favourably disposed towards the idea of confederation.

A more coherent justification for the British action was presented in a British Cabinet Paper in May 1880, even though it had, by then, become apparent that there might not, after all, be a sufficient number of the inhabitants in the area who desired to become the subjects of the Queen.

"The operations against Sekukuni, which were on a large scale, looking to the resources of the country, and were directed in person by the President, ended in disaster," the Paper announced. "The Republican field army melted away, a guerrilla war being continued, however, by a small mercenary force until a peace was concluded early in 1877.

"In the meantime the defeat of the Boers by an insignificant tribe of an unwarlike branch of the native race, and their inability to repair the disaster, were producing an amount of excitement in the native mind, which seemed to many and to Her Majesty's Government to imperil seriously the peace of South Africa . . ."

Shepstone, the Paper said, had been sent as Special Commissioner from Her Majesty "to watch events, and take such action as might be necessary to secure British interests and the interests of civilisation generally".

It was true, the Paper added, that the situation had changed somewhat by the time that he arrived in the Transvaal territory in January 1877, but:

> . . . still it was, to his mind, a very alarming situation, and it may be briefly described as follows: The peace with Sekukuni was but a hollow one, as the Chief declared that he had never assented to and knew nothing of its principal article, viz., that he should be subject to the Republic. The attitude of the Zulu king on the east was such that his irruption into the Republic with an overwhelming force might at any moment be expected. The Government had become paralysed beyond hope of recovery. The finances, which had never

flourished, had wholly gone to ruin under the strain of war expenditure and a foreign loan. The public servants were unpaid. The Treasury was empty. The public debt had risen to £295,071, an amount utterly beyond the power of the Government to pay or provide for. The people would no longer pay taxes, and the banks to which the Republic was heavily in debt, refused further advances. The coercive authority of the Government over its own subjects had ceased, and its defensive power against the enemies whom it had provoked was nil. In these circumstances – the Republican Government having in effect ceased to exist and being incapable of revival – Sir T. Shepstone conceived that no other course was open to him than to proclaim the Queen's sovereignty and set up a Government. This he did on 12 April by a proclamation which was approved in Her Majesty's name by a Despatch from Lord Carnarvon on 21 June 1877.

Shepstone's method of approach is however described in greater detail in his own letter to President Burgers in which he announced his intention of visiting the Transvaal.

On 20 December 1876 he wrote to Burgers from Pietermaritzburg that:

> . . . in consequence of the reports which reached England during my recent visit there, of the disturbed condition of affairs in South-Eastern Africa, Her Majesty's Government, having regard to the situation of the British colonies in South Africa, and the danger to which British interests were exposed by what was passing, thought fit to direct me to return to South Africa and to make special enquiry into the origin, nature, and circumstances of the disturbances, to the securing, if possible, the adjustment of existing disputes and difficulties, a settlement of the questions out of which they have arisen, and the adoption of such measures as may appear calculated to prevent their recurrence in the future. In accordance with the instructions I have received, I propose to leave Natal about 3 January next, for Pretoria for the purpose of conferring, on the part of Her Majesty's Government with your Honour and the Government of the South African Republic.

Shepstone said that he would be bringing a staff of six or seven and an escort of 25 men of the Natal Mounted Police as his personal escort.

As can be imagined, the letter caused a sensation in Pretoria where Kruger, predictably, declared that Shepstone's mission constituted interference in the internal affairs of the Transvaal and that Burgers should have forbidden it. It was certainly contrary to the provisions of the Sand River Convention in which Britain had undertaken not to interfere with the emigrant Boer farmers north of the Vaal.

Nevertheless Shepstone, who had spent the intervening weeks in priming the Zulus, set off from Natal a few days later without, of course, waiting for a reply from Burgers and, on 20 January, when he was but two days away from the Transvaal capital, Burgers held a conference of his Executive Council in his own house to decide how best to treat his unwelcome visitor.

Paul Kruger was present at this meeting as well as N. Swart, the State Secretary, and Eduard Jorissen, one of Burgers' Hollanders who had become State Attorney. The meeting decided that Shepstone as the Queen's representative should be received in a correct manner. (Kruger went so far as to recommend that as a precaution Shepstone should be escorted by a Transvaal commando wherever he went.)

So on 22 January Burgers sent the Presidential carriage, drawn by four greys, to meet Shepstone on the outskirts of Pretoria and carry him into the city. State Secretary Swart went one better. He travelled out to Erasmus' farm beyond the city boundaries and buttonholed Shepstone before the great man climbed into the Presidential conveyance. Swart later became Acting State Secretary and soon afterwards Shepstone gave him the post of Treasurer-General. Rightly or wrongly many people connected the two occurrences.

Shepstone himself was delighted with his reception and wrote in his diary:

Entered Pretoria. Met a large number of the inhabitants a few miles from the town. President had sent out his state carriage with the State Secretary, Mr Swart. Mr Lys welcomed me on behalf of the inhabitants – three cheers were called for and heartily given. On reaching the town, the horses were taken out of the carriage, and we were drawn in triumph by the working men. On alighting from the carriage, Mr Lys read an address of welcome to which I read a reply, whereupon he struck up, singing "God Save the Queen" in which the crowd heartily joined; the words "Send her victorious, long to reign over us" were sung with much emphasis and sounded strange in this yet strange land.

(So strange indeed that the Lys family were later subjected to some hard words from the good burghers of the town.)

The next day, 23 January, Burgers gave a public lunch for Shepstone and the Belgian Consul, Baron de Selys de Fauson, also newly arrived, as if to show that the Republic was used to receiving accredited diplomats and knew how to treat them.

The following day Burgers and Kruger called on Shepstone in the hope of discovering exactly what had brought him to their capital.

It was an uneasy partnership, since Burgers' official five-year term as President was drawing to an end, and the two men were running against each other for office. Kruger had been somewhat embarrassed in his campaign when it appeared that some voters in the Transvaal were considering supporting another candidate to oppose Burgers, namely F. W. Reitz, Chief Justice of the Orange Free State who afterwards became its President. Reitz was not only a distinguished lawyer, but also could write poems in Afrikaans, and the thought of running against such a candidate evidently upset Kruger.

In a letter to Joubert he wrote:

You are aware that I opposed the President's [i.e., Burger's] election, and you know the reasons for it. I feared his liberalism, which might cause the fall of Christianity. In particular I feared that the Education Act was a State measure which would deprive the Church of the children, and give them a secular education. During the last session, however, a motion by the President was adopted whereby the children were returned to the care of the Church. The cloud has thus lifted . . .

In the political field I have but one ideal – freedom. In this respect he [President Burgers] is equally determined. Hence I vote for him in the new election. [It was not unusual on such occasions for two opposing candidates to vote for each other.] Burgers is a liberal, a Freemason; Mr Reitz likewise. Mr Burgers champions our liberty. I doubt that of Mr Reitz. Mr Burgers wanted to fly. His wings are clipped [in Europe and in the Sekukuni campaign]. Now he will crawl with us. Mr Reitz in contrast still has all his wings. I fear that we will not be able to withstand another calamity...

Kruger concluded:

Dear Brother, ere I vote for someone outside the Republic or agree to federation, I would rather vote ten times for Burgers, for once my freedom is lost, the freedom of posterity is lost. One can always rid oneself of a President if he is no good. Brother, remind the people they should not vote for someone outside the Republic...

Kruger, in his own view at any rate, thus had the best of motives for his actions.

Burgers was indeed a less formidable opponent, and the campaign manifesto issued on Kruger's behalf accused him of being responsible for the near bankruptcy of the Republic (although Kruger had done his bit towards this by refusing to pay the war tax through which

Burgers had endeavoured to balance the Republic's finances). It also blamed him for defeat in the field although this was due in part to Kruger's absence from the field. The manifesto continued:

> How then is this retrogression to be explained? The word of God gives us the key to it. Look to the case of Israel; if the people have a devout King, everything is prosperous; but under an ungodly ruler the land goes backward and all the people must suffer thereby. Read Leviticus 26 with attention and see how literally its words have been fulfilled. In the days of the voortrekkers, a handful of people put thousands of Kaffirs to flight; so also in the war in the Free State. But see how when Burgers is President – he knows no Sabbath; he rides through every part of the country on Sundays; of Church and religion he knows nothing (Leviticus 26. 17).

Now we have the origin of the disease. What is the remedy? It was, of course, not to elect Burgers to a second term.

It did occur to some, and perhaps even to Kruger himself, that to oppose his own President at such a time of crisis might be playing into the hands of the enemy. But Kruger took precautions to protect himself from an accusation of this kind. He said in his memoirs:

> The President's term of office had at this time expired [meaning that it had been about to expire] and a new election had become necessary. I was asked by a great number of burghers to present myself as a candidate, and, although I at first refused, I at last accepted, in order to put a stop to the dissatisfaction which the burghers had shown at my refusal to stand. But I made this condition with the election committee, that, if Burgers obtained a majority, they must rest content and obey him, so as not, through open discords to give England an excuse for carrying out her plans of annexation. Already in the first week in which the votes of the several parties [not the official election] were recorded, it became evident that I should have a large majority. I went to President Burgers and said to him: "President, I promise to bring over the majority of burghers to your side, if you will promise me to take strong measures against the annexation and to defend our independence. If this is your intention, you must make it plain, so that I can emphatically assure the burghers that the independence of our country will be powerfully guarded. Otherwise, my arguments will, of course, make no impression. There is my hand on it, that I shall do what I have offered to do."

Both the straw vote and Kruger's manoeuvre took place, it is true, before Shepstone's arrival, but it could hardly have escaped the notice of the British that in view of Kruger's refusal to take part in the campaign against Sekukuni that there were already substantial discords in the ranks of the Afrikaners.

The stage was now set.

Chapter 5

Kruger Rediscovered

On 26 January 1877 Shepstone appeared before the Executive Council, which was, as we have seen, the Transvaal Government's Cabinet. According to Dr Jorissen who was present as State Attorney Shepstone presented his credentials and proclaimed that his instructions from Carnarvon, conceived in the most friendly spirit, were to go to Pretoria to support the Republic by word and deed. There was nothing about annexation in what he said, nor could anyone have inferred it from his manner, Jorissen declared.

Shepstone's report of the meeting took a different line. He reported that after stating the object of his mission "in general terms" he pointed out that in 1852 Her Majesty's Government had gladly granted "the request of her subjects then residing north of the Vaal river to be allowed to rule themselves", and that no interference with this had been desired so long as they appeared to be successful in their government. Lately, however, the weakness of the Republic has become a source of danger to itself and its neighbours. He, Shepstone, wished to confer with the Government and people of the Transvaal "with the object of initiating a new state of things which would guarantee security for the future".

It was agreed that both sides should nominate representatives to discuss the situation. Jorissen and Kruger were deputed to speak for the South African Republic, and Shepstone's secretary, Melmoth Osborn, and his son-in-law, John Henderson, would represent Britain.

"We met two or three times," Jorissen recalled, "but no real negotiations resulted." The British, he said, raised a number of questions about the Kaffirs, the difficulties of foreigners, etc., but when they began to meddle in our affairs we told them clearly that we were not inclined to answer any further inquiries. Kruger described the meetings in stronger terms. He said that the overwhelming majority of the voters had sent in memorials against confederation, and "I myself made a violent speech against any such plan, in which I said that this confederation would mean the absolute loss of our independence".

When it became clear that no progress was being made, Shepstone persuaded Burgers to send two envoys to Sekukuni on a fact-finding mission.

This in Kruger's opinion was a blunder of the first magnitude. He wrote:

As already mentioned, President Burgers had left several strong volunteer corps behind when the burgher commandos retired, and these had harassed Sekukuni so closely that he was now suing for peace. Some excesses committed by German and Irish mercenaries had already been reported to Queen Victoria, who expressed concern about them. But this did not suit Shepstone's plans, for if peace were concluded the principal argument in favour of the annexation of the Republic to the British Crown fell through. There would then be an end to his talk about the general incapacity of the Republic to master the Kaffirs or, as he phrased it, her "inherent" weakness. It was against my will that Burgers now agreed to his proposal to send two envoys to Sekukuni in order to investigate matters on the spot. This "duumvirate" Commission, which consisted of Englishmen, of course brought back the desired answer, namely, that Sekukuni had no "idea of making peace".

Shepstone was therefore on firm ground when he urged on Burgers that it would be desirable to call a special session of the Volksraad to consider the whole position of the Government on the native policy and to discuss the reforms which were clearly needed in the administration of the country's budget and its economy.

"I have today had a long personal interview with the President," Shepstone wrote on 31 January. "He is in a great dilemma, appears nervous and timid; he sees and acknowledges the condition of the country, but does not yet see his way to act in the direction of my mission, except that he has called a special session of the Volksraad to lay the state of the country before it." He might nevertheless have been warned by the arrival in Pretoria early in February of a commando of 400, who staged a demonstration by the people against Burgers.

When the Volksraad met on 13 February Burgers did his best for Shepstone (and the Transvaal) by claiming that a large number of burghers (Kruger among them) who had not paid the war tax should be excluded as defaulters from the debate. Kruger wrote:

During the adjournment I was chatting with the other members of the Volksraad on the veranda when President Burgers joined us, slapped me on the shoulder, and said: "Mr Kruger, you can't deny that the burghers who refuse to pay the taxes are in a state of rebellion against their Government?" I answered: "I deny it absolutely on the grounds which I have already stated. They don't refuse to pay their taxes; but they do refuse to pay a tax which you have added, without authority, to the already existing taxes. But, even if the facts were as you say, I should like to ask you a question. Would you consider it a proof of affection to accuse your wife – no matter what her faults – openly before her bitterest enemy? This is what you have done to the Republic in the presence of her enemy, and this to me is a proof that you do not love, but hate the Republic." The President was silent and left us.

At first the Volksraad refused to debate Burgers' Reform Bill designed to introduce efficient methods of administration. They did not believe Burgers' warnings that Shepstone really meant to annex the Transvaal, and sent a separate delegation to cross-question him. Later they debated a motion which covered both confederation and the reforms which might have made confederation unnecessary. Put in this form the motion was, of course, defeated. A week later Burgers again tried to interest the Volksraad in reform – without success. On 3 March he once more presented his proposals for reorganising the Government and delivered himself of a number of home truths which must seriously have prejudiced his chances of re-election. "We should delude ourselves by entertaining the hope that matters would mend by and by," he told his audience. "It would only be self-deceit. I tell you openly, matters are as bad as they can ever be; they cannot be worse. These are bitter truths, and people may perhaps turn their backs on me; but then I shall have the consolation of having done my duty." Burgers continued:

Do you know what has recently happened in Turkey? Because no civilised government was carried on there the Great Powers interfered and said, "Thus far, and no further." And if this is done to an empire will a little republic be excused when it misbehaves ... Complain to the other powers and seek justice there? Yes, thank God! justice is still to be found, even for the most insignificant; but it is precisely the justice which will convict us. If we want justice we must be in a position to ask for it with unsullied hands ... Today, a bill for £1,100 was laid before me for signature; but I would sooner have cut off my right hand than sign that paper, for I have not the slightest ground to expect that when that bill becomes due there will be a penny to pay it with.

Two days later Burgers warned the Volksraad that only a miracle could save the Republic. At one session Shepstone, according to

Dr Jorissen, who took a pencil note at the time, threatened to unleash Cetewayo and the Zulus on the Transvaal and said that it was his hand alone that had held them back. This was probably an exaggeration.

Most other writers deny that Shepstone would have been so unwise as to threaten to make an alliance with the natives against the Boers. But he undoubtedly pointed out to the Boers that they needed British help if they were to defend themselves against the Zulus, and this may certainly have influenced their thinking.

Finally on 8 March Burgers' new Constitution, providing amongst other things for a Supreme Court of three judges, a State police force, a regular army of 125 men and a Vice-President, was approved. Paul Kruger was sworn in as Vice-President and soon afterwards the Volksraad adjourned, having passed a resolution that independence must be maintained. They refused to consider the question of confederation which they said could be decided only by the sovereign people. The Executive Council were, however, empowered to take exceptional measures to balance the budget. "The Volksraad did not break up in a very happy mood," Kruger wrote. "Most of the members feared that the thread by which the sword of Damocles was suspended over the head of the Republic would break and end its independence. Although there were many who hoped that the new measures which the Volksraad had passed in its extraordinary session might avert the danger, it soon became evident that the pessimists were right." For the next month Shepstone continued to discuss the question of annexation with the President and the Executive Council but, on 3 April, he wrote to a colleague that it had now become impossible for him to retreat; that if he did so civil war would break out in the Transvaal, and that "the natives would consider this the sunshine in which they should make hay" in the Republic.

On 7 April Shepstone saw the Executive Council and told them frankly that he had been authorised and was prepared to annex the country. "I at once told him that I would never give my consent to any such step," wrote Kruger, "as I was bound by my oath to uphold the independence of the Republic. I would have to submit if the Volksraad agreed to the annexation and thus released me from my oath, but not otherwise. Shepstone thereupon asked me how long it would take to call the Volksraad together. I told him that I thought it would not take long if the President issued the summons at once. But here President Burgers intervened, saying that it would not do to try Shepstone's patience too far; and so the plan fell through."

By 10 April 1877 Burgers knew that Shepstone was writing his

Proclamation of Annexation and Shepstone knew that Burgers was preparing a formal protest. On at least one occasion they compared notes. Finally on 12 April the deed which Shepstone was anxious to perform before the Volksraad reassembled to elect a new President, was done.

In Shepstone's words to Carnarvon:

On Thursday last, the 12th instant, I found myself in a position to issue the proclamation necessary for annexing the South African Republic, commonly known as the Transvaal, to her Majesty's dominions . . .

Every step I have taken towards the accomplishment of my object was taken with the knowledge of the President. I thought it my duty to be perfectly open and frank with him from the beginning, and on the last occasion of my meeting with him in Executive Council, he took the opportunity to acknowledge and thank me for what he was good enough to call my considerate and frank behaviour to him and the Government.

After addressing this meeting, and in compliance with a request made thereat, I addressed the letter of the 9th April, copy annexed, informing Mr Burgers of my intention. He subsequently called upon me and informed me that he should be bound to make a protest, the draft of which he read to me. I agreed with Mr Burgers that from his point of view, he could take no other course, and you will observe that the wording of the protest is as moderate as was compatible with the object it was intended to attain.

On Wednesday the 11th instant, the Attorney General and Chief Clerk came and officially read the protest to me, and at the same time handed in a resolution of the Executive Council from which it appeared that a Mission to Her Majesty's Government and, contingently, to other Governments, which had acknowledged the independence of the State, had been determined upon. The resolution appointed the Attorney-General, E. J. P. Jorissen, D.D., and Mr Paul Kruger, Vice-President, to be members of this mission, with power to add a third person if required. I received these papers, but as they contained nothing to make me change the view I had taken of my duty, I said that while I recognised the propriety of their discharging what they conceived to be incumbent on them, I must ask them to do the same with regard to me; they expressed their acquiescence, and the interview which had been friendly throughout, ended.

Mr Burgers called upon me shortly afterwards, and explained to me the object of these documents. [They were designed to damp

down opposition and asked the Transvalers to await the result of
the Jorissen–Kruger mission.]

The following day at 11 a.m. the proclamations were read [by
Melmoth Osborn] to a small crowd of the inhabitants, mostly
English, in Church Square, by whom of course the most hearty
cheers were given for Her Majesty. [Rider Haggard (later to
achieve fame as the author of *King Solomon's Mines*), Shepstone's
clerical assistant, was among those who helped to hoist the Union
Jack.] Mr Burgers' protest and proclamation were immediately
afterwards read by Mr J. C. Juta, one of the Members of the
Executive government [he was Secretary for War & Public Works]
and were received in respectful silence. No excitement whatever
followed.

These, then, were the circumstances in which Paul Kruger rose to
be Vice-President or chief trouble-maker, patriot or purveyor of
subversion, according to whose view you accept. Shepstone's
opinions have been set out, as have Kruger's. But the account would
not be complete without the views of Burgers, who has been portrayed
in British accounts as something of a pawn, and in South African
accounts as a collaborator with the British if not an outright
Quisling.

Burgers' position was clear. He had been elected to office to reform
and modernise the Transvaal. He was therefore in favour of the
Transvaal remaining independent. Indeed his very job depended on
the Republic retaining a government of its own. In his view Kruger
and the Boers, by opposing reform, were jeopardising both the
independence of the Republic and Burgers' own prestige and future
career. To this extent he was the natural ally of the British.

Certainly the readers of *The Times* could hardly have thought
otherwise as they read Burgers' last address to the Volksraad. It was
preceded in the story by a significant paragraph:

The change of Government was effected [*The Times* correspondent
wrote from the Cape] without any disturbance, nor has the public
peace been interrupted in any way up to the present time. It was
known that British troops were on the borders of the adjoining colony
of Natal, but none were in the Republic. A number of the inhabitants
of Pretoria who supported the Special Commissioner's proceedings
formed a protecting force and offered their services to maintain
order, although fortunately there was no call for them. After the
Proclamation was read [in the Church Square] most of the officials
assembled in the Volksraad Chamber, when his Honour, Mr
Burgers thus addressed them:

"Gentlemen, officials of the South African Republic – You are no strangers in the land. You know what has happened and what is going on now. You also know what the Government has resolved to do. We bow only to the superior power. We submit because we cannot successfully draw the sword against this superior power, because by doing so we should only plunge the country into deeper miseries and disasters. We have resolved to appeal to England herself, and if we get no redress there, then we will seek the friendly intervention of other Powers that have acknowledged our independence. I have called you together to make one request to you. Continue to occupy your offices in abeyance of the result of this appeal. No other oath of office will be demanded from you, and you can continue to serve under the oath once sworn to the Republic. I have pledged my word for you and I know that I can depend upon you that you will not disappoint me. Serve the new Government with the same honesty and fidelity with which you have served our Government, for by that you will serve the people. I am leaving my office under protest on behalf of myself, of the Government, of the officials, of the Volksraad, and of the people. Grant me, therefore, this one favour that you serve the people so long and redeem the pledge that I have given for you . . ."

Burgers' own justification for his actions came to light when Mr Philip Watermeyer, a member of the Cape Parliament, forwarded a letter to the Editor of the newspaper *Volksblad* written by Burgers shortly before his death. After setting out the events which led to Shepstone's arrival in the Transvaal, Burgers wrote:

I foresaw the dangers which would accrue from this state of things for the Republic, and in order to upset Shepstone's design at one blow by uniting all parties, I proposed to Kruger that he and I both should withdraw from the candidature for the Presidency, promising at the same time that I would exert my utmost to get a man like Stockenstrom, and to assist him with all my might.

This Paul Kruger flatly refused to do, saying that I might withdraw, but that he would not. Fruitlessly did I press him by showing how our danger lay in our want of unity, how the English Government would have cause to step in on the ground of humanity to avert a civil war, to prevent a general rising of the natives, etc. He would not hear of retiring. Knowing that when I withdrew and left the field all to Kruger, my party would not be satisfied, I decided to stand in the contest, fully resolved to stick to the Republic whoever became President, and to save it from British rule, and I advised my party accordingly. Kruger, in spite of his having betrayed me, I treated as a friend for the country's sake. On the eve of Shepstone's arrival in Pretoria, I called the Executive [Kruger, Joubert and Holtzhousen with the Attorney-General, Jorissen] to my house [Mr Swart as State Secretary would also presumably have been included] in order to arrange upon a plan for dealing with Shepstone, and it was arranged on my proposal that not a single one of us should ever interview Shepstone privately or without at least one other of the Government members with us. It was also arranged that we should do nothing without the consent of the Volksraad, etc.

But what was my surprise when, the second day after, one member of the Government, Swart, went to meet Shepstone privately before he even arrived at Pretoria and had a long interview with him on Erasmus' farm; when Paul Kruger, whom I took with me when I went to meet Shepstone first, only remained a few minutes, and then left me all alone with Sir Theophilus, thus compelling me to retire sooner than politeness allowed; and then afterwards I learned that other members of Government, as well as several high officials and influential farmers, went repeatedly singly to call on Shepstone. This proved to me that but few, if any, had a faint idea of the danger the State was in, and I determined to trust no more to any one, but to face the danger single-handed. The meeting of the Executive [with] Shepstone, the appointment of a Commission from both sides to inquire into the alleged grievances of the English government such as slavery, etc., I foresaw, were only by-play, whereas the real thing was to be faced in a different way. Hence I met Shepstone alone in my house and opened up the subject of his mission. With a candour that astonished me, he avowed that his purpose was to annex the country, as he had sufficient grounds for it, unless I could so alter matters as to satisfy his Government. My plan for a new constitution modelled after that of America, of a standing police force of 200 mounted men was then proposed. He promised that he would give me time to call the Volksraad together, and that he would abandon his design if the Volksraad would adopt these measures, and the country were willing to submit to them and carry them out.

The Raad was called, and in the meantime the constitution drafted, prepared and then accepted by the Executive. In the opening speech of the Raad, which was already in print, I used the strongest language I could conceive to impress upon the representatives of the people the necessity of adopting the means of reform. During the night previous to the opening of the Raad,

I was aroused from my bed by Mr Bodenstein, the Chairman of the Raad, to whom I had, agreeable to custom, sent a printed copy of the opening speech. He was accompanied by one or two members of the Raad, the State Attorney and some officials. They told me that the speech was too strong, that it would create a disturbance, and cause needless uproar, that things were not so bad, etc., and finally prevailed upon me to alter or omit two or three paragraphs in the speech. This I ought never to have done. The consequence was that when the new measures were brought before the Raad, this body, almost without discussion, rejected them in toto, in spite of my passionate appeals. I then told them plainly that the Republic would be lost unless they were prepared to meet me in this, and warned them of the consequences, but in vain. The fate of Cassandra befell me. No one would believe, or could believe what I foretold them, and a great deal of valuable time was spent in idle talk. At last when members began to see that there was some danger, the enemies having commenced to talk boldly, a Committee of the Raad was appointed to confer with me about means of saving the Republic. In that Committee two members of the Raad were placed, of whom I knew that neither had paid either war tax or other taxes, and that one at least had dissuaded his constituents and other people from paying. I openly declared that I would not sit in committee with traitors to their country, and stated the case and my reasons fully.

To my astonishment, the Raad took these members under their protection, and made all kinds of excuses for their defaulting. About this time the Chairman, Mr Bodenstein, and some other members went to Shepstone, and from him they heard what they would not believe from me, that as the Raad had refused my plans for reform, he would be obliged to annex the country. This, of course, gave them an awful shock; and the Raad met in secret in a private sitting, at which it was resolved to censure me for having known the danger and kept it secret from the Raad.

After recounting how he survived the vote of censure, Burgers' account continues:

Paul Kruger was doing his utmost to make the Boers believe that I was aiming at becoming a dictator, and that the new constitution was a means of self-aggrandisement proposed by me and intended to be forced from the people now they were in danger. The English faction in and out of the House backed Kruger, and made the people believe it would be far better to be under the rule of Great Britain, than under that of a Dictator, as I was aiming to be, etc.

This was but too successful. The Raad began to flag in its zeal and only adopted half the measures proposed. Plans made by the Boers to mortgage their farms, and raise money to help the State, while the taxes were coming in slowly, as well as a solemn promise made to me by Pretorius that I would have £30,000 within a week to carry on the Government (made, as he said, in the name of 40 burghers of the State, who had decided to raise the money) were abandoned, and I never saw or heard of either Pretorius and his 40 Boers nor of the money ever since.

Constantly worried by calls for payment, while we had no shilling in the Treasury, harassed and pressed by the English party with memorials in favour of confederation or annexation, asked for payment by the Boers for losses sustained in the war while they refused to pay up their taxes, driven almost to despair by betrayal and corruption on all sides, ruined in my private estate as well as in health, I at last made a final attempt by boldly proclaiming the new constitution, as far as it was adopted, and by forming the new Cabinet. But there also I met with insurmountable difficulties. Joubert refused to accept, even for a time, the Office of Secretary for Native Affairs. Struben also refused, and so did one or two others, while those who would accept were objected to, on the ground that they were newcomers. Seeing my last attempt fail, the British Commissioner, having a handful of names fairly or foully obtained in favour of annexation, thought his time had come to act. The Volksraad had gone away having done nothing but harm. The members of the Executive had gone home, as if all were safe, and I sat with a half-new Cabinet and part of an old one, half discharged. Yet I made one attempt more, and drafted a letter to Shepstone, intimating that I would oppose the annexation by force of arms, etc., and showing this to two members of the Executive. The response to my appeal, however, was so weak (one of them being in league with the English) that I had to abandon the project, and try to prepare for the worst. When, therefore, Shepstone announced that he could wait no longer, that he had given us time enough to reform, and that he must issue his proclamation, I could do no more than advise a protest and an appeal to foreign Powers.

This having been agreed to by my Government, I met Shepstone in the presence of the Executive, and saved what could be saved for the country, namely its language, its legislature, the position of its officials, etc. Before issuing his proclamation, Shepstone desired to see copies of both mine and the Government protest. This, I promised, on condition that he showed me his proclamation before publication, to which he agreed. To one clause I greatly objected, namely the threat of confiscation of property for disobeying the proclamation. I pointed out that this was barbarous, and would be punishing a man's innocent family for his actions. The clause was omitted. This was the origin of the lie that I helped Shepstone in drawing up his proclamation.

After the annexation, Burgers left the Transvaal in an ox-wagon provided by Shepstone to return to private life owing £26,000, most of which, representing loans that he had raised privately to pay volunteers, was written off by the Government. He lived in poor health and outright poverty, the British Government having repudiated Shepstone's promise of an annual pension of £1,000 to be paid to him in compensation for loss of office. Eventually the British arranged for the Pretoria Government to pay Burgers an allowance of £500 p.a. provided he resided outside the Transvaal. So Burgers spoke the literal truth when he averred that he never took a penny from the British.

Apart from Shepstone, who considered that Burgers had acted in the best interests of his country, the former President was not in fact particularly well thought of by the overlords, and Sir Bartle Frere, the new High Commissioner at the Cape, noted with some surprise at the ball he gave in 1877 for Queen Victoria's birthday that Mr Burgers was there, dancing as if he were neither an ex-President nor ex-Divine. Sir Bartle went on to say – though whether with gratification or distaste is not clear – that "He drank Her Majesty's health with the most loyal of Her Majesty's British subjects . . . He is a singular and certainly a gifted man with great powers of attraction but I am much disappointed in what I have seen of him. There is to my mind more of the charlatan in him and less of the poetical than I had expected.

"I think he is not deliberately or of purpose untrue or treacherous, as he is often described; but very unreliable from the impulsiveness of a clever, vain man of no fixed or abiding principles, and little experience in any public life but one of temporary expedience."

No doubt Kruger would for once have been happy to agree with Her Majesty's High Commissioner at the Cape.

But people were beginning to sum up Kruger too.

In June 1877 the same Sir Bartle Frere wrote to Lord Carnarvon:

Mr Paul Kruger is about 55 years old; he was about ten or 12 when his father "trekked", and has always been a typical "Dopper Boer". I am assured by those who know him well that he is a very shrewd fellow who veils under an assumed clownish manner and affectation of ignorance, considerable ability – that he has natural eloquence and powers of persuasion. There is nothing in what is visible to a stranger to indicate a possible regenerator of the Transvaal.

Possibly Sir Bartle had been told not only the story of Kruger, Hugo and the lion but also another widely circulated anecdote according to which Paul Kruger celebrated the completion of the Rustenburg church roof by standing on his head on top of it. And Kruger might not have felt any more flattered than Burgers had been by Sir Bartle's assessment.

Lord Beaconsfield's opinion of Kruger, written to Lord Carnarvon a week before the annexation of the Transvaal, was expressed in shorter form but proved in the long run to be more accurate – from the British point of view. "Paul Kruger," Disraeli wrote, "is an ugly customer . . ."

Chapter 6

Reversing the Irreversible

"Silent, self-asserting, determined to oppose all innovation and division of his authority and very skilful in that sort of diplomacy which defers decisions and evades difficulties by postponed action..." That was how Sir Bartle Frere described the Transvaal's new ruler. If only Sir Theophilus had used his knowledge of Afrikaans to uncover the secrets of the Afrikaners, or his sense of history to interpret their movements, he would have realised that the Boers were weak because they were dispersed; that they were dispersed because they were determined to stay free; and that they remained silent because they believed that even if Queen Victoria failed to understand the justice of their case, either the Tsar or the Kaiser would be sure to do so.

But as the Boers withdrew "huis toe", i.e. to home sweet home in the countryside, Shepstone was only too ready to believe that their absence from his counsels was due to indifference rather than aversion. Besides, he had no patience for the old Boer who said on hearing of the annexation "Well now I must begin over again, as in my young days when I was also a British subject."

It is even possible that the British did not consider it necessary to cultivate the goodwill of the Queen's Afrikaner subjects. Paul Kruger, according to Mr W. Morcom, Shepstone's legal adviser, was "an elderly man, decidedly ugly, with a countenance denoting extreme obstinacy, and also great cruelty". He was also seen to comb his hair during a public luncheon and to put his napkin to strange uses. Moreover "his dirty wooden pipe was visible, for it stuck out of his breast pocket". This sort of person would never contribute to the kind of progress which the Imperial Government hoped to bestow on its new possession.

Meanwhile, now that the Volksraad had vanished into thin air, Shepstone's first care was to carry on the government – *his* government – with the aid of such members of the Executive Council who were willing to continue in his service. Piet Joubert was not willing, but Jorissen and Kruger both obliged, and on 14 May Shepstone was able to inform Carnarvon that although both men had left four days earlier to protest in England and elsewhere against the annexation, there would be every prospect of seeing them back at their posts in due course. Shepstone wrote:

> Mr Kruger is a member of the Executive Council for which he receives £200 a year, but holds no executive office. Dr Jorissen is a Doctor of Divinity, but nevertheless occupied the position of State Attorney or Attorney-General, in the late Republic, with £600 a year salary; he requested to be allowed to retain his office under the altered form of government, in terms of my proclamation, and that he might return to it on his coming back from Europe.

Shepstone continued:

> Both these gentlemen told me that they were going to Europe to discharge an obligation which had been imposed upon them, and that if their mission failed they would at least have done their duty, and Mr Kruger added, with the frankness which has always characterised his intercourse with me, that, in case of failure, I should find him as faithful a subject under the new form of Government as he had been under the old. [Why Kruger should afterwards have bothered to deny having made this highly equivocal statement is not clear since from the days of the Great Trek he had never considered himself to be a British subject.]
>
> Dr Jorissen, with equal frankness [Shepstone added] admits that the change [i.e. the annexation] was inevitable, and expresses his belief that the cancelling of it would be calamitous. It had been arranged that both these gentlemen should receive full pay during their absence, which they themselves tell me will not exceed eight or nine months, and I have not interfered with this arrangement.

Just why Kruger and Jorissen were so obliging is not so clear but one could suggest several reasons. Possibly they thought that refusal might amount to treason. Or they felt that the annexation would be a short-term affair and that it would be unwise in the meantime to absent themselves from the seat of power. They were, of course, leaving the country, and would not therefore be called on to demonstrate their loyalty to the British in public and, since it was at Shepstone's request that they were remaining in office, it would not do to be seen doing so voluntarily and without pay.

In any case they wasted no time. By June they were in the Cape where they saw Sir Bartle Frere at Government House. It must have been a galling experience for Kruger to have had to rely on Jorissen to interpret both his own words and Frere's answers. Sometimes Dr Jorissen gave replies that Kruger would probably have made far more effectively. For example, when Frere asked what body they represented or who had deputed them to protest to Europe against annexation, Jorissen was clearly stumped. "Dr Jorissen," the official report of the meeting said, "after some consideration replied that they were not representatives of any existing body, nor delegates from the Volksraad, or from any part of the Transvaal State. He was a member of the late Executive Government who had been empowered by the Volksraad to resist annexation to the utmost. The protest had in consequence been issued, and was 'necessary to prevent war'." On hearing this Sir Bartle enquired: "As Sir Theophilus at the time had no force with him, you mean to suggest that Sir Theophilus or any of his suite would have been put to death?" Jorissen was clearly nonplussed. Nor was he any more at ease on constitutional matters. "I further ascertained," Sir Bartle wrote, "that the deputation had no definite propositions to submit to your Lordship [Carnarvon] with regard to the future. Dr Jorissen seemed to have some difficulty in making the questions on this point intelligible to his colleague, and Mr Kruger observed that if the country were given back they would be ready to promise confederation for the management of the Natives regarding which Her Majesty's Government might dictate their own policy."

Sir Bartle afterwards discovered that the delegates were carrying a large number of signatures to a memorial which did not refer to the annexation but which supported the former Government's decision to oppose confederation . . . a discovery which did not help to explain what Kruger meant by "confederation for the management of the Natives".

Nor was Jorissen able to enlighten the Governor as to whom the country "should be given back". Jorissen's answer was that "this was a question of considerable difficulty which they would have to leave to Her Majesty to decide". Officially they regarded themselves as a Commission.

One could hardly expect that the red carpet would be unrolled in London for Kruger's reception. Nor could morale have been especially high among the members of the delegation. Kruger, speaking of Jorissen, said, "Dr Jorissen was appointed [to the delegation] by my wish, as he was a lawyer, and I was anxious to have someone with me who could speak foreign languages." He paid no tribute to Jorissen's ability or honesty and indeed clearly distrusted him as a Burgers man imported from Holland. At their first meeting Kruger had attempted to cross-question Jorissen on his religious views, and Jorissen told him he was not entitled to institute the inquisition. Kruger soon afterwards pointed out Jorissen to Mrs Kruger (known to all Transvalers as Tante Sanna) as "the man who has refused to tell me what he believes". Later Jorissen had made matters worse by expressing doubt as to whether in fact the Lord had created the world in seven days, and during the voyage to England he put forward certain advanced theories on the origin and behaviour of the stars. Kruger, according to the most widely believed anecdote, then held aloft the Bible that he had been reading. "If what you say is true, Jorissen, I might as well throw this book overboard." He then returned to his studies, and the discussion lapsed.

Jorissen for his part had no specially good opinion of Kruger, whose attitude he believed was "about the same as that of the Protestants of the 16th century", and was clearly convinced that his own superior education and knowledge of the world at large entitled him to play the leading part in the negotiations with the great powers, although it must be admitted that he had made no great reputation as a lawyer either in theory or practice. The two were a contrast, as the future Chief Justice Kotze noted when he met them just before they started out:

> Jorissen introduced me to Kruger, of whom I had already heard a good deal. The contrast between the two men was rather striking. The former was tall and spare with an intellectual face, the latter of middle height with thickset neck and stalwart shoulders, indicative of physical strength and a somewhat heavy countenance with quick observant eyes. Kruger wore a very short cut black jacket peculiar to the Dopper persuasion to which he belonged, and a black felt hat. This gave him a quaint appearance. After an exchange of a few words in conversation they passed on.

On 12 June, after Kruger, Jorissen and Edward Bok (whom they took with them as Secretary) had sailed for Europe, Sir Bartle wrote a further letter of assurance to Carnarvon:

> As regards the Transvaal itself, Sir Theophilus Shepstone has reported to your Lordship the general feelings of acquiescence, relief and satisfaction with which the announcement was received throughout the whole territory. I have little to add to what has been so reported, beyond bearing my testimony to the almost universal admission of the fact that there has been no expression of opinion in the Transvaal itself, from any class whatever, indicating the slightest desire to undo what has been done.

At the age of 52, Kruger was making his first trip abroad, a momentous event for a Transvaler but less momentous perhaps for those whom he was visiting.

In London that summer there was much else to preoccupy the citizens. Those present at the Queen's Theatre had been treated to the first public exhibition of the telephone and were enthralled by the fact that "The Blue Bells of Scotland" and "The Last Rose of Summer" could be played into one end of the line and be received at the other. The Emperor Pedro II of Brazil and the Empress Teresa Cristina were among the visitors to Britain; the Prince of Wales had unveiled the statue of King Alfred the Great at Wantage; a lady gorilla called "Pongo" was specially displayed at London Zoo; Russia had invaded Bulgaria; Irish terrorists were in full swing in Roscommon, and the dreaded Colorado beetle, potential harbinger of a potato famine, had appeared in Germany.

In these circumstances there was no great stir in the metropolis over the arrival of the men from the Transvaal, and the *Manchester Guardian*, which might have been expected to take a favourable view of their activities, contented itself with the speculation that "they are not likely to make a serious impression at the Colonial Office or indeed anywhere in Europe, if we except Holland where some feeling has been excited by the suppression of the Republic".

However they were received by Lord Carnarvon at the Colonial Office on Thursday, 5 July, soon after their arrival. They found him unassuming but also unbending. "I should only be misleading you," he said, "if I were to hold out to you the slightest expectation that the policy which has been adopted could now be altered, or that the annexation of the Transvaal could be undone." After speaking mostly on this theme for six or seven minutes, Carnarvon added:

I have heard it said that some of the Dutch Boers, under the influence of vexation at what has taken place, are thinking of leaving the country. I should be extremely sorry if they did so. I think they would be making a great mistake as regards their own interests, and so far as the conduct of the administration of the Government goes on, I think I can safely promise them that they shall have no cause whatever to leave the country. I do not desire to see the Dutch population reduced by one man. I am quite sure that they possess many of the qualities that make good citizens and render a country prosperous – I for one give them full credit for all this and desire to do everything that can promote their welfare and make them feel the present changes as little as possible.

He continued:

There is a great deal more that I could say, but I think those are some of the main points on which at this our first meeting I desire to dwell. I shall be very happy hereafter, if you desire it, to give you another meeting in which you can lay before me any particular questions to which you desire to draw my attention. I am only anxious that you should not be misled into supposing that the annexation itself is a thing still in doubt. It is settled; past recall. It is settled, and I simply desire to carry it out in the way which is most agreeable to the feelings of the Dutch population . . .

. . . after which the delegation, having thanked his Lordship for the kindly feeling which he had expressed, withdrew.

Kruger, of course, not knowing English, had understood hardly anything of what had been said, and the wonder of simultaneous translation into headphones was notably absent from the Colonial Office, but "the substance" of Carnarvon's words was translated for him by Mr Bok.

The result could hardly have brought much satisfaction. Nevertheless, after just over a week during which Jorissen and Kruger had had time to digest the shorthand note which Carnarvon had sent to them, the delegation was back again at the Colonial Office.

This time Kruger spoke, with Edward Bok again translating. Mr Kruger, Bok said, did not contest the annexation but wished to point out that Carnarvon's object, namely the prosperity of the Transvaal, could not be attained unless there was a general feeling of satisfaction among the Boers. "And," Bok continued, "he [Kruger] says that it is quite in the power of your Lordship to create such a feeling of general satisfaction among those Boers. That is what I am to say to your Lordship. He says that the means of creating the feeling of satisfaction to which he was alluding and which he thinks are quite in the power of your Lordship, consists of allowing a plebiscite to be taken on the subject of the annexation." If, following a plebiscite, the Boer party realised that they were only a minority, then they could be quiet and contented, and if Carnarvon would sanction this course he, Kruger, would return to Africa a happy man.

Carnarvon, however, was not ready to confer the necessary happiness. Quite the contrary. He said:

As regards the particular point which Mr Kruger mentions, the question whether a plebiscite can be taken, I am afraid it would be impossible for me to agree to anything in the nature of what would be a vote on the question of the fact of the annexation. That would be calling into question the act which Sir Theophilus Shepstone did with the sanction of the Queen and in Her name; and you must see at once that, while very desirous to meet you, I could not agree to such a proposal as that.

Carnarvon admitted, however, that it might be possible to allow a popular vote relevant to the new Constitution so as to give the Dutch population "the power of indirectly expressing their acquiescence in the new order of things".

At this point the interpretation broke down, though it is not clear whether this was because Kruger failed to understand what had been said or because he wished to express himself in words so forceful that he did not wish them to be recorded – and we find Bok saying, somewhat confusedly, "If you will allow me, your Lordship, to get correctly what he means. I do not believe that he caught now the real drift of the last proposal of the new form now given respecting the shape of the impossible part. He has said that he is quite willing to speak frankly with your Lordship, but he is rather anxious that what he now says should not be put into writing or printed." An unrecorded conversation then took place between Kruger and Carnarvon "on the question of the suggested popular vote", as the official Colonial Office record puts it.

Later the discussion turned to the possibility of the Transvaal being given responsible government such as prevailed in the Cape, and Carnarvon explained that this would be linked with his scheme for confederation and asked "Will you explain that to Mr Kruger now, or afterwards?"

Dr Jorissen: "Well, we had better explain it afterwards."

It is permissible to suspect that Dr Jorissen feared that Kruger might explode if he heard more about "the new order".

At any rate, at the end of the discussion Kruger asked if the next meeting with Carnarvon could be fixed in the near future "as we want to leave so soon as possible".

But the next meeting did not occur until five days later, and when it did so was even more inconclusive. Carnarvon revealed that he was preparing some written proposals for the delegation and that, in the meantime, they might like to consider the written report of the previous meeting with which he had now provided them.

Their contacts with his Lordship were not, however, confined to formal sessions at the Colonial Office. Carnarvon invited the delegation to his home at Highclere Castle near Newbury, and Jorissen noted that their host was a true aristocrat, "unpretentious", with courteous goodness, ready to shake the hand of his French chef "to whom he said that we were especially interesting people from Africa". Kruger, however, showed more interest in the coachhouse and the stables than in the lordly kitchens or for that matter in the Earl's own pedigree. What he thought of the Earl's crest – a wyvern wings elevated vert, in the mouth a sinister human hand couped at the wrist gules – is not recorded. Carnarvon, according to Jorissen, continued to maintain during this visit that plebiscites were part of the bad Napoleonic form of government and in conflict with the constitutional principles of Britain, and also "that we [the Boers] were our own worst enemies in not knowing where our own interest lay".

The final meeting with Carnarvon took place on 10 August and showed Kruger at his most persistent. As interpreted by Bok he again revived the idea of a plebiscite "by which the Boers may see how strong they are, or how weak they are, and what number they count, because he says he thinks that that is the only means to get happiness there, and that they may be quiet in future". Carnarvon once again said that it might be possible to arrange for a vote on some aspect of the new Constitution so that the Dutch could participate in making it, provided that it did not question what had already been done. Kruger answered that he fully understood the difficulty but said that Carnarvon had promised to "allow a vote for some measure by which the Boers could see those who were against the annexation and those who were for annexation". Carnarvon replied: "I am sure that Mr Kruger is much too intelligent a man to wish to put me in a position of doing indirectly what I say I cannot do directly. I must not do that." He then put a counter-proposal that there should be a vote on whether the Transvaal should unite with Natal.

But this did not suit Kruger as, in either case, the Transvaal would have to remain under the British flag, and speaking on his behalf Bok said:

Mr Kruger wishes me to translate literally, word by word, what he is saying. He says that from the very first meeting he has been aware, and he came to the conviction that the things that had been done could not be undone. He knows that, he says, but now he thinks that he can name a measure which will give happiness and good order to the country. He wants me to translate to your Lordship that he would like it to be a vote for the British Government or not.

Whether Kruger intended his words to be defiant or jocular is not clear from the official account. But Carnarvon took them seriously and replied with some resentment:

That, if I understand Mr Kruger rightly, is impossible for the reason that I gave before, namely that it would be a vote really for or against annexation. Does he not also see plainly that, supposing (I would put it merely for the sake of argument) there should be a majority against the British Government, what would be our position? I should have to undo that which he says from the first day that he came here he felt could not be undone.

There was not much more to be said, and Carnarvon promised to put in writing the various points he had touched on, in the hope that Kruger would use his influence to persuade his fellow-countrymen "how much better and wiser it is that they should join us in trying to do everything for the benefit and improvement of the province".

According to a paper prepared for the British Cabinet in May 1880, Carnarvon made two further points. When the delegation suggested that the dispute should be referred to a plebiscite, he replied that "it would be in the highest degree inexpedient to place on record that an extremely small minority of the community was opposed to an acceptance of the Queen's rule". "Since you left the Transvaal for England," he wrote to the delegates on 18 August, "the enthusiasm with which the vast minority of the people including the Dutch Colonists, have welcomed Sir T. Shepstone as the representative of Her Majesty has increased to the extent of absorbing apparently all other feelings."

The Cabinet Paper added:

It appears that the delegates supposed that this was founded upon information which had reached Lord Carnarvon, but had not reached them, that a great revulsion of feeling had taken place on the part of their fellow Boers. They thought in fact that the reason of their mission was gone.

This may well have been true. Kruger firmly believed that a plebiscite would support his views. In his memoirs he declared that when he was shown a letter from Dr Jooste, a young Minister of the Dutch Reformed Church recently appointed to Potchefstroom, first published in the *Zuid Afrikaan* in Cape Town, according to which "only a handful of irreconcilables, with myself at their head, had declared against the annexation, I denied this report with the greatest emphasis and said that it was easy to arrive at the truth by taking a plebiscite of the whole Republic . . .". But clearly, he did not wish to get ahead of public opinion among his own countrymen, and the delegation backed down slightly in their farewell letter to Carnarvon, dated 28 August. The tone was almost conciliatory as might perhaps have been expected in view of the fact that Kruger had successfully represented that the Colonial Office, in view of the delays, should pay the subsistence costs of the delegation. The letter read:

Although it did not please your Lordship to grant us a general vote of the population of the Transvaal, a measure which we still cannot leave off considering highly important, we may have the satisfaction that your Lordship gave the fullest consideration to this our proposition. Although we may have perhaps a different idea as to the number of the inhabitants of the Transvaal who should have preferred independence to the acceptance of Her Majesty's sovereignty, we think it quite useless after your Lordship's decision to dwell any longer upon this matter. In conclusion we are very happy to state that we feel ourselves quite able to report that we have found your Lordship quite desirous and willing always to give the fullest consideration to those wishes of the population of the Transvaal, which must be considered to be right and reasonable, and that we shall do our utmost to promote that general feeling of satisfaction in the Transvaal which we know is so much needed for the happiness of its inhabitants.

But although the Commission had achieved nothing with Carnarvon, and were unlikely to do so, they did not hurry home. They had hoped to promote their cause in the Netherlands, France, Belgium and Germany. But Carnarvon had kept them talking so long that on this occasion only the Netherlands was visited and it was November before they returned to the Transvaal, empty-handed under suspicion of having received bribes from the British.

Jorissen indeed resumed his post as Attorney-General and swore the oath required by the British, as if the Boers' cause was finally lost.

He was not dismissed by the British until 11 months later. But the British officials in the Transvaal had not long to wait however for signs of strong resistance and opposition to their authority.

On Saturday, 5 January 1878, at 1.50 p.m., Melmoth Osborn, the Colonial Secretary of the British administration in Pretoria, received a letter from Paul Kruger asking for permission to meet and address a number of Boers at 2 p.m. that day in the Market Square on the results of his mission to England. Lieutenant-Colonel Barnes, in his report on the incident, said:

Before the contents of the letter could be digested and an answer sent, a procession of about 700 mounted men, with a considerable following of others in ox-wagons, horse-carts, and other vehicles of a most nondescript assortment, was seen approaching the town, receiving as it passed some wagons outspanned near the entrance of the town, a salute from the occupants.

In due time the leaders of the procession, consisting of about 80 armed men, apparently acting as escort for Mr Kruger, who was in a Cape cart, were marshalled by the master of ceremonies in the Market Square opposite the Colonial Office, the remainder forming up in the rear as they came in, and making, in addition to another lot of Boers who had come into the town during the course of the day, a total of about 900.

Kruger was immediately summoned to Osborn's office to explain the meaning of the demonstration and why he had been given only ten minutes' notice of its being held. Outside in the square a report circulated that he was to be arrested and held in strict custody. Colonel Barnes wrote:

> On this, one of his followers, armed with a rifle and supported by a half-drunken German with a pistol, entered the Office and in a loud voice asked "Where is Paul?", at the same time pointing his rifle at the stomach of the Treasurer-General and late State Secretary [N. Swart]. In a few minutes "our Paul" (as he is familiarly designated) appeared, and mounting his cart, proceeded to address the meeting to the following effect: He remarked in a few well-chosen words, admirably suited to his hearers, with whom it is obvious that he has great influence, that he had come to give them an account of his mission to England, and hoped that they would be temperate and not interrupt him; that he had a few days previously requested his co-adjutor, Mr Jorissen, to prepare in writing their joint statement and meet him with it on that occasion, but that he regretted to say Mr Jorissen was not in attendance (here a voice in the crowd remarked "He has fled"), and that in consequence they would have to wait, he hoped patiently, until Monday, when they should receive a full account of what had been done and the result of the mission, which, he admitted, had failed to obtain from Lord Carnarvon any promise that the country would be restored to them.

Soon afterwards the meeting was adjourned till the following Monday. That Sunday various desperate remedies were discussed. Some thought that the Imperial Government should be given a week's notice to withdraw from the country; others that the Boers should leave after killing off eight selected individuals, and yet others that the Boers, having withdrawn from Pretoria on Monday, should return unexpectedly to make a surprise attack and seize the capital.

On Monday at 10 a.m. the Boers met again near the Dopper Church. Kruger and Jorissen (the latter having been "brought in from the country" where he was alleged to have fled for refuge) together with Mr Bok, and supporters from the different Boer parties, mounted a wagon-box and the day's proceedings then began. Bok read the reports of the interviews that they had had with Carnarvon and Kruger commented without stint on the main issues covered. Jorissen then got up to speak. According to Barnes he was evidently very nervous and excited. Jorissen said that he and Kruger had returned after eight months to find themselves received with suspicion and distrust. He could understand this, and therefore accepted the situation. He felt that as an honourable man he had done his utmost to carry out the object of his mission and obtain the restoration of the country. He finally appealed to Mr Kruger to corroborate his statement. "Mr Kruger, however, was silent on that subject, and merely requested the meeting to disperse till 2 p.m., digest what they had heard, and at that hour send to him the different representatives they had selected to confer with him on a course of action for the future." He suggested that they should draw up a memorial to be sent to Lord Carnarvon for submission to Her Majesty, which Barnes interpreted as a move to gain time and to prevent "an overt act on the part of the disaffected members of the assembly".

Not all the assembly agreed with Kruger's proposal and one of the most disaffected members of the audience was Mr Henning Pretorius, then a Field Cornet in the Heidelberg district and therefore a paid servant of the Government. (He later became commander of the Transvaal State Artillery.)

Pretorius told the meeting that a man could die but once and that he was ready to die for his country. "What has the British Government ever done for us?" he asked. "The Sand River Convention was initiated in order that the British Government might get rid of us, and we were bundled across the Vaal river for the purpose of being massacred by the different hostile tribes. What did they do during the Sekukuni war? Did they help us then? No! [Here a voice exclaimed: 'They were afraid to help us the d—— d——s'] I am a Transvaal braakhond [pointer dog] and will go throughout the land with my tail up, biting their heels wherever I find them." His words were met with some faint applause and waving of hats, and one man said: "I bow to the British yoke? No, never! Never will I bow, but shoot!" Another thought that Kruger had only fired a blank cartridge and it was suggested that Mr Jorissen should be cut up joint from joint. There was a feeling, too, that it would not do much good to send another memorandum when the one sent by Kruger and Jorissen had been set aside and the mis-statements of one man (referring to the letter of Dr Jooste of Potchefstroom) preferred.

Nevertheless in the end the delegates respected the advice which Kruger had already given once before to "sit still and not muddy the waters". A petition asking Carnarvon to "restore us our country" was prepared as "the last means to obtain our end by peaceable measures". It declared that "the undersigned cannot yet believe that it could be England's will and desire to reign over a people that will not be the subject of any power whatsoever. They would much rather believe the words addressed to them today by Mr S. J. P. Kruger, the employee of the deputation, when he said, 'Brethren, people in England really do not know the actual position here, and I am fully convinced that England's first Minister, Lord Carnarvon, acted in good faith when he spoke in his Despatch to the deputation of "that insignificant minority".' "

Thus Kruger's position was now established as the man of authority, responsibility and moderation with whom the British, if they had been so minded, could have done business.

Kruger made his position even more clear in a meeting held at Naauwpoort Farm on the Mooi river near Potchefstroom on 28 January. On this occasion Mr Bodenstein asked him in view of the fact that another Government was now in power whether he still considered himself Vice-President and Member of the Executive Council. This was an extremely awkward question for Kruger to answer, particularly since he was still receiving his salary as member of the Council. According to the account published in the *Transvaal* of 6 February:

> Mr Kruger gave an equivocal answer, but after a short pause asked if he must answer the question now or later?
> *Answer:* "The people are now together. Now is the best time."
> *Mr Kruger:* "I acknowledge that the law has not discharged me, and if there exists a majority for independence, then I am Vice-President (applause), but before we have won the case I am nothing. You cannot now summon the Volksraad. The Commission must have first completed its work. I do not wish to go beyond the law."

Three days later he wrote to Melmoth Osborn from Boekenhout-fontein informing him that he was organising a petition to determine whether there was a majority for the annexation:

> On my return to this country, I discovered with many of my countrymen a spirit of excitement and dissatisfaction on account of this alleged majority, and as I was sorry for my countrymen, and was afraid that they would adopt a wrong course, I did not hesitate to direct my countrymen to clearly indicate the majority to Lord Carnarvon in a petition. In case the majority should be for the annexation I have openly stated that I am prepared to stoop under and obey the authority of the Queen of England and it appears to

me that I shall succeed to convince my countrymen to reach their independence by a peaceful course.

In this spirit I am now labouring, and many with me, being persuaded that this method is the only one for Her Majesty's Government as well as for my country to bring peacefully to an end the discord at present existing.

But the Colonial Secretary was far from being reassured by Kruger's professions of moderation, and replied on behalf of Shepstone that "His Excellency can scarcely believe that you can be aware of the full meaning of what you have done, and of the heavy responsibility which you have laid upon yourself by the course which you have adopted. You said at the meeting that you did not wish to go beyond the law, but you do not appear to have felt that you were doing a great deal to induce other people to go beyond the law, and that for this you should be held answerable."

Kruger, however, was not the man to let such a promising correspondence drop. In a letter dated 4 March to Shepstone (whom he privately called the old rascal) he claimed that he had no intention of taking "any steps that may be offensive to Her Majesty's Government, a Government that once gave us our freedom, and in whose justice I place the fullest confidence". He argued that the people were "disturbed and embittered in the highest degree", and that there might have been bloodshed if he had not directed public attention to the petition which had in fact been proposed not by himself but by a Mr Vorster. And besides, "As the people assured me that the documents which showed a majority in favour of annexation were untrue, it is not illegal, in my opinion, to prove their untrue. What civilised being could consider it a transgression to make known [i.e. expose] an untruth?" It would be very unjust, Kruger said, if the cause of discontent should be placed on his shoulders because he found this state of affairs already existing when he returned from London to such an extent that he had been accused of defending the British Government and even of having been bought over by them.

On 9 March Shepstone issued a warning about the meeting which it was planned to hold the following month at Doornfontein to deal with the petition against annexation. It proclaimed to all "mischievous and ill-disposed persons" that meetings called to weaken, resist or oppose the power or authority of the Government were contrary to law. This seemed to have had some effect for, on 28 March, M. W. Pretorius, M. J. Viljoen and Kruger issued a notice on behalf of the "Committees of Pretoria and Potchefstroom". It said that the signatories "having heard there are burghers who will attend the meeting at Doornfontein on Thursday, 4 April, next, for what purpose so ever, and whether armed or unarmed, hereby warn those burghers not to do so, and most strictly forbid it", as the resolutions taken at Naauwpoort provided only for a meeting of Committees to deal with the petitions.

Shepstone's own view was that the Boers would not "go beyond talk", but he nevertheless asked for more troops to be put at his disposal and the Colonial Office ruled that a show of force would be necessary.

Indeed a Colonial Office minute of 3 April, agreed by the Secretary of State, said, "It will be hopeless ever to pacify or conciliate the class – 'The Doppers' whom Mr Kruger represents. The real chance of preventing disturbances is to make all classes feel that there is nothing to gain but a great deal to lose by it." The questions pending with the Zulus would afford a pretext for sending the troops without offending the Boers, the Colonial Office minute continued.

Nevertheless the meeting at Doornfontein was held and passed off peaceably, and Wilhelm Kok kept open house there for three days under the big oak tree which stood in front of his homestead.

The Commission duly met at 1 p.m. and its first business was to discuss an accusation which had appeared in the *Volkstem* of 2 April, based on the official Government organ, that Kruger, Pretorius and Viljoen had taken the oath of allegiance to the British Government. Pretorius resigned from the main committee in order to defend himself. He said that there was not the slightest truth in the charge and that he was ready to sign and publish a declaration to this effect. The Chairman, Mr S. Prinsloo, said that he had never doubted this.

Kruger was somewhat more forthright and biblical. "I know, and they know," he said, "that he that lies is a devil. There is not a shadow of truth in it, and Sir Theophilus never alluded to it." Viljoen made a similar protestation of loyalty and the meeting declared itself satisfied with these statements. Pretorius was appointed Chairman of the combined Commissions of Pretoria and Potchefstroom.

In all, 157 petitions were presented, of which 125 were opposed to the annexation and 31 in favour. One other petition remained in doubt since only a copy and not the original had been sent. A further petition launched in the Crocodile River Ward appeared to have foundered, it was presumed, because of an outbreak of fever in the area. A total of 6,591 had signed against the annexation and 587 were in favour.

In the afternoon of the final session on 6 April Kruger and Joubert were elected to take the petition to London. According to the report of the session Kruger in his speech of acceptance said that his life was at the disposal of his country and he was under the impression of having given proof of this. To cut the matter short he would accept the call. The Lord would give His blessing to the cause. "Where is the hope if it is not on God, who holds the hearts of kings and princes in His hand?" Kruger added. No doubt he meant to include the hearts of Her Majesty's ministers in his prayers.

Mr M. W. Vorster said he hoped that the two delegates would not be angry with him if he said that he hoped the message brought back by the gentlemen would be the same as the message brought by Joshua to Caleb.

On 8 May, presumably after having heard of the proceedings at Doornfontein, Shepstone wrote again to London. He said that despite the notice issued by the three leaders, a crowd of Boers estimated to have numbered between 500 and 1,000 had assembled at Doornfontein. Kruger, he said, had encouraged the Boers to believe that if it could be shown that the majority were against annexation, then it would be annulled, and that faulty information given to the British Government was the real cause of the annexation. Shepstone continued:

I can find nothing to justify either of these assumptions in the conversations which Lord Carnarvon held with Messrs Kruger and Jorissen in London; but on the contrary, his Lordship distinctly declined to give assent to a general vote on the ground that should there even be a majority against annexation it could not be annulled.

When reminded of this, Mr Kruger explains his conduct away by saying that the plebiscite referred to in his conversations with the Secretary of State was to have been an authoritative vote, and that this having been vetoed, he had submitted, but that the votes now taken are intended to show that Her Majesty's Minister was mistaken in supposing that those against the annexation formed but an insignificant minority instead of, as would now be shown, an overwhelming majority. He appears to consider that any other ground for the measure must give way to the wish of a majority thus questionably ascertained, and that Her Majesty's Government will not fail to agree with his view.

Shepstone pointed out that the new mission was not, like the former one, a deputation sent by the Government but "is the outcome of a meeting at a farm of a number of persons estimated at from 500 to 1,000, who themselves contributed and undertook to collect contributions to defray the cost, and the object of the mission is to procure the withdrawal of the act of annexation".

On 14 May Kruger and Joubert, shortly before boarding the mail-coach for Cape Town, called on Shepstone and left a letter saying that they could not state what action their deputation would take after its return from Europe as this would depend on the result of their mission "and the will of God and the people".

Things were beginning to hot up. Shepstone saw Kruger's latest letter as a direct threat, and sent a scornful reply to their forwarding address in London to a Mr Pratt of 79 Queen's Street, Cheapside. "No two men in the Transvaal have done more to make the general ruin you deprecate possible than you have, and upon no shoulders will the responsibility of averting it press so heavily as upon yours," it said.

It was only to be expected that Shepstone would no longer wish to have Kruger as a member of the Executive Council and it was convenient that his three-year term of office had expired the previous November. On 20 May Osborn, on his instructions, wrote the letter of dismissal:

After the line of conduct which you have thought it right to pursue with regard to this Government, and especially after the undisguised notification which you have given it in the letter addressed by you and Mr Joubert of the 14th instant to the Administrator that you intend to persevere in an agitation that threatens, as you yourself believe, danger and ruin to the country, his Excellency sees no advantage and does not feel justified in suspending the operation of the law any longer for the purpose of enabling you to retain that office and the pay attached to it.

I am also under the necessity of calling to your attention the fact that on 8 January last, when you personally applied to me at Pretoria to be paid the arrear salary due to you, which according to law was at the rate of £200 a year, you demanded salary at the rate of £300 on the ground that you had been promised that increased rate by the Administrator before your first departure for Europe, and that I, relying upon your word and influenced by your urgency as well as by a desire to avoid appearance even of any breach of faith on the part of his Excellency, who was then absent from the seat of Government, paid you at this increased rate without further question and without authority.

I now find that the only ground you had for preferring this claim was a private conversation with the Administrator, in which you complained that your salary was inadequate, whereupon he told you that he wished to retain your services to aid the new Government, and that he would recommend that you should be retained permanently as a member of the Executive Council to be called up for your advice when required, at a salary of £300 per annum instead of £200 to which you were then entitled.

The reply you made was that you were a representative man and must act according to the feelings of those you represented, but that when you were relieved from those trammels you could act according to your own convictions. You neither accepted nor rejected the proposal, and nothing has since passed to renew or confirm it; therefore you were not justified in making the demand you did, and I have made myself responsible for the payment to you without authority of the amount in excess of your usual salary.

Melmoth Osborn was thus roughly £100 out of pocket. Kruger might perhaps have argued that he had genuinely believed that he had been promised the money, or even that it was illegal for the upstart British Government to have withheld it. And it was probably to be used for the legitimate purpose of paying the expenses of his first trip to London. But he did not trouble to state his case in his memoirs and so it goes by default. In the Cape, Sir Bartle Frere had tried to persuade them that the Cape Colonists had everything they wanted and the Transvalers could have the same – all in vain. In vain he told them that whatever they did the Union Jack would continue to fly over the land. "Over the land, possibly," retorted Joubert, "but over the people *never!*"

Meanwhile the deputation was on its way north with Joubert suffering from sea-sickness and Kruger his usual self, and on 22 June Donald Currie, founder of the Castle (later the Union Castle) Line, cabled to the Colonial Office that "Our new steamer, *Conway Castle*, arrived Madeira today, bringing Cape Town news to the evening of the 4th instant. Transvaal deputation aboard. I may call this afternoon."

Currie did indeed call, and accompanied the Boers on the rest of their voyage. They invited him to come with them on 10 July on their first visit to the Colonial Office where he introduced them to the new Secretary of State for the Colonies, Sir Michael Hicks Beach, the man sometimes known as Black Michael, who sported a beard as bushy as any Boer's. Sir Michael had replaced Lord Carnarvon the previous January when the latter resigned over the Turkish question and, as was usual in Whitehall, had been receiving contradictory advice from various quarters about matters pertaining to South Africa.

Sir Bartle Frere, in a private letter to Hicks Beach which reached

London at the end of June, listed at least six real grievances of which the Boers could rightly complain.

Under Shepstone's system:

1 There was no protection of the just rights of the Transvaal on the Zulu border.

2 There was no visible Government to redress complaints.

3 There was no Volksraad or any attempt at a substitute.

4 Promises regarding the preservation of the Dutch language had not been kept.

5 The Railway tax was still levied although no railway was being built.

6 There were too many officials from Natal in the administration.

Frere suggested that a new two-chamber Volksraad should be set up with the right to send members to the Cape Parliament when there were questions of common interest to be decided.

Even so, Hicks Beach was unsure whether it would be wise to summon a new Volksraad – which might officially declare independence. He would have preferred a nominated Council.

But on 26 June Mr (later Sir) Robert Herbert, Permanent Under-Secretary for the Colonies, wrote on an internal minute intended as advice to Hicks Beach: "I think that Paul Kruger has been weak and cowardly like a true Boer, and when he found that he dared not tell his people the truth as to the absence of any hope of a reconsideration of the assumption of British Sovereignty, he advocated the taking of a popular vote to gain time and avoid censure." Three days later, Herbert wrote another minute: "There is *no* hope of Messrs Kruger and Joubert behaving loyally or honestly when they return, and it is, I think, desirable to be very firm and explicit with them, with, of course, all proper courtesy." Herbert continued:

It is not impossible that, knowing how hopeless any attempt at rebellion will be when we are fully prepared, they may, before their own return, let their friends know of the failure of their mission in order that advantage may be taken of any favourable moment for a rising.

I think it, therefore, desirable that there should be no delay in stationing a considerable force of additional troops in Natal and the Transvaal; and looking to Sir T. Shepstone's strong arguments as to the comparative inefficiency of English troops for native warfare, it would seem expedient to send some of the Indian troops from Malta or from Aden to the Transvaal.

Whether the advantages of using Indian troops for "native war-fare" would have been decisive in defeating the Boers – or in provoking a rising by the Boers of the Cape – will never be known.

What is certain is that the reputation of Carnarvon, with whom the Boers had originally hoped to deal in their second visit to London, had been in the meantime destroyed for good.

Once upon a time, in December 1875, Disraeli had written to Lady Bradford: "Carnarvon is in Somersetshire and worries me to death with telegrams of four pages; he is a very clever fellow but the greatest fidget in the world."

Just over two years later Montagu Corry, "Dizzy's" Private Secretary, wrote from 10 Downing Street to Sir Henry Ponsonby, who for 25 years was the Queen's Private Secretary:

Lord B. is extremely dissatisfied with all that has taken or is taking place at the Cape. The troubles [were] commenced by Lord Carnarvon who, he says, lived mainly in a coterie of editors of liberal papers who praised him and drank his claret sending Froude – a desultory and theoretical littérateur who wrote more rot on the reign of Elizabeth than Gibbon required for all the *Decline and Fall* – to reform the Cape, which ended naturally in a Kaffir War.

Later that summer Disraeli, again in a letter to Lady Bradford, wrote:

I am not in a state of consternation about Afghanistan and if anything annoys me more than another, it is our Cape Affair where every day brings forward a new blunder of Twitters. The man he swore by was Sir T. Shepstone whom he looked upon as Heaven-born for the object in view. We sent him out entirely for Twitters' sake.

Consequently the atmosphere when the Boers met Sir Michael was not the most propitious. Nevertheless Mr Bok, interpreting for the delegation, opened up in a restrained manner.

As the official record has it:

Mr Bok: "Mr Kruger says, Sir Michael, that he has been introduced by Mr Donald Currie, and he wants to express his gratitude for having been so soon received by you and he takes the liberty to consider it as a good omen for the objects of the deputation; that is what he says. What Mr Joubert says is that he quite agrees with the former speaker, and that he only hopes that you will allow me to read what he has to say."

No sign of rebellion so far and Sir Michael expressed himself as agreeable to listening to what the deputation might have to say.

Mr Bok thereupon read "a lengthy statement of the views of the deputation", which he duly handed to Sir Michael, whose reception of it was, however, the reverse of encouraging. "I confess," said Sir Michael, "that I regret, and I am to some extent surprised that, so far as I have been able to gather its purport, the memorial which you have read should have consisted merely of a re-statement of the arguments upon those general questions which have long ago been met, and should re-open the question which last year was dealt with and actually settled."

Hicks Beach said he could not accept some of the statements in the memorial as accurate and that he had nothing else to say about it at the moment but that he would send a written answer. After a formal "Thank you" the deputation retired.

The Boer memorandum added little new material to the controversy but inferred that the sense of justice of the British nation would no longer oppose the restitution of independence which had been recognised by the Great Powers, and the general impression in Whitehall was that the Boers had put their case with great ability and that in composing it they must have been helped by an Englishman of some political experience. (The culprit was almost certainly Leonard Courtney, the member for East Cornwall, who was afterwards to lose his seat because of his opposition to the Boer War. It could well have been Courtney who, as an English friend of the Boers, presented Kruger with a gold ring engraved with the words, "Take courage, your cause is just and must triumph in the end." Kruger continued to wear this ring throughout his life as his only ornament.)

After waiting for nearly a month without having received an official reply – the British needed time to prepare themselves for the struggle which they expected to break out when or even before Kruger and Joubert arrived back in the Transvaal – the delegation wrote again to Hicks Beach. Their letter said:

It is very disagreeable for the deputation, by the many and important affairs which they know rest upon you, and which, under the present circumstances, exact all your attention, to be obliged to trouble you also. However the deputation should not fulfil their duty, and act unwarrantably, if they did not take notice of what happens presently in the country, the interests of the inhabitants of which they here defend. It is therefore that they beseech you not to take amiss when they implore you to send the promised reply to the protest and complaints of the people of the Transvaal delivered to you. The actual state of their country compels them to fulfil the mission with which they have been charged, with the utmost speed.

From the language in which the letter was couched it does not appear that on this occasion the deputation received the advice of an Englishman; nor on the other hand was there any clear declaration of independence. But in fact the letter need never have been written at all, for it crossed one from Hicks Beach to the deputation dated 7 August.

Sir Michael's reply was lengthy and contentious, and it, too, added nothing fresh to the controversy. But the Boers' rejoinder, sent from the Albemarle Hotel, introduced a new ominous note:

The sense of injustice [prevailing in the Transvaal about the annexation] may be said, perhaps, to be one of sentiment; but the effects of it are none the less substantial, and this feeling will not be removed except by arguments that have fact for their foundation.

After stating that there was now a conflict of opinion on matters of fact between the two sides, the letter concluded:

We beg in the meantime to state, that it would be misleading in use to hold out any hope that the policy you have indicated will be such as will tend to soothe or to satisfy the now prevailing discontent, and that, for our own part, we feel bound to decline the responsibility of accepting it as such on behalf of those we represent.

Most accounts of Kruger's visit to London in 1878 mention these two letters as the sum total of what happened. There was however a private interview between Hicks Beach, Kruger and Joubert on 18 July about which Hicks Beach wrote without delay to Frere:

I have today had a private interview with Kruger and Joubert. I pointed out to them the impossibility of renouncing the Queen's Sovereignty over the Transvaal. They attempted to argue this – but, after an hour's discussion, I got them to the point of admitting the possibility of our protectorate over the country, with control over its dealings with foreign, i.e., native neighbours. I propose to try and build up something on this idea which they may take back to their constituents, as a kind of alternative to independence which they have brought and which I shall of course distinctly and plainly refuse . . .

It was not enough.

On 23 August the Deputation sent an exhaustive elaboration of their position in which they declared that:

It is made clear to us that no argument based on the terms of the convention itself, on a refutation of the allegations or assumptions contained in the proclamation of annexation, or even upon the question of abstract right, is any longer of avail to us.

Hicks Beach's reply sent on 16 September was that there could be no advantage in continuing the discussion. The Boers, however, continued it on the Continent. Mr Bok, who was a Hollander, made them feel at home in The Hague; the German press was already attacking the annexation and the deputation was much encouraged in France, where Kruger met the President and was lofted up in a balloon so high that he wondered whether the pilot could not take him the rest of the way to the Transvaal. They were back in London on 19 October in time to fire a parting shot. In their final letter they concluded:

It is these circumstances which force us to the conviction that it is only by the redress of its wrongs and the re-establishment of its independence, that the Transvaal can co-operate with the adjoining States for the permanent welfare of South Africa.

Chapter 7

Prelude to a Battle

To the British, Kruger was an irreconcilable who would, nevertheless, be compelled to submit to their authority.

To the Boers, his image was less clearly defined. Here was a man who had left his native land twice to negotiate with the enemy, on each occasion without success. On his first mission he had neglected to take with him to London any written proof of his countrymen's opposition to the annexation, and their case had thus been fatally weakened. During his second visit he was able to offer to produce the evidence of some signed petitions, but it should have been clear that these were going to be treated as irrelevant and that in collecting them he had, in Carnarvon's words, been encouraging vain hopes among his supporters.

He was not entirely trusted by the Boers, who were willing to suspect that he might be in the pay of the British (which in a technical sense he had been). Nor could they have considered him a really effective advocate of their cause.

Kruger, on the other hand, could not rely unhesitatingly on the kind of commando with which the Boers normally fought their local wars – an undisciplined semi-volunteer force good only for a short campaign at the end of which they expected to be paid off in cattle if not in new territory. A war of independence against the British would not bring rewards of this kind, since the Boers would be fighting only to hold what they already had. Nor was the need to take up arms apparent to all, for they were being asked to fight not a native tribe which, if unsubdued, would murder, burn and plunder, but a civil administration that most Boers would have preferred to ignore or escape from rather than attack.

Kruger himself could have had no doubts. He had not jumped on the British lion's chest; but he had looked fairly closely into its mouth. For him there was no choice. It was independence, the survival of the Afrikaners' attitude towards life, of their language, their beliefs and their livelihood. Or it was nothing.

Kruger would have preferred not to have been forced to take up arms – not, at any rate, when the odds against winning were so formidable. Besides, he had learnt in his dealings with the natives and with other Boers that there was much to be gained by negotiating with the enemy, by wearing him down with talk, offering the chance, even, of putting one's opponent in the wrong. It should be possible, Kruger thought, to prove that the British were more culpable in refusing to respect their undertakings under the Sand River Convention than the Boers would be if they tried to recover their independence by force of arms. Surely it was better to argue thus than to shed precious blood in a land already inhabited by far too few fellow-Christians.

In his talks with the British Kruger appeared, at times, to be adopting a highly respectful if not obsequious tone, but it is difficult to be sure whether this was due to a natural respect for authority or to a desire to appear as a moderate, law-abiding burgher anxious to hold back the extremists who would otherwise commit excesses. It is even possible that the interpreter may have translated Kruger's rough and ready phraseology into something that he, Bok, thought more appropriate to the occasion.

Certainly Kruger was capable of speaking to the Boers and of speaking for them. He reacted as they reacted. He shared their prejudices. He displayed their obstinacy. He was disputatious and a good debater. He revered the same Bible and could draw profit as well as instruction from it. Part of his value was that he was a human landmark of memorable appearance, easily recalled to mind by those who had no television screen and few photographs to aid the memory. There can be little doubt that Kruger was respected by his contemporaries.

Whether he was ever popular is another matter. There were no polls to prove it. Public figures as we know them today were not to be found among the Boers. They met each other too infrequently for that, and when they did so they were not on show. There was no "society", apart from Church gatherings and cups of coffee taken together, and the last thing expected of a leader was that he should be a good fellow. Perhaps, indeed, the Boers were glad to discover in Kruger a streak of stubborn harshness, of ill nature and even meanness which proclaimed him as a fighter who would afford little comfort to his friends and none at all to his foes. The situation called for such a man. Yet it was two years before he was able to send them into battle.

Finding that Sir Bartle Frere, the High Commissioner, was not in Cape Town but had gone to Natal, Kruger and the delegation sailed on to Durban and disembarked there. His first duty was to report to the Boer Committee and he met them at Rietvlei (Reedlake) Farm near Potchefstroom. After listening to and agreeing with the final warning which the delegation had given to Hicks Beach, the Committee decided to call a mass meeting at Wonderfontein on 10 January.

There, Kruger was startled to find that the British Commander-in-Chief, Lord Chelmsford, was asking for help as to the best way of waging war against the Zulus. Kruger did his best. He warned them that whenever they halted for the night they should form a laager or movable fort with wagons and should use plenty of scouts and spies to warn them of enemy movements. He asked Lord Chelmsford, "How have you arranged your troops . . . Ah well, that is very good. There are too many troops as we Dutch fight but not too many for you." Then Kruger said, "Ask what precautions the General has taken to see that his orders are carried out *every* evening, because if they are omitted, one evening that will be fatal." Sir Bartle asked Kruger to accompany one of the Commander-in-Chief's columns as adviser and leader. "I at first refused," Kruger afterwards said. "But when Sir Bartle Frere pressed me and declared that I might name my own reward for this service, I said 'Very well, I accept. I will take 500 burghers and hand Zululand over to you, if you will give me the reward I want.'

"Sir Bartle Frere was a little offended when I offered to do with 500 men the work for which the English had placed so many soldiers in the field, and asked: 'Do you mean to say that your people are so much better than our soldiers?' 'Not that,' I replied; 'but our method of fighting is better than yours, and we know the country.'

"Sir Bartle now asked what reward I required. I said, 'The independence of my country and people,' whereupon the High Commissioner refused to discuss the subject further." Thus Kruger refused to fight as an ally of the British but was equally unwilling to aid the Zulus by declining to advise the British.

The disasters of Isandhlwana and Rorke's Drift followed,* and the Boers began to realise that, in a short campaign, they might not, after all, have much to fear from the British.

About 3,000 assembled at Wonderfontein and, according to Kruger, there would have been still more if it had not been the season of flooded rivers and horse sickness. After Kruger had spoken on the theme of "unity is strength" and had listened to various protestations of burghers impatient to "shoot the English" or anxious to die for their country, it was decided that they should all continue to protest against the annexation and would consider other means which the people as a whole might adopt for regaining their independence,

* At Isandhlawana an entire British army was encircled and wiped out, and at Rorke's Drift only the bravery of desperation saved another British force from a similar fate.

although the time for using force had not yet arrived. Soon the Boers were raiding ammunition stores and buying gunpowder at gun-point from those stores which still had it.

In February 1879 Joubert was sent down from the Transvaal to Natal to tell Frere of the new developments. Frere would offer only self-government under the British flag but promised to come to the Transvaal to meet the Boers face to face.

When this news got round, the Boers assembled en masse at Kleinfontein on the road from Newcastle to Pretoria, between Pretoria and Heidelberg. They arrived there on 18 March and out-spanned, in some cases with their wives and children, and settled down to await Sir Bartle's arrival. Once more there was talk of "shooting the English" and once again Kruger made a speech in which he urged the Boers not to break ranks, but to leave policy matters to the Committee who would certainly let them know as soon as it thought that the chances of a peaceful settlement had vanished.

Frere had written home that Joubert had been "afraid to tell his Boer friends the truth and wants me to do it for him", but he seemed in no hurry to do so. He and his advisers considered that the assembly of such a large number of Boers constituted a threat to the Pretoria garrison, especially since, after waiting for a fortnight, the Boers moved camp to be nearer the town. He therefore waited for re-inforcements to arrive in Natal before setting out on 15 March on his journey of about 300 miles.

Frere arrived at Heidelberg on 9 April and the Boers sent him a note which implied that he had kept them waiting because he was afraid to come and meet them in camp. So, after breakfasting at Ferguson's hotel two or three miles away from the Boers, the 64-year-old High Commissioner borrowed the fastest of the horses ridden by his staff and galloped into the camp ahead of his staff. The camp was pitched on a slope by the roadside with a wide passage in the middle between the wagons. The Boers were drawn up on either side of this passage – about 1,200 of them perhaps – in two rows, three deep. Frere rode slowly between the two lines and raised his hand to his sun-helmet in salute. Not a man acknowledged it and there was dead silence as he passed by, and the Committee received him correctly. Frere, an unusually tall man with a quiet friendly voice and a cour-teous though at times sarcastic manner, soon impressed the Boers.

The meeting took place in April 1879 in a large open-flap tent with Frere and his staff sitting on one side of a large table and the members of the Committee on the other three sides. The Boers crowded round the opening of the tent, watching and listening to every word. A friendly atmosphere was eventually established, but no new ground was broken. It was Thursday in Passion Week and the two sides agreed not to meet on Good Friday but to hold discussions again on Saturday, this time at Erasmus' farm about six miles from Pretoria. Here Frere got off to a good start by getting his interpreter, the Revd G. W. Stegmann, to open the proceedings with a prayer in Dutch, but for five hours the two sides repeated the same arguments, at the end of which Joubert said, "We have a last request to put before your Excellency: Will your Excellency be our advocate for our interests to the British people assembled in Parliament, and tell them that the people of the South African Republic abhor the annexation?" Frere refused to be their advocate but agreed to send home a memorial and, in answer to a question from Kruger, said, "I will not only send home the memorial, but show Mr Kruger what I will write regarding it." "Is the meaning of this," Kruger asked, "that your Excellency will give your support to the case as it will be stated therein?" "Now, my good friend Mr Kruger," Frere answered, "after all I have said, do you think that I can give such support, that I can say one thing now here, and another there?" However the memorial was prepared and sent off and, with it, Frere's own summary of the Boer arguments, initialled by Kruger and four other members of the Committee.

This did not entirely relax the tension, and some of the younger Boers were in favour of entering Pretoria and attacking the garrison. The townspeople mounted night patrols, put up barricades and handed out arms and ammunition. But in the end the Boers went away of their own accord almost at the very moment when the world heard that Frere had been publicly censured for his plans to annex Zululand.

After nearly six months, during which no response came from Whitehall, Frere was replaced by Wolseley who came to the Transvaal as Governor of Natal, the Transvaal and Zululand, to announce at the end of September that the territory should be and should remain permanently an integral part of Her Majesty Queen Victoria's dominions.

He toured the Transvaal speaking at every dorp, and at Standerton he told his audience, "So long as the sun shines, the Transvaal will be British Territory; and the Vaal river shall flow back to its sources before the Transvaal is again independent."

The Boers, however, decided to hold yet another of their mass meetings, this time on 10 December 1879, again at Wonderfontein. When Wolseley got to hear of this he issued a warning proclamation from his temporary field headquarters at Fort Weber. In it he claimed that the proposed meeting was aimed at undermining the authority of the Government and would lead to unrest. He warned those taking part that they and their families might face prosecution for treason. Nevertheless, according to Wolseley's own report, about 2,000 Boers arrived in 500 wagons. Kruger was obviously emerging as the national leader, and, before the discussions began, Gerrit Scheepers and Nicholas Smit appeared at the head of a procession of 400 mounted Boers in front of Kruger's tent, carrying before them the Vierkleur (literally: "four colour") flag. "The flag flying before your eyes is the symbol of our unity and on behalf of my friends and followers here," Scheepers said, "I confirm that we are ready to sacrifice our blood and all that we possess in order to see it flying again over our free and independent land." Smit added: "This flag is the flag of our fathers, precious to them and doubly precious to us. Let us show that we wish to preserve it and that if asked we will shed our blood for it."

Kruger then set the tone of the meeting by asking those of little faith to withdraw. "I take this opportunity," he said, "to tell you that I have heard that there are some men here who have been brought here through intimidation and duress. Sir Bartle Frere and Sir Garnet Wolseley have promised these men their protection. We do the same. I stand surety for their safety. But let them leave us. We do not wish to keep them. Let neither fear nor false modesty hold them back and let it not be said that a single person remained here against his will." Then the leaders tried to decide on the next step. Joubert said that resolutions, deputations and meetings were obviously leading nowhere; the Committee must be given further instructions. "We wish to know what the people want. Are you to submit, and if not what course do you suggest taking?" Someone proposed that they should "take the country, elect a President and assemble the Volksraad". But Kruger warned that taking on the British Empire was no light matter.

Joubert turned down a proposal that the Committee should spend another two months in an effort to find a peaceful solution. He was not advising them to regain independence by force of arms, yet he knew of no other way which would lead to independence. "It is true that England is mighty," he said, "but do not lose sight of our goal. It is a sacred cause, and God will help us . . . Our freedom has been taken from us and we want it back. Consult your God, but remember that the Lord takes revenge on those who cause the downfall of their land and people through irresponsibility."

Kruger himself might well have written these words, as also Joubert's warning to the waverers: "It is not for you to say 'Kruger and Joubert advised us.' You must come to your own decision."

Kruger, in his memoirs, records having done some "market

research" by eavesdropping round the camp-fires of Wonderfontein after dark:

> Late that night, I walked through the camp to listen to the conversations which the burghers were holding at their camp-fires. I was anxious to find out how my warning [that the British Empire was a formidable opponent] had been taken. Many of the remarks that fell upon my ears were very characteristic. For instance, I heard one man say:
> "I think Kruger is betraying us."
> "No," said another. "I will never believe that of him, for he has done too much for us and he is still working too hard to deserve being accused of that sort of thing."
> "But," replied the first, "if he doesn't mean to betray us, why won't he let us shoot the Englishmen?"
> "Aye," said the other. "I think his plans are wrong, but I won't believe he is betraying us."

From this Kruger rightly concluded that the Boers would be glad to shoot the Englishmen under his guidance, and keep on shooting.

The meeting's decisions were put on paper on 15 December. It was resolved that "the people of the South African Republic have never been, and do not wish to be, Her Majesty's subjects and that everyone who speaks of us as rebels is a slanderer." It was also recommended that Kruger should be promoted from Vice-President to President; that he should convene the Volksraad (i.e. set up a rival Government to the British Authority); that nothing less than independence would suffice; and that "We solemnly declare that we are prepared to sacrifice our life and shed our blood for it. If the Committee could think of any better suggestions they should consult the people about them."

They planned to meet again on 6 April, which would allow time to set up the new Government before 12 April, the anniversary of the annexation.

Wolseley, telegraphing from Pretoria on 15 December, commented: "I intend to retain the King's Dragoon Guards here for some time to come, in addition to the garrison of a battery of artillery, and three battalions of infantry already determined upon."

Later he added that Kruger had refused to accept office as President, but that he, Wolseley, had instituted proceedings for treason against Pretorius and Bok who had signed the letter notifying him of some of the resolutions passed at Wonderfontein.

The meeting was not overlooked by *The Times* of London, a newspaper which, then as later, was not particularly noted for its partiality to the Afrikaners. In a leader published on 17 January 1880 it pointed out that although the meeting had broken up without any breach of the peace, the Boers had arranged to reassemble and that one of the resolutions to be put before them "disclosed a very serious and determined spirit of disaffection among the Boers". One resolution, it pointed out, was that if the British Government continued to repress the independence of the people, and refused to remove the grievances due to the annexation in a friendly way before 6 April next, the people would then consider themselves bound to burn, or otherwise destroy, all texts, books or documents in English within their reach; to take away all their children from English schools; to forbid the English language in their houses, and to oppose its use elsewhere as much as possible; to refuse hospitality to Englishmen or their allies, and to give them no assistance or protection on the roads.

The Times commented that in default of evidence to the contrary it must be admitted that the majority of the white inhabitants of the Transvaal were now opposed to British rule and that it was a pity that Sir Garnet had pre-empted what should have remained an open question by declaring immediately after Wonderfontein that the territory would hereafter be administered as a Crown Colony. This, *The Times* considered, was ill-advised, particularly since the threat to the South African Republic from the surrounding tribes had now been removed.

Sir Garnet was, however, no less peremptory in pushing ahead with a revised constitution designed to reconcile the Boers to their new lot, and, on 10 March, the first meeting was held in Pretoria of the so-called "Assembly" set up under a new Whitehall constitution. London began to receive rather more optimistic accounts not only from Wolseley but also from Owen Lanyon who had succeeded Shepstone as Governor of the Transvaal.

It is difficult to find the basis for such optimism – unless it could be ascribed to the fact that a drive by the British tax collectors had succeeded in raising more money than had previously been wrung out of the Boers. (Joubert, for one, lost a plot of land which was seized and sold by the tax authorities because he refused to pay his dues.)

If Pretorius had ever possessed claims to lead the Boers against the British he would have had to abandon them as a result of his conduct after Wonderfontein. He was lodged in Potchefstroom jail accused of treason and had been refused bail. His first move was to send an appeal to the Boers not to rescue him by force. This was a sound enough decision since an armed rescue might have precipitated counter-measures by the British before the Boers were ready to fight back. Kruger, who was on his way to Potchefstroom to persuade the

British to release Pretorius on bail, took the same line when he heard that, despite Pretorius' appeal, a rescue party of 350 armed Boers was already on the way. "I galloped after them as fast as my horse could carry me and caught them up close to the village [of Potchefstroom]. After many arguments, I at last succeeded in persuading them to give up their plan," Kruger recalled.

Pretorius was certainly released on bail but in the meantime the British had "got at" him and persuaded him that since violence would not pay, acquiescence should. So Pretorius agreed to set out on a mission of pacification with transport provided by the British. Wolseley's decision to arrest a relatively weak member of the Boer opposition had paid off – temporarily.

Pretorius' first meeting was with the Boers who had come to rescue him, and who were still gathered at Naauwpoort not far from Potchefstroom. Kruger was present when Pretorius arrived and heard him read out the British proclamation to the effect that though the annexation could not be reversed, self-government was on the way.

For Kruger, this was going too far, and when Pretorius had finished he spoke. "Burghers," he asked, "do you understand what the British Government offer you? I will try to explain to you what this self-government, in my opinion means. They say to you, 'First put your head quietly in the noose, so that I can hang you up: then you may kick your legs about as much as you please.' That is what they call self-government."

Thereafter Pretorius discontinued his campaign and refused the seat that he was offered on Wolseley's Executive Council.

Two things interfered with Kruger's plans to hold the mass meeting in April.

The first was the strong support which the Boer cause was already receiving from the Liberal Party, and in particular from Leonard Courtney to whom the Boers had been indiscreet enough to pass a public vote of thanks at their meeting at Wonderfontein.

In February 1880 Lord Hartington, a traditional Whig and Leader of the Opposition to Disraeli, declared in Parliament:

It is perfectly clear now that the annexation of the Transvaal was a measure adopted by the Government and sanctioned by the House, under wrong impressions and incorrect information. We were informed that a large majority of the European settlers and inhabitants of the Transvaal were in favour of that annexation. It is now proved conclusively that a large majority of the Boers are bitterly against it. We were told that we could not permit the foreign policy adopted by the Government of the Transvaal to be continued. We have ourselves been compelled to adopt precisely the same line of policy [he meant the war against the Zulus] and under these circumstances I think it ought not to be regarded as a settled question simply because the annexation has taken place. If it be proved that it is for the advantage of the district and for the peace of the whole community of South Africa that the Transvaal should continue to be governed by us, by all means let it be so. But if, on the other hand, we find it would be more advantageous, and more honourable, to restore the former Government of that country, then I say that no false sense of dignity should stand in the way.

It looked, therefore, as if the Boers could count on Liberal support but might lose it if they set up their own Government on 12 April.

The second obstacle to the April meeting was an attempt by Hicks Beach to revive the interest of the Cape Government in a scheme for confederation.

The Transvalers felt that if ever South Africa were united under the British flag their chances of independence would have vanished. The Cape Parliament had been under pressure from Whitehall for nearly a year and had withheld their support for confederation largely because they did not wish to become involved in the expense of a Zulu war. With the Zulu problem settled, there was now a danger of their acquiescing to Hicks Beach's proposals. In March Kruger insisted that he and Joubert should go to the Cape to speak against the proposals. They held meetings at Paarl, Worcester, Stellenbosch and Malmesbury as well as at the Cape itself, and Kruger, perhaps in an effort not to appear too patronising, told the Cape Town audience, "I would prefer to be a British subject [as the members of his audience were] than to accept the independence of the Transvaal with conditions which will bind it to British policy and the wrongs which are committed under British rule."

Kruger declared that the Republic would never accept confederation under the British flag and would not allow foreigners to determine their future for them. At the end of his campaign Kruger made a final speech and which he appealed to the Cape Dutch: "Do not wash your hands in the blood of your brothers."

The Cape Parliament rejected Hicks Beach's proposals.

The decision to send Kruger and Joubert to the Cape was taken on 6 March, almost on the very day that Disraeli, whose Government's popularity had dwindled with each new colonial war, decided to hold a General Election in Britain. Disraeli expected to be returned with a comfortable majority, and the Boers were as surprised as their

Liberal friends when Gladstone came back to power. Gladstone, when accounting for his victory, said: "I do believe the Almighty has employed me for His purposes in a manner larger, or more special, than before, and has strengthened me and led me on accordingly" – an explanation greatly to Kruger's taste.

But in his Midlothian campaign Gladstone had said many things – as politicians in opposition often do – without suspecting that he might have to carry his proposals into effect. He had described the annexation as "the invasion of a free people" and an attempt "to coerce the free subjects of a republic and to compel them to accept a citizenship which they decline and refuse". And at Peebles on 30 March he declared, "If these acquisitions [Cyprus and the Transvaal] were as valuable as they are valueless, I would repudiate them, because they are obtained by means dishonourable to our country." Consequently it was with some impatience that Kruger waited for Mr Gladstone to complete his Cabinet and fulfil his promises.

But among the legacies left to the new Cabinet was a paper written by Wolseley shortly before Wonderfontein setting out the arguments for retaining the Transvaal. Not one of the British pro-consuls summarised as clearly as Wolseley the considerations which made it desirable for Britain to keep the territory. His despatch, marked "Confidential", was sent on 13 November 1879 from Fort Weber in the Transvaal. He began by giving a preliminary warning about the meeting to be held the following month and the consequences which were likely to follow it. He then made it clear that if the Transvaal was to be held, it would apparently be against the wishes of the majority of the white population. This, however, was due in part to intimidation of the more responsible Boers, and because the British, who formed the most influential part of the population, were silent for fear of losing their trade with the Boers, who were twice their number. Wolseley wrote:

> Although the members of the trading community will tell me in private how destructive to them and to commerce in general would be any reversal of our policy here, they are not prepared to come forward as a body and take any actively open part in support of this Government, as by doing so they would incur the lasting enmity of the Boers who are now their best customers. If nine shopkeepers out of ten were to actively assist the Government and the tenth man to remain cowardly, inactive, expressing no opinion, or traitorously advocating the Boer cause, he would monopolise all the Boer business in the district to the ruin of the nine others.

Civilised government, it appeared to Wolseley, would never be forthcoming if the Boer had his way:

The Boers are essentially the most ignorant of people, easily led by the few designing men who appeal to their instinctive dislike of English rule and the English race generally. They resent all and any form of Constitution which restricts their individual power to do as each man lists. Each individual wishes to govern, I might say to bully, the natives in his immediate neighbourhood as he thinks fit, and hates the establishment of a strong government over him such as we are endeavouring to inaugurate, by which the native will be protected from violence and by means of which order will be maintained and taxes collected. The condition of affairs most agreeable to the Boer is that of having such a weak executive over him that he can resist it effectually whenever he thinks it is in his own individual interest to do so. Before the annexation, if the Volksraad passed a law that was disliked by any clique in the surrounding district, it was no uncommon practice for a party of 50 or a 100 armed Boers to ride into Pretoria, "off saddle" in front of the Council Chamber, enter it, and insist upon the obnoxious law being instantly repealed.

Wolseley went on to say:

The Transvaal is rich in minerals; gold has already been found in quantities, and there can be little doubt that larger and still more valuable goldfields will sooner or later be discovered. Any such discovery would soon bring a large British population here. The time must eventually arrive when the Boers will be in a small minority, as the country is very sparsely peopled, and as yet the land is made but little use of. Would it not therefore be a very near-sighted policy to recede now from the position we have taken up here, because for some years to come the retention of 2,000 or 3,000 troops may be necessary to reconsolidate our power?

As these troops are now here, the expense of maintaining them in the Transvaal will be but little in excess of what their cost would amount to elsewhere. When the grass is high enough to cut, Kaffir huts can be quickly constructed for them at a small outlay, as was done in Natal when its permanent garrison was increased in 1876. The presence of these troops in the Transvaal will tend greatly to establish a good healthy English feeling in it, and so be the means of largely increasing the number of its inhabitants of British descent.

Wolseley concluded that: "Under a Boer Government the great resources of this splendid territory can never be developed as the

Boers, one and all, are ignorant of even the first principles of governing."

On 14 May 1880 the Cape Prime Minister, Gordon Sprigg, announced the receipt of a telegram from Lord Kimberley, the new Secretary of State for the Colonies, confirming that the Queen's Sovereignty over the Transvaal could not be relaxed. On 20 May Gladstone delivered the Speech from the Throne of his new administration. In it he spoke of "self-government" for the Transvaal rather than independence. And Gladstone, replying on 8 June to a letter from Kruger and Joubert, claimed that:

Looking to all the circumstances both of the Transvaal and the rest of South Africa, and to the necessity of preventing a renewal of disorders [i.e. the Zulu war] which might lead to disastrous consequences, not only to the Transvaal, but to the whole of South Africa, our judgement is that the Queen cannot be advised to relinquish her sovereignty over the Transvaal.

Wolseley, by then, had left the Transvaal but he had won his battle and, as the months wore on, it became more and more clear that the Boers, too, would need to win a battle if they were to regain their freedom.

Chapter 8

Majuba

A wrangle over a farm wagon started a small Boer war in 1880, 19 years before the great Boer War broke out.

Piet Bezuidenhout, the owner of the wagon, had already clashed with the collector of taxes earlier in the year and had gone to prison for a week rather than pay a fine of £5 for buying gunpowder without a permit. Now the tax authorities were dunning him for £27 5s – roughly £13 more than he said he owed them. He would pay £14 into Court, he told the magistrate, but only on condition that the money would be handed over to the South African Republic if its independence were to be restored by the following January.

The magistrate, Mr A. Goetz, naturally referred the case to Pretoria and was told that he should accept £14 in payment of taxes due, if Bezuidenhout also paid costs amounting to £13 5s (which, Bezuidenhout could not fail to notice, raised the total to exactly what the tax authorities had originally demanded).

Bezuidenhout refused to oblige and Goetz seized his wagon and gave notice that it would be sold at eleven on the morning of 11 November as lien for the debt.

But, on 7 November, four days before the deadline, Goetz received a visit from Piet Cronje, a seasoned warrior who was also a tax defaulter. Cronje rode in at the head of 130 mounted Boers, who claimed to represent the district of Schoonspruit. They handed Goetz a written declaration affirming their refusal to pay taxes demanded by an illegal Government. Their dues would be forthcoming only under the same conditions as Bezuidenhout's.

Goetz duly reported this visitation to the authorities, who insisted however that the sale of Bezuidenhout's wagon must go on.

On the appointed day Cronje reappeared outside the Courthouse with about 100 armed supporters. Speeches of a rebellious nature were made, after which the Boers repaired to the Market Square where the wagon was to be sold. They shouted down the Court Messenger, Moquette, who had started to read out the conditions of sale, bundled him off the wagon, and had it in-spanned and driven away to Bezuidenhout's farm.

There was no garrison at Potchefstroom to restore law and order, and the alarm signal had to be sent to Pretoria where Colonel "Long-John" Lanyon was now Administrator.

Lanyon sent Commandant Raaff to Potchefstroom as Acting Superintendent of Police with power to enrol volunteers. He also ordered Colonel Bellairs, the Area Commander, to rush a detachment of 140 men, under the command of Colonel Winslow, to Potchefstroom to support the police. Warrants were issued for the arrest of Cronje, Bezuidenhout and some other disaffected Boers, but the number of British troops in the Transvaal had been so greatly reduced since Wolseley's departure in May that it was thought inadvisable to make any arrests.

The Boers began to mass on Cronje's farm, and sent a message to Rustenburg telling Kruger that they were now ready to start the War of Independence. Kruger in turn summoned Joubert from Wakkerstroom in readiness for a meeting of the People's Committee. He also arranged to go with Cronje to see Raaff at Ventersdorp. The British were heavily outnumbered there but Raaff proposed, nevertheless, that Cronje and the other wanted men should give themselves up to the Magistrate, and promised that if they did so they would be treated leniently.

Kruger clearly held the key to the situation. He pointed out that he had not been involved with Cronje, that he had arrived from Rustenburg only the previous night and that he had not come on his own initiative but had been sent for. He had come to try to prevent bloodshed, but he was disturbed to find how serious the situation had become. The Boers were armed and determined to fight, and this must be his final effort to keep the peace.

The best he could do was to arrange a meeting between Cronje and George Hudson, the Government Secretary, who was then in Potchefstroom.

Colonel Winslow put it to Kruger that Cronje's action amounted to open rebellion. Kruger replied, "I should agree with you if we had acknowledged the annexation; but that is not the case. We do not look upon ourselves as British subjects, and the question of tax is not a private problem of Bezuidenhout's, but one of principle which concerns the whole country."

Kruger's meeting with Hudson took place on 1 December at Labuschagne's farm at Kaalfontein in the presence of the Boer Committee, but Hudson had no more to offer than Raaff, and Kruger advised him to leave quietly before the Boers got out of hand.

From then on the tempo speeded up. The British had a Basuto war on their hands and the Boers thought they would seldom have a better opportunity of launching their own war of independence. It was decided to hold a mass meeting of Boers only seven days later at Paardekraal. On 10 December 32 members of the People's Committee resolved to carry out the resolution of 16 December 1879 and resurrect the Government of the South African Republic.

Kruger was asked to call a meeting of the Volksraad, and 12 of its members met on 13 December. The Executive Council of the new Government voted to entrust the Government of the country to a group of three men, Paul Kruger, Piet Joubert and Marthinus Wessel Pretorius (although Pretorius was largely a figurehead included to conciliate the "moderates").

As a symbol of solidarity they built a memorial to their new-found freedom.

Each man gathered a stone or rock and brought it as his contribution. One by one, walking by in single file, they laid the stones together to form a huge cairn, on top of which the Vierkleur was planted to flutter once more openly in the breeze.

At Kruger's suggestion, Joubert was appointed Commandant-General. Kruger set up his own headquarters and "capital" at Heidelberg, then a town of about 250 inhabitants. There he was well placed to prevent any British forces which might be sent up from Natal from reaching Pretoria. Heidelberg was occupied without a shot being fired.

The Boers then presented a lengthy proclamation setting out the reasons for the re-establishment of the South African Republic. The text was drawn up by Dr Jorissen who, following his dismissal by the British, had rejoined the new Boer Government as Attorney-General. In their communications to the British, the three-man committee continued to express the hope that bloodshed would be avoided and that the transition from dependence to independence would proceed peacefully.

The proclamation issued at the end of the rally did, in fact, offer the prospect of peaceful co-existence between the Boers and the British. It acknowledged the right of the British Government to appoint a Consul or diplomatic agent to safeguard the interests of British subjects. It agreed to submit disputes about boundaries with neighbouring native tribes to arbitration, and to consult with the Colonies and States of southern Africa on native policy. Finally, it stated that the South African Republic was prepared to enter into a confederation in consultation with those Colonies and States.

Piet Cronje was sent to Potchefstroom with a detachment of 400 men to take over the town and its printing works, which were needed to print copies of the proclamation for general distribution. Arrangements were made for copies to be sent to Sir Gordon Sprigg the

Cape Prime Minister, to Colonel Lanyon and to Sir George Colley, Commissioner for South East Africa and Governor of Natal.

The meeting at Paardekraal which authorised these irreversible decisions was stage-managed in near-professional style. It needed a Rembrandt, Dr Jorissen said, to sketch the scene.

On the topmost ridge stood the tents of the leaders looking down into the great amphitheatre below. The Boers and their families in scattered groups – some on camp stools, others stretched out on the ground – waited patiently for the next move. High up on the edge of the plateau stood a pulpit with an awning above and a small table with a Bible on it in front. A prayer was said and a hymn sung. Then the preacher read out an appeal made three months earlier to the ministers of all Churches for help in the coming struggle. Waving the paper backwards and forwards he cried, "I cannot resist such an appeal: Here I am, and I shall go with you and stand with you."

The Boers sent a covering letter to Lanyon with their Proclamation. It read:

Excellency, in the name of the people of the South African Republic, we approach you in order to fulfil a grave but inevitable duty. We have the honour to send you a copy of the Proclamation settled by the Government and the Volksraad and generally promulgated. The will of the people is evident, and needs no explanation. We declare in the most solemn manner that we have no desire to spill blood, and that from our side we do not wish war. It lies in your hands to force us to appeal to arms in self-defence, which may God forbid. If it comes so far, we will do so with the deepest reverence for Her Majesty the Queen of England and her flag. Should it come so far, we will defend ourselves with a knowledge that we are struggling for the honour of Her Majesty, for we fight for the sanctity of the treaties sworn by her, but broken by her officials . . . In 1877 our then Government gave up the keys of the Government offices without spilling blood. We trust that your Excellency, as representative of the whole British nation, will, not less nobly, and in the same way, place our Government in a position to assume the administration. We expect your answer within 24 hours.

But already, before then, the war had commenced. At Potchefstroom a trigger-happy British soldier had fired a shot from the fort in which the heavily outnumbered British garrison had taken refuge; it wounded a farmer, Frans Robberts, who came from Wijsfontein Farm near Rustenburg. From then, during the next two months, the British made almost every mistake it is possible for the military mind to commit.

As the Boers had foreseen, British reinforcements were despatched to the principal towns in the Transvaal, and Colonel Philip Anstruther, with three Companies of the 94th Regiment, nearly 300 officers and men and dependants, was ordered to proceed from Lydenburg to Pretoria together with a train of water-carts, ambulances and wagons loaded with provisions, ammunition, camping equipment and other stores. It was Christmas week and the men were in good spirits. They were not apparently expecting any trouble although their Commander had been warned about the possibility of attack, and in fact the wires between Durban and Pretoria had been cut on the night of 15–16 December. Nevertheless, the British made no attempt at concealment, and the band was playing.

All went well until about 2.30 in the afternoon when the column reached Bronkhorstspruit – a group of farms situated about 36 miles short of Pretoria. Suddenly the leading officers caught sight of armed Boers. The band stopped playing and the troops halted. Almost at once a Boer rode up carrying a white flag and a note. It called on the British Commander to halt his advance at a small stream near by and gave him two minutes to make his decision.

Colonel Anstruther repeated that his orders were to proceed to Pretoria and the messenger then returned to his Commander. Almost immediately Anstruther realised that he had been ambushed, and that the Boers were closing in to his rear. It was too late to deploy, and, in a few minutes, there were 120 casualties and the remainder compelled to surrender. Colonel Anstruther, who had tied a white handkerchief to his sword "so that at least some should survive to tell what happened", had been hit in several places and died soon afterwards from his wounds.

Bronkhorstspruit was only a skirmish but a decisive one. It raised Boer morale, disconcerted the British, and made it more difficult for them to relieve not only Pretoria but other isolated garrisons at Potchefstroom, Standerton, Rustenburg and elsewhere.

Nor were the British more successful in their set battles. Their Commander, General Sir George Pomeroy Colley, was one of those brilliant eccentrics whom the British Army occasionally throws up. He composed poetry, was an admirer of Ruskin, played the flautina and carried a sketch book with him on his campaigns. He had passed out of Sandhurst brilliantly, had served as a Border Magistrate in the Cape Eastern Province, and also with his regiment in Peking. He had been selected for training at the Staff College where it was said his examination papers eclipsed those of any other previous student. He had become Professor of Military Administration at Sandhurst. It was unfortunate that he was called on to sustain such a reputation by results in the field. He proved quite incapable of performing the task. At Laing's Nek, the key pass leading up from Natal to the Transvaal, he sent his men charging across open ground towards a trench bristling with Boer rifles. One in three of his men were hit. Ten days later, on 8 February, in an effort to keep open his line of communications, he allowed his men to be caught on the wrong side of a ford over the Ingogo river and was lucky not to lose all of them. Finally Colley performed what he considered would be his master-stroke. On the night of Saturday, 26 February, in an attempt to break through the mountains lying between Natal and the Transvaal, he sent his forces in single file up the side of a steep slope leading to the plateau on top of Majuba Hill, which commanded the Boer positions. But his men were driven off in disorder the following morning by the Boers in a skilful attack made up the other, less steep, approach to the summit. Colley's judgement of slopes and contours was so poor that he had not believed it possible. He was killed by a bullet in the head while leading his men.

Of course Majuba was not one of the great battles of the world, but its moral effects were considerable. The atmosphere of the engagement was vividly described by a 19-year-old officer, Percival Marling, who was afterwards awarded the VC during the Suakin campaign.

His diary entry for Sunday, 27 February 1881 reads:

A fine day till about 5.30 p.m. I shan't forget it in a hurry. We were awakened by firing about 6 a.m. which went on in a desultory manner till 11.30 a.m. when it became very heavy. Our riflemen were all on the left of a plateau at the foot of Majuba, and we couldn't see whether the Boers were on the top of Majuba Hill or not. The guns (two nine-pounders) were ordered out of camp about 12.30 to shell the Boers. The first intimation we had of our repulse was a wounded rating, who came in about 2 p.m. saying we were being driven off. He said it had taken him five b——y hours to get up Majuba, but he only touched the ground five b——y times on the way down. Then two or three more stragglers came in, who said the General was shot. By this time the camp was thoroughly alarmed. The forts were manned, all the ammunition divided amongst them and the Gatlings and rockets got ready. I had command of Nr. 4 Fort, with about 20 men and 12 sailors with the rockets. The firing kept coming nearer and we could see our people coming down the hill like blazes. We covered their retreat.

It came on to pour with rain about 5 p.m. Beaumont and I volunteered for picket although it was not our turn. There was an officer in each fort. It was far and away the worst night I ever had. I couldn't even see the entrance to the fort which was only about 30 feet in diameter. I had on my field boots, waterproof breeches, greatcoat, and mackintosh. Twice the relief lost themselves; you literally couldn't see your hand in front of your face. All night long the wounded kept coming past our fort. We expected to be attacked every minute. The fort was about 18 inches deep in mud and water, and in the morning the men were so stiff and cramped they could hardly move. Essex, the Brigade Major, who had wind up badly, came out and said I was to keep an extra sharp look-out, as the Boers were coming down to attack the camp disguised in the 92nd's kilts and the 58th's red coats! The only bright spot that night.

It was so dark you couldn't see a man three yards off. Twice I was nearly shot by my own sentries . . . I never slept the whole night and didn't come off picket till 8.30 a.m. . . . . Major Fraser [afterwards Major-General Sir Thomas Fraser] had an extraordinary story to tell when he came into camp. He said he fell over a 40-foot precipice when he was escaping from Majuba Hill, and that he caught glow-worms, which he put on his compass, and eventually found his way back to our camp . . .

Later: Everybody was sorry about Colley, he was a most lovable person, but his death was a most fortunate thing for him, and as someone said, for the Natal Field Force too. After Ingogo he hardly slept at all, and used to be writing, always writing, in his tent half the night.

Kruger, for once, had not been in the front line. No doubt he felt it was more essential to organise resistance in the country as a whole rather than to interfere with Joubert's defence of his eastern frontier. He visited the areas round Potchefstroom, Sanderton and Rustenburg to encourage the Boers to stand firm (and the Kaffirs to remain neutral).

He had already issued a Petition of Right to the Orange Free State (which was still an independent republic), appealing to its President, Sir Johannes Henricus Brand, and to its Volksraad for help against the alien British. "Whether we conquer or die," Kruger's letter said, "freedom will come to Africa as surely as the sun rises through tomorrow's clouds – as freedom reigns in the United States. Then shall it be from the Zambesi to Simon's Bay, Africa for the Afrikanders." Although Brand remained neutral, it was not long before a contingent of volunteers rode northwards across the frontier from the Free State into the Transvaal.

Kruger, as the chief organiser of the resistance movement, was obviously the man to negotiate any peace settlement which might follow the conflict.

But neither he, nor the Boers, realised that their victories delayed rather than hastened a peace settlement, for there were many in Britain who had been ready for negotiations before the fighting started, but who felt with Queen Victoria that once hostilities had begun they could not negotiate except from a position of strength.

As early as 10 January, on the very day when Colley set out to join his troops for the campaign, Lord Kimberley, Gladstone's Secretary of State for the Colonies, had got in touch with Brand and asked him to tell Kruger that he might be able to make a satisfactory arrangement if the rebels ceased "armed opposition to the Queen's authority". Both he and Gladstone still hoped to interest Kruger in a confederation with the Cape, Natal and the Orange Free State.

Colley, on noting these signs of appeasement, was far from pleased, and his dissatisfaction grew as further messages, aimed at securing peace before he had had a chance to win the war, continued to flash between London, Bloemfontein and Heidelberg.

Soon after his defeat at the Ingogo, Colley himself was compelled to join in the ignoble traffic of peace.

Kimberley instructed him to tell Brand that Her Majesty's Government would be ready to give all reasonable guarantees as to the treatment of Boers after submission if they ceased from armed opposition, and that a scheme would be framed "for the permanent friendly settlement of difficulties".

On 12 February Kruger, possibly on Brand's advice, wrote saying that he was willing to make one more effort to avoid bloodshed and to co-operate with the British Government for the good of South Africa. He was sure that the English people would support their case if the truth reached them. He would not fear the inquiry of a Royal Commission which his people knew would give them their rights. Therefore he would give free passage to British troops withdrawing from "our country", and in this case his own would withdraw from their own positions.

(One wonders, if the British garrisons had been withdrawn, whether any verdict favourable to Britain given by the Royal Commission could have been enforced.)

On 16 February, 11 days before Majuba, Kimberley went one step further by sending a reply to Kruger through Colley. In it Kimberley agreed not only to a Royal Commissioner, but also to a suspension of hostilities if the Boers also "desisted from armed opposition".

It was left, however, to Colley to decide for how long the offer should remain open and Colley, never one to shirk a fight, insisted on the proposal being accepted "within 48 hours". According to one interpretation this gave the Boers 48 hours after the receipt of the offer in which to consider it. But to Colley it meant that their acceptance must be received by him within 48 hours.

He did not deliver his note to the Boer headquarters till 24 February when Kruger was thought to be at Heidelberg 120 miles away (in fact he was on his way to Rustenburg, still further from the front line). A reply within the 48-hour limit could not have been expected, but Colley was not prepared to wait any longer.

His troops scaled Majuba before the 48 hours had expired.

After Majuba there was a lull. The Queen of course was horrified and the defeat intensified her dislike and distrust of Gladstone. But the Grand Old Man had slipped on some soft snow and cut his head open. He was still in bed and escaped the struggle in the Cabinet between the hawks and the doves, and also some of the criticism that he would otherwise have met at first hand. The War Office, too late, ordered six infantry battalions and three cavalry regiments to South Africa. Sir Evelyn Wood, who, though senior to Colley, had agreed to serve under him, was placed in temporary command while Sir Frederick (later Lord) Roberts, of Kandahar fame, was sent for to take over from him. It was essential for the Boers to make peace before the full might of the imperial machine could be mobilised. Kruger, however, was still unavailable, and on 4 March Joubert, prompted by Brand, offered to meet Wood to arrange an armistice, and the latter, on his own responsibility, agreed on 6 March to an eight-day's truce which he calculated would give him time enough to prepare to accomplish, with his substantial reinforcements, the victory which had eluded Colley.

On 7 March Kruger's reply to Colley's 48-hour ultimatum arrived and was forwarded to London. It was relatively mild in tone and Wood realised that he might not be allowed to avenge the defeat at Majuba. London would press ahead with peace negotiations rather than towards the military success he felt certain of being able to offer them.

About the same time Kruger issued, in imperial style, an Order of the Day to commemorate Majuba. The text in true Boer tradition attributed the victory not to human power but to "the God of our fathers to whom for the last five years we have addressed our prayers and supplications".

The British saw matters differently. They had been astonished to find themselves in the field against men who were anything but cowardly and who advanced undeterred by shell-fire. They noted that the Boers could pick off their opponents one by one without having to fire indiscriminate volleys as was the practice in the British Army.

Kruger's first act, after announcing his satisfaction with the Lord's work at Majuba, was to criticise Joubert's. He deplored an armistice which, among other things, allowed Wood to take food supplies to the besieged garrisons in Pretoria and elsewhere. Kruger maintained that these concessions, if granted at all, should have applied only to military personnel and should have excluded all civilians.

He started the negotiations at a disadvantage, for the longer the ceasefire lasted, the more difficult it would be to prevent the Boers from breaking camp and returning to look after their farms.

But in the end the Boers were able to prove that they were no easier to defeat at the conference table than they had been in the field. They made difficulties from the start. For example, the British had proposed that the two sides should meet at O'Neill's cottage, set on a hillside half-way between the British camp at Mount Prospect and the Boer lines at Laing's Nek, on the Natal side of the border. At first the Boers refused to advance so far ahead of their lines as O'Neill's cottage – it was an hour's ride – and insisted on the meetings being held in tents pitched on more open ground where, it was implied, they could not be ambushed. There was also a long discussion about the number of armed men each team would be permitted to bring to the meeting place.

Each side also questioned whether the other was duly authorised to negotiate a settlement, and Wood made a good start by showing the Boers the telegrams he had received from Whitehall granting a general amnesty to those who had taken part in hostilities and agreeing to negotiate with anyone truly representative of the Boers.

It was a strange meeting. On one side there was Wood, a fox-hunting, lawn tennis enthusiast, wearing a white military helmet, riding boots and a scarlet tunic to which were attached a double row of medal ribbons – the Victoria Cross among them – and on the other the Boers, looking like Old Testament prophets in borrowed clothes. Some wore frock-coats, others greatcoats and yet others mere shooting-jackets. Their hats were normally soft wide-brimmed felt hats which could be turned up in front or at the side to suit the style of the wearer, but, on more formal occasions, black top-hats, grey top-hats, bowlers and stove-pipe hats decorated with ostrich plumes were to be seen above the regulation bandolier slung over one shoulder.

And then there was Kruger himself. Charles Norris-Newman, whose work *With the Boers in the Transvaal and Orange Free State in 1880 and 1881* was published a year later, wrote of him as "the most peculiar man of the lot". Norris-Newman correctly described Kruger as being of middle height (he was certainly shorter than either Pretorius or Piet Joubert), and added that he possessed black whiskers and a beard but no moustache, a prominent heavy nose, high-arched eyebrows, very loose clothes and a hat thrown far back over his head. A photograph taken outside O'Neill's cottage does indeed show the black whiskers, and the loose clothes are there. The hat, a solar topee, is in the act of being removed from Kruger's head, but on a warm day there would be every reason for Kruger, like many other Boers, to wear it off the back of his head. The eyebrows in the photograph are not arched, probably because Kruger was looking directly into the sun, and the moustache at this time was clearly visible, though he did not always wear one.

O'Neill's cottage, where the peace terms were eventually negotiated, was uncomfortable enough to make all concerned anxious for the negotiations not to be too long drawn out. It was an undistinguished double-fronted building built of hewn rock. Set on a lush green slope, it had a small front garden. The roof was of corrugated iron, and there was a small balcony in front which allowed the Boers to step out to whisper among themselves when things looked grim. Thomas Fortescue Carter of the *Times of Natal*, whose *Narrative of the Boer War* is one of the classic works on the 1880–81 campaign, called the building a miserable, wretched place at best. "Its floors of the bare earth trampled into mud, its darkness and desolation, were depressing to the last degree."

Referring to a meeting held there on 18 March, he wrote:

The day of this meeting was bitterly cold, with a driving rain, which pierced to the very marrow, defying thick clothing, mackintoshes, blankets or any other wrappings. It was necessary to ride right in the teeth of it to go from Mount Prospect [the British Headquarters] to the little farmhouse lying right under the Majuba . . . Four small sticks in a very large fireplace distributed all the warmth we could muster in the kitchen whilst waiting for the result of the interview in the next room.

But on Wednesday, 16 March, the first day of substantive talks, there was deadlock over the powers to be given to the Royal Commission. Kruger believed that its one function should be to re-examine the Boer case against annexation, and that it should include both British and Boer members. The British believed that all its members would be nominated by the Crown and that its main purpose would be to advise the British Government. This, Kruger refused to accept. Then there was the question of timing. Should all

British troops be ordered out of the Transvaal before the Commission started its work? Or should they, as Wood insisted, stay until the Convention had been ratified by both sides? Equally, should the Boers continue to remain on the Natal side of the border or should they disperse at once to prove that they had ceased armed opposition? Should they lay down their arms, and what kind of standing army should the new State have for its own self-protection? Negotiations on the first day lasted from eight in the morning until six in the evening, at the end of which Wood told correspondents that they were no nearer peace at the close of the day than they had been at the beginning. Negotiations would break down if the Boers did not lower their sights, he said. A further two hours had to be spent drafting telegrams to London setting out Kruger's views.

Then both sides sat down to wait for the answer from London. The armistice had already been prolonged from Monday until midnight on Friday, 18 March. But when Friday morning came no reply had been received; Kruger was said to be unwell, and the armistice had again to be prolonged, this time for three days until Monday night. Kimberley had in fact telegraphed his answer on 17 March, but his attitude was much stiffer than had been expected. He said nothing about the Constitution of the new State and very little about peace terms. These, together with native affairs and the Transvaal boundaries, were to be left to the Royal Commission whose members were to be nominated by Britain.

Faced with this the Boers made preparations to resume the battle. An Order of the Day, known as the Third Proclamation, was prepared, calling on the "Dutch" in South Africa to resume the struggle. After recounting all the efforts made by the Transvaal leaders to secure peace in the face of British obstinacy, the Proclamation concluded, "It is for you to say who shall rule Africa, the Afrikaners or a pair of idiots in Downing Street."

The latter part of Sunday, the day before the armistice was due once more to expire, was spent in an argument between Kruger and President Brand of the Orange Free State who had hurried up from Bloemfontein to mediate between the two sides. Brand appealed to Kruger for concessions. Kruger refused to budge. Finally Kruger ordered Jorissen to read the Proclamation aloud to Brand, adding that they had a messenger willing to take it to the Free State where volunteers were waiting to join their brothers in the Transvaal. There, in the semi-darkness of a tent with lamps set on upturned chests, Brand gave way.

Rather than see his own Republic dragged into the struggle, he would tell the British of the dangers they risked if they refused to make concessions. Brand rose early on the morning of the 21st and rode over to see Wood alone before Kruger arrived at 8 a.m. at O'Neill's cottage.

Brand was able to get one significant concession: the British guaranteed to restore the Republic within six months. In return the Boers withdrew their claim to be represented on the Commission, and their demand that the British garrisons should be withdrawn from the Transvaal at the same time as the Boer forces, still in position on and over the Natal border, dispersed. A compromise was reached whereby Wood agreed that, if the Boers dispersed, he would not follow them up, nor occupy Laing's Nek, nor send ammunition into the Transvaal.

There were other provisions of course. In the first place, all that the two sides had signed was a draft agreement which had to be put into legal form. The triumvirate were recognised as the lawful representatives of the people of the Transvaal then under arms but they accepted Queen Victoria as their suzerain which meant not only control over the foreign relations of the Transvaal but also the right to move troops through the country in time of war.

The Royal Commission, consisting of Sir Hercules Robinson (the recently appointed British High Commissioner for South Africa), Sir Henry de Villiers (Chief Justice in Cape Colony and a man of the Cape), and General Sir Evelyn Wood, was to determine not only the boundaries of the new State but was also to consider measures for the protection of the natives. Furthermore, although the Republic was to be restored within six months, the territory would remain under British rule until the report of the Royal Commission had been approved by the British Government.

Kruger was largely responsible for the concessions which the Boers obtained. The British report of the negotiations made Wood and Kruger the two spokesmen for their respective sides and Buller, who first met him at this time, said: "Kruger is the strong man and, I fancy, the power. [Piet] Joubert is the clever one, but not altogether trusted by his party." (Joubert enjoyed reading English newspapers and was a non-smoker.) Kruger had refused to be thawed by Wood's charm and affability or to share in the jokes at which Joubert sometimes laughed with the British. Wood wrote: "Kruger was without culture, untutored, impulsive and ready on the least occasion to lose his temper." He was inclined to put the worst construction even on offers which would benefit the Boers. And at one point he had threatened to recall the burghers to arms unless a written agreement setting out the conditions under which the armistice was to be extended, was signed.

What the two sides thought privately of the agreement was an open secret. Wood would have preferred the judgement of Mais to that of President Brand, and at one point, when the talks looked like failing, he told Joubert that if they did he would add a tenth medal to the nine that he already had. "That is the difference between us," rejoined Joubert. "You fight for honours and we for our rights." During the first week of March Wood had told Kimberley, "When I move, I am confident, with God's blessing, of success." But, in the end, Wood felt bound to follow the instructions of his own Government.

Queen Victoria was if anything still less satisfied than Wood.

On 20 February Sir Henry Ponsonby prepared a draft note for her to send to Lord Kimberley which said, "The Queen observes that Sir Hercules Robinson considers a concession of everything before a victory has been won would seriously increase our difficulties in S. Africa." She added her own view that disastrous results would follow peace obtained by an apparent confession of weakness "such as the admission that we could not take Laing's Nek". On 6 March she wrote in her journal, "President Brand, of the Orange Free State, sends a proposal; I do not like peace before we have retrieved our honour."

On 9 March she wrote still more strongly to Kimberley from Windsor Castle: "I find that an impression prevails that we are about to make peace with the Boers on their own terms. I am sure you will agree with me that even the semblance of any concessions after our recent defeats would have a deplorable effect."

Two days later Ponsonby reported to the Queen that he had told Lord Kimberley, Lord Granville (Foreign Secretary) and Mr Gladstone of the *impossibility* of listening to demands for independence or entering into terms with the Boers while they are still in Natal.

The next day Mr Gladstone told Her Majesty the nature of the terms which, without consulting her, he had already offered the Boers (before they had left Natal), and claimed that the general outlines of the permanent arrangement he would propose for the territory had been given "in what the Cabinet deem safe and general terms" of which Lord Kimberley would inform her, although the message had already gone off.

Later the same day Ponsonby told Kimberley that "The Queen did not like your telegram being sent off before being submitted. She fears it looks weak and as if we were yielding to the Boers . . . A humiliating peace would ruin our position in South Africa."

Kimberley waited until 17 March to inform Queen Victoria of a telegram "which he was compelled from shortness of time to send off at once" on 15 March, and expressed the hope that "a peaceful settlement may follow on terms honourable to this country and as advantageous as the difficult nature of the questions to be dealt with will permit". "It is very satisfactory that the Boers accepted at once the suzerainty of the British Crown," Kimberley added.

But the Queen was still unconvinced, and on 22 March she ordered Ponsonby to write to Kimberley that she had been given no time for considering the final terms of the agreement. The letter continued:

> Her Majesty can scarcely understand them. It would appear that the Boers have obtained all they fought for, viz. independence within their borders; while we on the other hand, although we publicly refused their demands and have sent a large army to oppose them, have now undertaken not to advance into the Transvaal with our troops, and not even to occupy the positions on the soil of Natal taken by the Boers.
>
> If the Queen has read this telegram correctly, she feels sure that these conditions will be considered humiliating both in England and at the Cape . . .

No wonder Gladstone never became her favourite Prime Minister.

But the Government felt justified in its attitude. They were convinced that, if fighting continued the conflict would spread and that Afrikaners in the Cape as well as the Free State would join in. Besides, one Ireland was enough.

Whether Kruger regarded the rights of the burghers as safeguarded is less certain. Perhaps he felt – and to a certain extent he was later proved right – that he would in due course be able to wring concessions from the Royal Commission because of the realities of the situation in the Transvaal.

At any rate, for the time being, he announced to the Boers only that a preliminary treaty had been signed and that at last they could go home. Wood shook hands with Joubert.

Sir Evelyn Wood wrote in a private despatch to the Queen that:

> Mrs Smit, wife of the "Fighting General", dished out breakfast which consisted of huge pieces of beef weighing 8–10 ozs in a curry sauce, chops, a pie with a most formidable paste, vegetables, preserved peaches, butter, "hard Bake" bread, set off by wild flowers picked that morning by Mrs Smit, as she said, in Sir Evelyn's honour.

There were "hurrahs" and rifle shots, and the British officers in their white helmets looked on in wonder while the Boers, with much hand-waving, got under way. Three young couples, who had post-poned their marriages until peace had been declared, ate their wedding breakfasts. And soon, as far north as the eye could see, the roads were white with the hoods of covered wagons travelling home.

Chapter 9

The Lull

Queen Victoria's subjects, for whom the Government published the inevitable self-justifying White Book on Majuba, received the settlement with every appearance of dissatisfaction, and Earl Cairns (leader of the Conservative opposition in the House of Lords) laid bare the Government's shortcomings in dealing with the Transvaal problem in his memorable speech on 31 March 1881.

Cairns argued that the arrangement now proposed was quite different from that set out in the Speech from the Throne. If this arrangement was what was intended, why had not the Government given it at once? Why did they spend the blood and treasure of the country like water, only to give at the end what they had intended to give at the beginning, he inquired. The "suzerainty" which Britain had reserved for herself was an equivocal term, and in any case, Lord Cairns maintained, since the garrisons were to be withdrawn and not in the meantime supplied with ammunition, neither the peace terms nor the findings of the Royal Commission would be enforceable.

But the peace terms were no more acceptable in the Transvaal than they had been in London.

Kruger's first step after the dispersal of the commandos was to get the Government of the Republic working again, and he summoned a special session of the Volksraad to meet in Heidelberg on 15 April. At this gathering he endeavoured to present the terms as something for which thanks should be given to Queen Victoria as well as to "the God of our fathers, who has been near us in battle".

"I consider it my duty to declare plainly before you and the whole world," he said, "that our respect for Her Majesty the Queen of England, for the Government of Her Majesty, and for the English nation has never been greater than at this time, when we are enabled in this treaty to show you a proof of England's noble and magnanimous love for right and justice." By this, Kruger no doubt intended to convey that the terms which had not already been settled could confidently be left to the discretion of the Royal Commissioners but he went further and appealed to the Transvalers: "Let all citizens offer and accept the hand of reconciliation in order to establish a happy state."

His speech met with a mixed reception, and after several members had criticised it he proposed an adjournment.

Nevertheless on 24 May he went still further.

Before he realised that almost every question of importance would have to be referred by the Royal Commission to Downing Street, Kruger addressed a message of loyalty to the Queen through Sir Evelyn Wood on the occasion of her birthday:

May it please your Excellency – We the undersigned representatives of the people of the Transvaal, herewith beg to tender our most hearty congratulations to your Excellency as the representative of Her Most Gracious Majesty Queen Victoria, on the anniversary of Her Majesty's birthday.

A short time ago we had occasion publicly to state that our respect for Her Majesty the Queen of England, for the Government of Her Majesty, and for the British nation, had never been greater than now, that we are enabled by the peace agreement to produce proof of England's noble and magnanimous love of right and justice.

And we beg now to reiterate those sentiments, and to add that we are convinced that the relations which will for the future exist between the Crown of England and the people of the Transvaal will be the best guarantee of a sincere and everlasting peace.

We are thankful that your Excellency has afforded us the opportunity of expressing our sincere desire to maintain the most friendly relations with Her Majesty's Government.

But the most telling words of the address came in the last paragraph. It read:

We respectfully request that your Excellency may be pleased to convey to Her Majesty our deepest respect, and the assurance that our prayers are that the Almighty God may shower His blessings upon Her Majesty for many years, for the welfare and prosperity of Great Britain and the whole of South Africa, and more especially of the Transvaal, who hails and respects Her Majesty as her future suzerain. We have the honour to be, your Excellency's most obedient servants . . .

Kruger's name heads the list of those signing.

Outside the building, however, leaders met to protest against the possibility that the Royal Commission might deprive the Republic of frontier territory as in fact happened in the Western Transvaal, or even partition the Transvaal with the object of "protecting the natives".

When, in due course, the Commission met at Newcastle in Natal in the house of Rider Haggard who had, not long before, helped to annex the Transvaal, Kruger, though not a member, was allowed to attend sessions and make "representations" against proposals of which he did not approve. In particular he objected to the Commission's habit of referring to his Government as the Transvaal State rather than as the South African Republic, and he protested at the limitations imposed on the Republic by the rights reserved to the suzerain power. Kruger realised that when writing to foreign Governments, even to those which had previously recognised his Government, he would have to do so through the British Resident in Pretoria. The Resident would have to forward the communication through the High Commissioner at the Cape who in turn would pass it to the Foreign Office in London and so through the local British Embassy or Legation to the Government concerned. The answer would have to travel along the same channels.

He was not successful either in changing the name of the State or in securing direct communication between it and foreign Governments, and the Convention of 33 Articles was concluded with the Commission in Pretoria and signed (subject to ratification within three months) on 3 August 1881 in Church Square, Pretoria, on a makeshift platform of planks and straw bales. From the Boer point of view it contained several unsatisfactory features. In fact one Boer said that the Convention was a glass of milk with 33 dead flies in it. For example the "Transvaal State" was to be liable for the balance of debts due by the South African Republic at the date of annexation; natives might acquire land to be registered through the Native Location Commission and might move freely through the territory; grants of land previously issued by the Transvaal Government outside their newly agreed boundaries were no longer valid; and Swaziland was to be independent. Immigrants were to have freedom of entry, freedom of movement, trade and residence and could hold property including factories, warehouses, etc., and establish businesses of their own. This was hardly self-government and certainly not independence as the Boers understood it.

Britons were not to be subject to discriminatory taxation and, by registering with the British Resident, they could be exempted from liability for commando service. Furthermore, although government would be handed over to the triumvirate on 8 August (it was already functioning in practice since the Boers in most cases had commandeered the taxation and other records) British troops were not to be withdrawn until ratification had taken place.

The three-man Boer Government duly assumed power on 8 August

1   President Kruger with one of the marble lions presented to
him by "Barney" Barnato

2 From Wellington: Paarl, Drakenstein Valley and Simonberg
(J. T. Haverfield, 1863)

3 Samaganga's village on the Botletle river (T. Baines, 1863)

4 Eno's "Caffer" warriors charging (Lt-Col. C. C. Michell [from the album of Lady Francis Cole])

5 Morning Market, Johannesburg (A. E. Huitt, *c.* 1893)

6 President Kruger "at home" (C. E. Fripp, 1899)

7 Kruger explaining to young John Bull that "Suzerainty is Sovereignty with the bottom knocked out". (Many people in Britain, Lord Cairns in particular, were unhappy when Gladstone agreed to replace British "Sovereignty" over the Transvaal by "Suzerainty")

8   Pritchard Street, Johannesburg (F. L. Emanuel)

9   Commissioner Street, Johannesburg (K. G., 1893)

10 President Burgers   11 Cecil Rhodes

12 Willem Johannes Leyds

13   Joseph Chamberlain

14   Lord Milner

15   Dr Leander S. Jameson

16　President Kruger, President Steyn and Sir Alfred Milner
at the Bloemfontein Conference, 1899

and the Vierkleur was legitimised. A further special meeting of the Volksraad was held a few days later after Kruger had recovered from a bout of fever. On this occasion his way with the members was short. He told them that a Convention had indeed been signed but that new elections would have to take place before its terms could be laid before them for their approval. This meant in practice that the new Volksraad would not be in session for another six weeks.

When it reassembled on 21 September, however, Kruger found that its fighting spirit had by no means evaporated.

He held off making his main speech until the second day of the session when he announced that the terms of the Convention and details of the negotiations which led up to it would be published in the official State newspaper. He maintained that even if the terms were not entirely satisfactory, the negotiators had felt compelled to sign them in order to prevent further bloodshed.

Then came the comments of the individual members, as given by T. F. Carter in a summarised report:

Mr Spies expressed himself in strong terms against the injustice of the Convention. He dared not say that the Triumvirate had betrayed the people. Mr Van der Heven presented a memorial signed by himself and thirty others protesting against parting with any territory. He [Van der Heven] said that if he dared approve the Convention his constituents would stone him to death. Mr Fouché said that the Convention was in direct conflict with the peace negotiations. It [now] seemed as if the burghers were the losing party. Mr Pretorius had truly remarked that a Kaffir has more liberty. Mr Otto declared himself against accepting Clause 1 of the Convention [which limited the boundaries of the "Transvaal State"]. Mr Labuschagne pointed out that the Sand River Convention [which had fixed other boundaries for the Transvaal] was still in force. Mr Van der Heven intervened again to ask whether it was just that their own flesh and blood who had gone over voluntarily to the British side should be pardoned. No country and power would allow this. His constituents were dead against it. Mr Lemmer said he was ashamed to say more about the document. It was a child without a father. Mr Birkenstock was sorry to say that the Annexation Proclamation gave more privileges [to the Boers] than this Convention. Mr Minaar said that Mr Birkenstock is so far right, but the Annexation promises were never carried out. Mr Taljaard declared that Article XXVI [dealing with freedom of entry, residence, trade, profession, etc.] "was an insult in so far as it implied that these freedoms did not previously exist". And so, according to Mr C. L. Neethling, was Article XXVII which provided free access to the Courts of Justice to all inhabitants of the Transvaal for the defence of their rights. Mr Lemmer commented, "We struggle every day to explain this document but we shall never succeed. I could almost swear to it."

(They were speculating on whether the British could be compelled to buy their exemption from commando service.)

Kruger does not appear to have said much, and when he intervened it was usually to correct some obvious misinterpretation, to supply a missing fact.

He was being "blooded", to use the huntsman's phrase, in the sport of politics, and was learning that it often paid to let the Hon. Members of the Volksraad blow off steam before proposing the course of action which he wished them to follow.

Frans Joubert, the "victor" of Bronkhorstspruit, made one of the most effective attacks on the Convention. He said:

Two days ago I swore to maintain the independence of the Republic. It is impossible for me to confirm the Convention as it now stands. I am not speaking for myself alone, for I can go to Damaraland if my freedom is signed away; but I speak for the widows and orphans, for those who are reduced to poverty by the war and are to be deprived of their land for the benefit of others who have no right to it. This is called a Convention, a term which I understand applies to a mutual agreement; but this document represents nothing more than terms dictated by a conqueror to barbarous and untrustworthy subjects. It endorses every calumny which drove us to desperation and reduces us to a condition worse than before. We took up arms in defence of our liberties and good name. We want to be friends of England and England to be our friend. These terms open up every wound of the past instead of, as we hoped, closing them for ever. We have no desire to throw off the suzerainty, for we look to England to be the protector of our liberties and of our defence against foreign invasion, but it must be within limits dictated by justice. If the Sand River Convention can be thus set aside, what is the value of this one . . .?

Then came the moment of truth. Mr Neethling suggested that Her Majesty's Government be asked to state what the position would be if the Convention were not ratified. The Chairman, Mr C. H. Bodenstein, said that the Volksraad had decided to pass no resolution until the Convention had been disposed of. Piet Joubert then intervened to point out that if the Convention were not duly ratified it would fall to the ground but that the Volksraad would not. He imagined that General Wood must know what he will do if the Convention is rejected, but he would certainly not tell them.

Eventually the House formed itself into a Committee with Frans Joubert as Chairman and went into secret session.

On 5 October it sent a telegram to Gladstone informing him that the Triumvirate had been instructed by the Volksraad to declare that in their opinion the Convention was contrary to the "treaty" of Sand River in 1852. The telegram continued:

> The Convention is in many respects an open breach of the peace agreement between Sir E. Wood for Her Majesty, and the Boer leaders, who, trusting that the principles laid down there would be executed, laid down their arms. The Volksraad request that Articles II and XVIII (dealing respectively with foreign relations and the competence of the British Resident to deal with native affairs) be altered. The suzerain has no right to the conduct of foreign affairs, only the control . . . The suzerain has no right of approval over our laws. The Resident, being a foreigner, cannot be a trustee of property belonging to our citizens [i.e. the natives owning property].

It also asked for "proof and vouchers" for the debts claimed and for the deletion of articles XV, XVI, XXVI and XXVII dealing respectively with freedom of religion, "slavery", freedom of residence, etc., and access to the Courts. These it claimed were "superfluous – calculated only to offend". It further stated that the British Government, which proposed to annul grants of land made by the Transvaal Government, should be responsible for paying compensation to those who would have benefited.

But Gladstone was facing the disapproval of the Queen, the Army and the loyalists in the Transvaal, not to speak of General Colley's widow who would not keep silent. Whitehall felt that it could yield no further and the reply was that "the Convention having been signed by the leaders who agreed to the peace conditions, and they having undertaken that the Convention shall be ratified, Her Majesty's Government can entertain no proposals or modifications of the Convention until it is ratified and the practical working thereof tested".

But even this did not satisfy the Volksraad who made clear when it ratified the Convention that its assent was provisional. The resolution embodying the ratification stated that:

> The Volksraad is not satisfied with this Convention and considers that the members of the Triumvirate performed a fervent act of

love for the Fatherland when they, upon their own responsibility, signed such an unsatisfactory State document. The Volksraad finds itself compelled to ratify it by the same motives which led the Triumvirate to sign. These motives they dare to proclaim to the world, without any reservation, and they may be expressed in two [i.e. a few] words: "The fear of renewed bloodshed between people who are bound mutually to forbear and respect each other and the fear of new disunity between the white races in South Africa."

The resolution continued, in a somewhat stilted official English translation:

Therefore is it that the Volksraad hereby unanimously resolves not to go into further discussion upon the Convention, and maintaining the objections to the Convention as made before the Royal Commission or stated in the Volksraad, and for the purpose of showing to everybody that the love of peace and unity inspires it for so long, and provisionally submitting the articles of the Convention to a practical test, hereby complying with the request of the English Government contained in the telegram of 13 October 1881, proceeds to ratify the Convention of 3 August 1881.

Once again Kruger had justified his policy to his countrymen.

But for the moment, once the ratification had been secured, the "strong man" retired to his farm at Rustenburg.

It would perhaps have been natural to suppose that Kruger on his farm, or rather farms, would have found contentment and prosperity. And so perhaps, but for a number of obstacles, he would have done.

One was the fact that he had little time to farm – or indeed to pursue any other gainful occupation. Wars against the natives could, of course, be profitable, but civil war, or war against the British, did not offer the same rewards. And Kruger had been drawn into both these last two forms of conflict for much of his working life.

Then there were various kinds of fever which attacked man and beast – and Kruger was clearly not immune. A third disadvantage from his point of view was the low salary which office brought him – and the difficulties of getting it paid promptly.

Sometimes Kruger suffered from all these handicaps in the same year.

Thus in September 1858 we find him writing to Pretoria to the President and the Executive Council about his debts which he put at 3,000 Rand, a considerable sum for those days. He was afraid that he would soon be taken to court which would expose him to considerable embarrassment. His immediate request was for a payment of £100 salary.

But five months later he was still in difficulties.

In the summer of 1866 he wrote to Pretoria to tell them: "All my horses are dead. My fruit lies rotting under the trees. I can hardly get any game, and lung sickness has broken out among the cattle. I am pursued by creditors. My son is overworked and no one can look after my affairs. My report as Commandant-General is a long one, and as I have no great secretariat things have got into a tangle and I have had no time to put them right."

Three years later in April 1869 he excused himself to President Pretorius from attendance at the Executive Council "as I am still so unwell", and a year later he explained a further absence as being due to "circumstances at home mainly because of malaria", from which his wife and family also suffered.

Two years later (February 1871) he wrote to Pretoria: "I must tell you that I am really ill. I am suffering from head and neck pains and don't see any chance of travelling."

In July of the following year we hear that his 14-year-old son Antje had been at death's door for five days, that his wife was sick and that his other children look as though they were sickening.

In March 1873 he had to tell the Executive Council: "My wife is seriously ill. She has been in bed for two days and her pulse stopped. We expected to have to give her up at any minute. Now she is a little better."

And in 1875 we hear that one of his children was sick and getting weaker, that his father-in-law had been sick for two months with little hope of recovery, and (in September) that some of his cattle were still down on the Crocodile river, that others had escaped and had been impounded, and that he was unable to look after them because of an attack of fever.

In 1876 he wrote that he was still under doctor's orders and not "fris" (fresh), and in the following year, just a week before the Transvaal was annexed, he wrote to tell President Burgers: "I am in a lamentable state. One of my children is seriously ill and my wife is ill too."

So the wonder was not so much that he was chosen at the age of 53 to lead his country, but that he was able to do so continuously for more than 20 years.

Chapter 10

Kruger Fenced In

Kruger's triumvirate had inherited a bankrupt State. The war expenses had been Himalayan, and his Government borrowed £48,000 from the Cape Commercial Bank, £85,667 for the Railway Loan and owed a further £27,226 15s to the so-called Orphan Chamber (which administered the estates of those who had died intestate or were bankrupt). These debts, he had agreed, should be a first charge on the revenue. And there was also a little matter of £265,000 which the British claimed to have spent on governing the Transvaal after they had seized it. Kruger had agreed to accept this as a second charge on the revenue.

He had hoped that, given independence, it might be possible for the Church to take over education, thus preserving a Christian spirit in the classroom. But there was no money for this either. He was hampered by the presence of a British Resident in Pretoria, fettered in his foreign relations and shut off from a large slice of territory to the west in Bechuanaland (now Botswana) which he had hoped to occupy. The natives were no longer fully under his control.

But this was not the time for regrets, for the burghers decided, after a lengthy debate, to replace their three-man team with an elected President. Joubert and Kruger were both asked to stand, and each agreed to recommend the other to the voters. Kruger's programme was semi-traditional, semi-revolutionary. He promised to govern according to God's word, to develop agriculture and to oppose foreign immigration into the Transvaal. But, on the other hand, he held fast to the plan for linking the Transvaal with the outer world by building a railway to the sea, and he undertook to introduce new industries into the country. The mixture appealed to the electors, and Kruger scooped two-thirds of the votes. British observers were right when they reported that Joubert was not fully trusted by the solid mass of Boers, and his mock-modesty and high-pitched reedy delivery helped to talk him out of office.

The election was fought during late January and early February 1883, and it was hardly over before Kruger was making efforts to annul the despised Pretoria Convention.

From the start he had cavilled at hearing his country referred to as the Transvaal State, and in his letters to the British Resident, Mr George Hudson, he spoke persistently of "the South African Republic". Kruger wrote in his memoirs:

One fine day Mr Hudson came to me to complain about this, saying that the name of the country was the Transvaal State and not the South African Republic.

"How do you prove that?" said I.

"Why," answered Hudson, "by the Convention which clearly says 'Transvaal State'."

"Very well," I rejoined. "If I sell you a farm and, in the deed of sale, I say, 'Paul Kruger, hereinafter called the Vendor, and so on,' then, in what follows, I am no longer Paul Kruger, but the 'Vendor'. Even so in this case. In the Convention, just as in drawing up a deed, the Republic is referred to as the 'Transvaal State'; but that does not make it her real name, but only her specification. Her real name is, and remains, the 'South African Republic'."

Hudson laughed and said, "Well call her as you please, only do not mind if I keep to the name of the Transvaal State."

Already in April Jorissen was in London and had two "unofficial" interviews with Lord Derby, the new temporising and over-cautious Colonial Secretary, whom the Queen disliked even more than his predecessor, Lord Kimberley. Jorissen had been asked to express Kruger's dissatisfaction with the Pretoria Convention – particularly the limitation of the frontiers, the interference in native affairs and the problem of the debt – and to ask for a return to the days of the Sand River Convention of 1852 under which the Transvaal had originally been granted independence, at a time when the western frontier was virtually undefined.

Derby, understandably, fought shy of renouncing the Pretoria Convention so recently negotiated by his own party; yet he was equally unwilling to face the expense of reoccupying the Transvaal by force in order to keep the Boers within their allotted boundaries.

But perhaps Kruger might be satisfied with a revision of the Pretoria Convention and, after a good deal of manoeuvring, Derby agreed to receive a three-man deputation consisting of Kruger, General Nicolas Smit and the Revd S. J. du Toit, one of the founders of the Bond, the Afrikaner political party in the Cape.

And so Kruger set out on a fine spring morning and after a picnic lunch among the thorn trees near the road to Kimberley, sang a hymn and stepped into the mail-coach bound for the Cape.

It was not perhaps the most propitious moment for a mission of this kind. Gladstone was preoccupied with the problems of Ireland

and Egypt, and Queen Victoria was completely lacking in the respect which Gladstone considered to be his due. She had been especially unfriendly over the matter of a cruise which he had taken in company with the poet Tennyson in one of Sir Donald Currie's yachts, during which, without informing her in advance, Gladstone had been so thoughtless as to pay a visit to Denmark.

Her feelings were expressed in a letter to Lord Granville, her Foreign Secretary:

> The Queen believes everyone is much astonished at this *escapade*. But what would they say if they knew that the Queen knew nothing of it? Indeed he told the Queen he was not going on a cruise this year, and his private secretary informed us he was not to cross the border as he was not to go to Midlothian!
>
> The Queen must say she is very indignant. Will Lord Granville convey the substance of what she has written to Mr Gladstone, or should she write direct to him?

It was not the most favourable moment for the solution of the Boers' problems. But even Gladstone, weighed down as he was with these burdens, could see that the real difficulty with the Transvaal at that moment concerned the western frontier. The Boers were anxious to escape westwards out of British control, even if they had to leave the Transvaal in order to do so. They were establishing themselves in new territories to the west by making alliances with some tribes against others. But this in turn involved fighting the enemies of their new friends. And it also left them controlling the main road between the Cape and the north, an artery used by both missionaries and traders . . . the Suez canal, as it were of South Africa.

But there were many unanswered questions: "How were the Boers to be kept on their own side of the trade route?"; "Who was to protect the natives who wished to remain free?"; "Would the Cape Dutch approve if Britain intervened to hold back the Boers?"; "If the Cape Dutch disapproved, did they care enough about their trade route to the north to intervene themselves?"

The missionaries, and in particular the Revd John Mackenzie, feared that Derby would surrender everything to avoid a new war with the Boers.

Kruger and his companions had sailed in the *Roslin Castle* from Cape Town on 10 October (Kruger's birthday) on their mission to Lord Derby, and made some effort to improve his English with the help of a Bible with the High Dutch and 17th-century English texts set out side by side. They landed on 30 October 1883 in Plymouth, where Kruger was presented with "an address of welcome on behalf of 53 students studying at Edinburgh". Finding no officials on the quay-side, the Boers had made their way to the train and arrived at Paddington the same evening at 6 p.m., whence they betook them-selves to the Albemarle Hotel.

They met Derby for the first time on 7 November and were asked to put their case in writing. Their reply was ready a week later, and on that day they had a 20-minute interview with Gladstone. Their proposals, however, were vaguely worded both on the position of the frontiers and on the arrangements for policing them, and, when pressed, the Boers repeated that they really wanted to return to the "old" frontiers of 1852.

Derby, however, did not abandon all hope of an agreement. He even went so far as to offer to set up a joint protectorate with Kruger over Bechuanaland. But Kruger countered by offering to hold a plebiscite there to see which tribes wished to come under Transvaal rule. But this was too much even for Derby. He realised that any vote conducted by the Boers themselves would inevitably lead to the result they wanted. He realised too that there would be criticism in the House of Commons of any arrangement which simply abandoned all the inhabitants of Bechuanaland to Boer rule, especially if, at the same time, the Boers were to be left straddling the trade route from the Cape to the north. And, on 18 December, the Boers were told that unless the delegation agreed to the boundaries Derby proposed there would be no revision of the Pretoria Convention.

For once, Kruger had overbid his hand. He tried once more, just before Christmas, to interest Derby in a scheme to let the Chiefs of Bechuanaland decide their own future, but Derby's only answer was an impenetrable silence which lasted until 9 January 1884, when he merely repeated his previous offer. Derby's courage had been forti-fied by Sir Hercules Robinson, Governor of Cape Colony and High Commissioner for South Africa, who had extracted from Sir Thomas Scanlen, Prime Minister at the Cape, an assurance to the effect that, if Britain set up a Protectorate over Bechuanaland, the Cape might be prepared to share in the expense of administering it.

Kruger realised from Derby's manner that the tide in the nego-tiations had begun to turn against him, and Derby, for his part, realised as more and more Boers flooded westwards from the Transvaal borders, that Kruger, no matter what agreement he might sign, might be unable to contain the flood. Nor would the Cape Government, dependent as it was on the goodwill of its Dutch voters, use force. Britain herself would have to take responsibility for Bechuanaland.

These arguments stiffened Derby's determination to reject totally the Boer proposals on the frontier, and, when Kruger turned from the frontier to other matters, Derby said he assumed from this that the problem of the frontier had now been settled.

But Kruger was not finished yet. In his reply delivered on 5 February he completely ignored all reference to the frontier, but raised instead the whole question of Derby's good faith by asking for the negotiations to be speeded up. Three days later, however, he was still asking for time to think. And a week later he retreated to his old attitude which was that "the [Boer] deputation regret to say that they cannot accept without modification of some of the articles of the proposed new Convention".

In between bouts of bargaining the delegation was not socially ignored. The members lunched at the Royal Pavilion at Brighton on the invitation of Councillor William Hall; they were invited to Birmingham, and to a dinner given by the Dutch residents in the Princes Banquet Room in the Criterion building at which "several dishes peculiar to the Dutch cuisine" were served. Most likely it was after this entertainment that someone, knowing the President's horror of bare arms and low cleavage, asked him that question about the ladies' dresses.

It has been suggested that during this visit Kruger was presented to Queen Victoria and was invited to dinner at Windsor. But there is no record in the Royal Archives at Windsor of such a meeting having taken place at this or any other time. The Queen, from Majuba onwards, regarded Kruger as "one of the rebel authorities" and was unwilling, even after Kruger's "magnanimous" gestures after the Jameson Raid, to allow his grandson, Lieutenant Eloff, to be presented to her. Her subsequent references to Kruger do not suggest that she had ever set eyes on him.

The closing stages of the negotiations were not without drama and at one point Kruger, seldom over-courteous, lost his temper, picked up his hat and prepared to leave the room. "Tell him," he said turning to du Toit who was interpreting, "that we have hammered the British out of the Transvaal once and will do it again." But the interpreter remained dutifully silent.

Whenever it was safe to do so Kruger raged and stormed. Kruger afterwards wrote:

During the negotiations Sir Hercules Robinson and I had the misfortune to come into collision. I was pointing out and insisting that certain farms, among others Polfontein and Rietfontein, should come within the boundaries of the Republic, especially as they had formerly belonged to us. When I made this statement,

Sir Hercules Robinson, who was present at the negotiations, whispered to Lord Derby: "It's a lie."

I jumped up, quite prepared to fall upon Sir Hercules. Lord Derby and other gentlemen present interfered, and Lord Derby said:

"Gentlemen, you are not going to fight?"

I answered that Sir Hercules had insulted me and that I did not intend to put up with it. I accepted his apology, however, and his assurance that "no offence meant".

Despite this incident, Sir Hercules and I afterwards became very good friends and remained so until his death.

But eventually, after Derby had made several major concessions, Kruger decided that he would have to live with the British proposals and, on 27 February 1884 (the anniversary, incidentally, of Majuba), he signed the new London Convention.

The new agreement certainly had solid advantages. It no longer spoke of the Transvaal State but of the South African Republic. There was no longer any mention of British suzerainty, and a British Consul would replace the former British Resident in Pretoria. The debt to Britain had been drastically reduced, and Mackenzie, who was supposed to govern Bechuanaland and keep the Boers at bay, had been allotted a police force of exactly ten men.

Nor was Kruger unduly dismayed about the clause in the new agreement which forbade him to conclude treaties with any state or nation other than the Orange Free State before the Queen had signified her approval.

The very next day after the signing Kruger and his party set off for Rotterdam aboard the Dutch steamer *Batavier*.

From Rotterdam they travelled to The Hague and were given a banquet at De Oude Doelen.

The message they brought was that the Boers had been inspired to fight the British by the war of independence which the Dutch had waged against Philip II of Spain, and Kruger made it clear that Dutch immigrants – and, of course a Dutch railway loan – would be received with open arms. The day after the banquet the Prince of Orange, heir to the throne, gave a second feast for the delegates, this time at Delft, and Kruger and his delegation visited the tomb of William the Silent, the founder of the Netherlands' independence.

At Amsterdam he spoke to an audience which one report put at 100,000:

We are the lost tribes of parents left by you in the Cape Colony. We settled amongst strangers but have preserved all that may remind us of our forefathers. First the flag; the flag of Holland, to which we have merely added green, the colour of hope, symbolic of the energy of a young nation. Secondly the language. People have tried to force various languages on us, but we have clung to the Dutch language, at any rate to its fundamentals, even if, now and then, you may not be able to understand me. We have kept our own language, the language of the Netherlands people, who fought 80 years for faith and freedom. Our people in the wilderness have kept their language and their faith through every storm. Our whole struggle is bound up with this. Though forgotten by our mother-land, we have risen out of the dust and have let our voices be heard.

On 7 March Kruger, wearing his Presidential sash of office for the first time in Europe, had an audience with King William III of the Netherlands. There, as in Britain, the President had to contend with the problem of women's low-cut dresses. At one banquet, a woman sitting on the opposite side of the table and next to General Smit wore a particularly provocative gown and insisted on leaning forward over the table to ask questions of Kruger. The President refused to look at her and answered all her inquiries with his eyes on his own plate. At last she turned to Smit and said, "It seems the President can't bear the sight of bare arms and low necks?" "That's right," said Smit, "he can't. But as far as I am concerned, the more naked the better." The lady jumped up and went to change, after which she was reported to have had an agreeable conversation with Kruger.

Then, after travelling through Belgium, the Boers arrived in France. There it was pointed out that men like Joubert and du Toit were clearly of French descent, and France's President Grévy received his brother President with a view to the two nations concluding a commercial treaty. The French Geographical Institute gave a banquet at which Ferdinand de Lesseps presided and proposed Kruger's health, and Kruger expressed a desire to see a French line of steamers which would run from Marseilles and call at Zanzibar, Réunion and Delagoa Bay.

In Lisbon, King Luis I of Portugal received Kruger in audience and lent him one of the State coaches in which to see the sights of the city. Here the plan for the railway from the Transvaal to the sea through the Portuguese colony of Mozambique gave them a common interest. Next, King Alfonso XII of Spain received Kruger in Madrid.

The Derby talks had taken so long that at one time Kruger had given up the idea of visiting Germany, and was prepared to discuss the question of a trade treaty through the German Ambassador at The Hague. At the last moment, however, he learnt that the Volksraad would not be meeting until July, so that there was a week to spare for a visit to the Kaiser's Reich.

The party arrived in Berlin on 8 June and were received by Kaiser Wilhelm I in special audience the following afternoon. In his address to the Emperor, Kruger laid somewhat less emphasis on his country's Dutch connection than he had when in Holland. "May it please your Majesty," he began, "it is an honour and real joy to have been received by your Majesty in so friendly a manner, all the more as a large proportion of the population of the South African Republic and of all South Africa are of German origin. I myself am proud of the fact of my being of German origin, though I regret my inability to address your Majesty in the language of my ancestors."

As a mark of Imperial favour the Boers were invited to a gala dinner given at the Palace on the occasion of the investiture of His Royal Highness Prince Henry of Prussia with the Spanish Order of the Golden Fleece. (What made Lord Derby think that Britain would have control of the Republic's foreign relations?)

Bismarck was greatly impressed by Kruger and afterwards told the story of how when the other guests sat down with the Emperor, Kruger alone remained standing. He asked that Grace might first be said before the meal as was his own invariable custom. He also insisted on drinking the Emperor's health in milk. The two came to a close understanding as Bismarck could talk the Low German dialect of Germany's North Sea coastline – a tongue not far removed from Kruger's Afrikaans.

But what must have most interested the Foreign Office in London was a report in *The Times* according to which the Transvaal delegation:

... were waited on yesterday [10 June] by the Society for Promoting German Colonisation who indulged in compliments to the Boers on their "heroic struggle with England for their independence"; and expressed the hope that it would be vouchsafed to Germany and the Transvaal Republic to carry on together the work of civilisation and colonisation. President Kruger reciprocated these good wishes, referred to the warm welcome which had always been extended to German missionaries in South Africa, and said that "just as a child sought support from its parents, so the young Transvaal state would seek, and he hoped also find, protection from its strong and mighty mother country Germany in her glorious reigning house".

These were not the words of reassurance for which Queen Victoria was hoping. Indeed they foreshadowed the speech he was to make in January 1895 at a celebration of the Kaiser's birthday when he claimed that the Transvaal would have to turn to Germany because Britain was offering children's clothes to a nation which was no longer an infant.

Something short of a hero's welcome awaited Kruger when he got back to Pretoria towards the end of July. The written address which he received from his Executive Council was markedly noncommittal. It ran:

> When, ere long, the High Representatives of this Republic will judge of the work performed by you in Europe for the welfare of this country and its people, we hope and trust that the explanations and information you will then give, and of which the undersigned are as yet entirely ignorant, will clearly show that the work performed by you will tend to the prosperity and welfare of this country and its people.

Kruger had to reply that although his report was not yet ready he could undertake to say that the country had obtained absolute independence, that suzerainty had been withdrawn and that the British Resident was a thing of the past. He added, with scant regard for accuracy, that provisional treaties had been arranged with foreign powers by which the Republic had been received among the nations of the world.

To the Raad itself he delivered a very lengthy report and commented:

> I wish briefly to say this. We have got back our independence – that is the chief matter. The suzerainty is abolished and Her Majesty has nothing more to say within our land. Secondly, the Deputation, with the consent of Her Majesty's Government and Lord Derby, have thought it well to enter upon provisional negotiations with other powers with a view to being received among the list of the nations. That has happily been accomplished with mutual recognition in four cases. These are the two most important matters.

(One wonders whether Derby would have agreed with Kruger's account and, if not, why he did not protest at the time. This omission was all the more singular since the Colonial Office knew that the *Volkstem* newspaper had called the special attention of members of the Volksraad to what it considered an important divergence between statements made by the President in the Raad on two occasions as to the effect of the new Convention on suzerainty, and the words of Lord Derby in the House of Lords on the same subject.) Kruger continued: "If our report is accepted in its entirety not a penny more of taxation will thereby be imposed upon the burghers, even if the railway should go through." His main defence against accusations that he had not got enough was to say that "Die Deputasie kon geen berge versit nie" (the deputation could not overturn mountains), and to add that he would put forward other claims later: "The English took £1 away from us; the Pretoria Convention gave 10/- back and the London Convention another 5/-. We still want 5/- more."

Back in London the British were resisting Kruger's efforts to break through to the sea with considerable success, despite the fact that he had brought back with him from the Netherlands a brilliant new attorney, 25-year-old Dr Willem Leyds, who was to cause almost as much embarrassment to Queen Victoria as Kruger himself.

At home Kruger was treated with even less ceremony, for Tante Sanna, on seeing the President about to try on the pair of pyjamas with which he had been presented, ordered him "to throw away that rubbish and put on your nightshirt".

Kruger's immediate internal problem was that the Boers who had emigrated from the Transvaal had already set up two small independent republics – known as Stellaland and Goshen – alongside the western border of the Transvaal. Yet he had just signed an agreement surrendering any claim to a large part of these territories, and Britain was about to take them over as a protectorate. Furthermore, John Mackenzie, who had been chosen to administer the new British territory of Bechuanaland, was not the man to let the grass grow under his feet. One of his first acts was to depose Gerrit van Niekerk, the President of Stellaland, and to declare Goshen to be a British territory.

Kruger was embarrassed. But the Cape Dutch were even more shocked, and the British Government too were alarmed at the prospect of having to send troops to maintain their authority in the South African hornets' nest. In August 1884 Mackenzie was compelled to resign, and Cecil Rhodes, already a member of the Cape Cabinet, was sent north with the rank of Deputy Commissioner to sort out the mess with methods that he always favoured – persuasion and cajolery. Rhodes succeeded in reconciling the Boers of Stellaland to British rule by guaranteeing them the farms they had occupied. He put it to them that if the British left, the Germans would walk in instead from the base they already possessed on the west coast. But the Boers in Goshen stood firm, and Kruger unwisely allowed himself to be persuaded by du Toit into a piece of rash adventurism. He announced to the world in the Transvaal official gazette of 18 September that he had annexed both Stellaland and Goshen provisionally "in the interests of humanity" and subject to the approval of Queen Victoria. Du Toit hoisted the Transvaal Vierkleur flag in the new territories "to draw attention to the proclamation".

On the day of the Proclamation Kruger sent a telegram to Lord Derby stating that General Joubert had succeeded in restoring peace on the western boundary of the Transvaal, that all the combatants had laid down their arms and that the necessary steps would be taken, subject to Her Majesty's approval, to ensure a permanent peace. Next day he sent a further telegram reminding Derby that Montsioa, one of the Chiefs in the territory concerned, had asked to come under the protection of the Transvaal. A third telegram in support of Kruger's action was sent on the following day.

But Kruger had backed a loser. He probably realised that the Queen's approval would not be forthcoming. But he may have hoped that his friend Mr Gladstone, her doughty opponent on most matters, would support the Boer cause. Alas, Gladstone had been alarmed by the German landings on the west coast of Africa and the possibility of a link-up between the Goshenites and the Kaiser's imperium. As for Lord Derby, he sent no reply of any kind to Kruger's three telegrams. Instead he ordered Sir Hercules Robinson "to call upon the Government of the Transvaal to disavow the recent acts by which the South African Republic has assumed jurisdiction over Montsioa as a violation of the Convention of 1884".

It was a difficult situation to talk oneself out of, but Kruger managed it. On 16 October he issued a fresh proclamation in which he stated that his "provisional" announcement of the previous month had succeeded in its object of restoring peace on the western border, that he wished to preserve this state of affairs, that there was now opportunity for the Governments concerned to establish a permanent friendly arrangement for the future, and that in so far as his provisional proclamation might be an obstacle to progress, he, Kruger, acting on the advice and consent of his Executive Council, withdrew it.

Too late alas. For the British Government had decided that a military expedition would be needed to establish its authority in Bechuanaland and had commissioned General Sir Charles Warren to lead it, and it was mooted that Kruger might have to pay for the whole cost of the British expedition. Furthermore, Warren was to be advised by Mackenzie whose view it was that no Boers whatever should be permitted to settle in the new British possession of Bechuanaland.

There was, as it happened, no question of a fight. Most of the Boers, when they heard of Warren's approach, absented themselves from the field and rode back over the Transvaal border.

On 24 and 26 January 1885, while Warren was still in charge, a conference was arranged with Kruger, Warren, Mackenzie and Rhodes at Fourteen Streams near the Transvaal border.

Kruger was still on the retreat. Before leaving Pretoria he called his Commandants to a meeting and told them to pacify the burghers. He blamed du Toit for what had happened. He said that when du Toit had reported that he was about to raise the Vierkleur, he had warned him that this could not be done without the approval of the British Government. But du Toit had not waited. The flag was already flying when Kruger's reply arrived. But it was hauled down at once. Thus when Sir Hercules' telegram arrived alleging that the flag was still flying, Kruger was able to retort that orders to lower it had been given ten days earlier.

To a meeting of the burghers of Goshen he said that his mission was to obtain a recognition of their rights by peaceful means. He urged them not to make matters more difficult for him by creating disturbances. "Do not blow on the fire," he said, using, as usual, a homely metaphor.

At the Fourteen Streams meeting Rhodes, who preferred to make his own arrangements with the men on the spot rather than as a pawn of the Colonial Office, did his best to make himself agreeable to Kruger. Kruger's first reaction was: "This young man will cause trouble if he doesn't leave politics alone."

But he eventually came round to Rhodes' view that the most practical solution might be for the Cape to annex the disputed area, which of course was also Derby's hope. But Warren, on Mackenzie's advice, maintained that no Dutch colonists should be allowed to live in Bechuanaland. He was recalled in August 1885 after it had been announced that his mission had been completed, but, by then, any immediate chance of the Cape accepting Bechuanaland had vanished. The following month Britain annexed the lower half of the territory as a Crown Colony and the upper half as a Protectorate.

Kruger had been frustrated in his first attempt to break out of the British "Kraal".

The President and his Republic were now corralled in on the west and north-west by the Bechuanaland colony and protectorate. The Portuguese colony of Mozambique confronted him on the north-east. Two other possibilities of expansion remained. One road lay directly north towards Mashonaland and Matabeleland in the territory now known as Rhodesia. The other lay eastwards from the south-eastern corner of the Republic along a corridor running across Swaziland between Mozambique on the north and Zululand on the south.

Kruger tried both possibilities, and even Rhodes felt compelled to express his reluctant respect for the old man's spirit. "I have acquired an admiration for Oom Paul Kruger," he wrote, "for did he not conceive the noble scheme from his point of view, of seizing the interior, of stretching his republic across to Walfisch Bay, of making the Cape Colony hidebound, and of ultimately seizing Delagoa Bay, and all this without sixpence in his Treasury." Rhodes indeed was far more likely to have seized Delagoa Bay than Kruger but the two could certainly have worked together if Kruger had been prepared to adopt Rhodes' methods.

As it was, they ran a close race in their efforts to expand to the north. Already in 1887 Lobengula, Chief of the Matabele, had sent an envoy to Kruger to propose that the President should send a representative to foster good relations, and Kruger duly sent Piet Grobler north to act as Consul. Grobler succeeded in drafting an agreement giving freedom of movement to anyone entering Matabele territory with a pass signed by the President of the South African Republic. The Chief asked for a few days in which to consult his Council, and Grobler decided to leave the court to meet his wife who was on her way north to join him. It was a fatal decision, for Grobler was ambushed and killed on his way south by tribesmen acting, Kruger always believed, on instructions from Rhodes.

From then on Lobengula was open to offers from elsewhere, and Rhodes went post-haste to Grahamstown, where Sir Hercules Robinson was opening an exhibition, and persuaded him on Christmas Day 1887 to send a communication to Sir Sidney Shippard, the Deputy Commissioner of Bechuanaland who was a close friend of Rhodes. It instructed Shippard to spur on his Assistant Commissioner, the Revd J. Moffat, to come to terms with Lobengula. And on 11 February Moffat was able to sign a treaty by which Lobengula gave Britain the first option for a protectorate over Matabeleland, the more northerly of the two territories.

So far so good. But there was no certainty that the Imperial Government would take advantage of this golden opportunity. So Rhodes prepared a second line of advance. He sent his partner, C. D. Rudd, his Compound Manager, F. R. "Matabele" Thompson, and Rochfort Maguire, a fellow of All Souls, the Oxford College composed entirely of dons, to negotiate a more specific agreement. They met with only moderate success until Rhodes had the idea of sending Moffat and Lobengula's favourite missionary, the Revd C. D. Helm of the London Missionary Society, to join them. Within a month Rhodes had his agreement. It allowed him to dig for minerals anywhere in Lobengula's territory and to exclude rivals in return for a payment of £100 a month, 1,000 Martini-Henry rifles, 100,000 rounds of ammunition and an armed steamboat on the Zambesi.

And that was the end of Kruger's hopes in the north.

But still the President did not give up hope. Indeed he put it to the British that since he was prepared voluntarily to hold back his burghers from trekking northwards he should be allowed some special privilege to the east.

The Swazi territory extended almost to the sea, and between it and the sea there remained only a narrow strip of unattractive fever-ridden country belonging to two Chiefs, Zamban (or Sambane) and Umbegesa, who paid tribute to the Swazis. Swaziland therefore would be a magnificent prize for Kruger, and his abilities as a negotiator were employed to the full in endeavouring to get possession of it. Both Britain and the South African Republic had undertaken to maintain Swazi independence in return for Swazi aid in previous campaigns – a pledge recorded in both the Pretoria and London Conventions. But, before then, under Kruger's rival President Burgers, the Boers had established some kind of protectorate over Swaziland and, more recently, some of the Afrikaners who had left the Transvaal had received concessions of land from Umbandine, the Swazi king. Another Stellaland operation seemed to be in the offing, and King Umbandine turned to the Natal Government for help. He asked them to recommend a reliable "adviser", and Theophilus Shepstone, Junior, son of the original Shepstone, was sent up. But "Offy" proved unsuitable and, in October 1889, when King Umbandine died, it was clear that a new relationship between Swaziland and the Republic would have to be established, if only to deal with the problem of the Boer concessions there. Accordingly, in March 1890, Kruger agreed to meet Henry (afterwards Lord) Loch, who had succeeded Sir Hercules Robinson as Governor of Cape Colony, together with Rhodes, at Blignaut's Pont on the Orange river.

Striking hard, Kruger tried in the talks to gain control of both Swaziland and the territory of Sambane and Umbegesa. And his negotiating technique on this occasion was so remarkable that I have thought it worth reproducing some of his exchanges with Loch in a separate appendix (see p. 251).

Eventually, on 4 August 1890, Kruger signed a Convention and agreed to joint control of Swaziland; the UK approved a strip of ground not more than three miles wide for a railway through Swaziland and Amatongaland to Khosi Bay in return for which Kruger promised not to oppose the extension of the railway line from Natal into the Transvaal. But a proviso which Loch introduced at a late stage of the talks (and apologised for not having mentioned before) remained. The South African Republic would have to agree within three years to join a customs union with the Cape, and this, as Kruger rightly foresaw, was a step on the path to political union. He argued, in addition, that forcing a customs union on the Republic amounted to interference in its internal affairs.

Naturally the customs union did not materialise and consequently negotiations had to be restarted in 1893, first at Colesberg and later in Pretoria. On this occasion Kruger got new concessions. The British agreed that he could negotiate with the Swazis to acquire full rights of jurisdiction for the Transvaal in Swaziland, although the territory was not to become part of the South African Republic.

This agreement never came into force partly because the Volksraad ratified it only with reservations which would have destroyed its effect. And in the meantime trouble had arisen between the Queen and the Queen Mother of the Swazi King, who was a minor. The elders of the tribe refused to ratify either the 1890 Convention or that of 1893 lest they be put to death by the King when he came of age.

Finally, in 1894, a third Convention was signed under which Kruger was given direct responsibility for administering Swaziland, without the formality of negotiating first with the Swazis, and had no difficulty in procuring the agreement of the Volksraad to ratifying this arrangement.

But in May 1895 Lord Rosebery's Government, persuaded by Loch, annexed the whole of Amatongaland (the disputed territory between Zululand and Mozambique) thus making it impossible for Kruger to proceed with his plan for a seaport for the Republic. It had taken 12 years to fence him in.

Chapter 11

Kruger at Home

The Pretoria in which Kruger reigned was an Arcadian township. Hares, partridge and wild guinea-fowl ran wild through the orchards between the houses, and snipe could be shot off the swamp in the centre of the town. Water was plentiful, and almost every garden displayed fig and apricot trees. But most of the houses were of unburnt brick and unpretentious. The side-streets were rides of grass straddled by unmade roads which rolled hither and yon. There were no drains, and Church Street, already the centre's main thoroughfare, was flanked on each side by an open furrow bridged with paving-stones only at the crossroads.

The Boers who came to the town with their produce were happy to barter it for voerchitz (printed linen), molvel (moleskin), or other consumables such as sugar and coffee. In the early years of Kruger's presidency they distrusted money. There were no theatres, and strict laws prevented shooting, digging and other forms of husbandry on Sundays.

The first car to reach Pretoria was a two-seater Benz with a $1\frac{1}{2}$-HP engine and candle-lamps, which arrived in 1896. Kruger saw it in the Berea Park. He also saw the first film show in South Africa – a news-reel of himself going to Raadzaal. He stayed up late to see it, but insisted first on having the piano which was to have provided suitable accompaniment replaced by an organ.

Those who lived around Pretoria did not however lose touch with life on the veld. Many of them went on shooting trips and some, during the colder four or five months of the year, moved their flocks and herds off the plateau, where there was little for them to eat, down to the bushveld which, though unhealthy for livestock in the heat of the summer, offered good pasturage. During this excursion the Boer and his family camped out in tents. They took everything with them – bedding, kitchen-ware, some furniture, chickens and even the household cat – just as they would have if they had been setting out once more on the Great Trek. Boys from the home farm tended the sheep and cattle, and the farmer himself seized the chance to meet and entertain relations, sometimes even holding a dance under the sail-flap of the wagon, with a local fiddler or accordion-player for the band.

Kruger's house in Pretoria was built by Charles Clark, an English-speaking builder who had settled in Pretoria in the days of President Burgers; Kruger described Clark as one of his tame Englishmen. The house was a mixture of styles. The moulding around the front and the moulded plasterwork were in the style of the later Renaissance period, whereas the verandas were oriental.

The house had a large carpeted reception-room to the left, furnished with two settees, four armchairs, 12 chairs and two round tables – a harmonium stood against one wall. The curtains were of heavy damask with an interwoven floral design. The wallpaper, too, had flowers in red and gold, and was topped by a white and gold ceiling.

The Krugers' was one of the first houses in Pretoria to have a telephone, and electric light was installed in the days when the switches were still marked "Light" and "Dark".

There was also a dining-room, a bedroom, a stone-paved kitchen and a small room which served as an office and led to a private study used by the President alone. The stoep, or veranda, used for receiving visitors ran along the front wall of the house.

When he moved into the house in 1884 the President gave a house-warming party for 60. It began at 7.30 and ended exceptionally late at 10.30.

Up until 1889 no sentries were posted outside the President's home, and when two were eventually provided it was understood that as far as the President was concerned they had his permission to smoke.

Sometimes they were invited into the kitchen for a cup of coffee or into the parlour to hear an anecdote that the President felt inclined to tell them, or even, if it happened to be raining heavily, into the dining-room for a bite of supper. It was not unusual on these occasions for the President, as a special mark of favour, to demonstrate as a parlour trick that he could grip as firmly with the second and third fingers of his left hand as if he had never lost a thumb.

Several evocative accounts have come down to us of what it was like to visit the President in those days. One was written by Melina Rorke, daughter of the British Consul in Mozambique who afterwards became a nurse in the Boer War:

The next morning, when the sun was still lingering behind the rose and purple clouds in the east, we once more started on our way, turning frequently to wave farewell to the kindly Boer family, who had assembled on the stoep to bid us god-speed.

It was a beautiful day, and the pleasant, well-watered valley through which we wound our way, with its woods and its rich cultivated farms, was a welcome contrast to the bleak, windy ridges of Jo'burg.

By ten o'clock our wagons were thundering up the broad, tree-shaded avenues of Pretoria. It was a quiet, sleepy little town, with few people on the streets and little traffic, and in spite of the fact that it was the capital of the Transvaal it looked more like an English city than a Dutch one.

Father had told us that we must pay our respects immediately to President Kruger, who was a good friend of his, for one of Oom Paul's small vanities was his delight in having newcomers call upon him. Mr Kruger's house was in the very centre of the town – a two-storeyed white colonial building with large columns and a wide, hospitable veranda. Although Oom Paul had a salary of seven thousand pounds a year, he had the simplest of tastes, and would have been quite as contented to live in any sort of rude shack, had not the Republic presented him with this more suitable residence. Just across the street from his house was the little chapel of the so-called Dopper Sect, in which the President himself sometimes preached to his people.

The Hottentot boy who answered our knock informed us that his master was not at home, but that the "missy" was, and promptly led the way across a side hall into a big, white-washed room. Mrs Kruger, a plain, dumpy middle-aged woman dressed in a voluminous black skirt, with a basque waist, and a "cappy" that almost concealed her dark hair [parted habitually in the middle] was sitting in a huge wooden armchair with a cushioned back, her short slippered feet and bare legs resting on a square footstool. She welcomed us in shy Dutch monosyllables, and, explaining that her husband was presiding at a meeting of the Volksraad, but would soon return, motioned to us to sit down. The room was plainly furnished with massive wooden chairs and tables and along the walls there were several couches which, instead of being upholstered, were woven in criss-cross strips of cowhide. I sat down rather gingerly on one, and was pleased to find it more comfortable than it looked. Mrs Kruger spoke very little, contenting herself with a nod of understanding at Bassy's explanations of who we were and why we had come to Pretoria, and nervously pinching and fluting the black cotton lace that edged her black silk apron. My knowledge of Dutch at that time was rather limited, so while Bassy was carrying on his difficult one-sided conversation I looked round the room, but there was little of interest in it, except the beautiful animal-skin rugs scattered over the white scrubbed boards of the floor.

Presently another Hottentot servant appeared with coffee in komikies – crockery basins, decorated in appallingly gaudy designs, with a bowl-like bottom and a wide rim. It required considerable skill to drink out of them without having the coffee trickle down one's chin, and I had to make hasty recourse to my handkerchief several times before I acquired the knack. I learned later that a huge brass kettle of coffee was always kept on the stove, for Oom Paul kept open house, and at any hour of the day or night a way-farer was certain of receiving a hearty welcome and a komikie of hot coffee.

The drink seemed to loosen Mrs Kruger's tongue a little, and when she noticed my interest in the footstools which stood in front of each armchair she explained that the reason they had an open top was that in cold weather, a pan of coals was placed in the stool to warm one's feet. As she talked I realised with surprise how illiterate she was, and that the reason she confined herself to monosyllables with strangers was that she was afraid of disgracing her husband. Not that Oom Paul minded – he was perfectly satisfied with his ignorant, plump Hausfrau, and his noisy, healthy brood of sixteen children.

Mrs Kruger could neither read nor write, but she had a great respect for anyone who could, and whenever her husband had a document to sign would shriek through the house, "Stil, kinders! Papa vell ze nam tieken" (Quiet, children! Papa wants to sign his name). And then she would watch with breathless pride while Oom Paul's big awkward fingers traced his signature.

Just before noon Oom Paul himself came striding into the house. He seemed even bigger and stouter than I had remembered him in his black frock-coat, his black trousers, and top-hat, with his little sore, pouched eyes and his straggly beard that fringed his jaw from ear to ear. His face lit up when he heard who we were, and as he crushed my fingers in his big hand I noticed his missing thumb and remembered hearing that when it had been crushed he had himself hacked it off. Impatiently he looked round the room: "But what are we doing indoors on such a fine day, eh? Let us go outside." He led the way to the stoep; Mrs Kruger, Bassy and I swept along in his mighty wake. Before we had even found seats he had thrown himself into a chair and was shouting for the boy to bring coffee.

While the young Hottentot was padding rapidly to and fro with more komikies Oom Paul lit his pipe, and began talking to Bassy about conditions in South Africa, the curse of the diamond- and gold-mines, and the depravity of Jo'burg with its cafés, its dance-halls, and brothels. He punctuated his sentences by spitting in the general direction of a huge brass cuspidor, but I noticed with fascination that only about once out of five times did he hit the mark.

Mr Kruger insisted that Bassy and I must stay under his roof as long as we were in Pretoria – our father was his friend; a fair, just-minded man, unlike most of the uitlanders. His booming voice, extolling father's virtues, drowned our protests.

I discovered during the next few days that Mrs Kruger had only one interest outside of her home, her husband, her children and her step-children, and that was the Nagmaals. Her stolid face became almost animated when she spoke of the annual Nagmaal, which I should be privileged to attend on the following day. I had no idea what a Nagmaal was, and I was reluctant to admit my ignorance of what to her was obviously of vital importance.

A Nagmaal, I discovered shortly, was an annual confirmation of the young Boer boys and girls, the great outstanding event in the whole year, for not only did it hold tremendous religious significance, but it was usually the occasion of many marriages, and a great social gathering for Boers from all over the country. Before it was light I was wakened by the sound of heavy ox-wagons rumbling past the house on their way to the market-place and the baaing of sheep, the crowing of roosters, the lowing of cattle and the shouts of the native drovers and drivers; the excited voices of men and women.

When after a hurried breakfast, I reached the centre of the town, the quiet market-place was unrecognisable; it was surrounded on three sides by rows of great wagons from which the oxen had been unharnessed and driven to pasture on the outskirts of the city, and all the wagons had been transformed into stalls displaying piles of carefully polished vegetables, glowing fruit, jars of home-made preserves and pickles, loaves of bread and cake, presided over by proud and excited women and girls, all dressed in their best gowns and aprons. Beyond the wagons the big bearded Boer farmers displayed crates of chicken and geese, herds of frightened sheep, stolid cows, restless, pawing bulls, and a few sturdy horses – all for sale or barter.

After due time had been given to the business, the long elaborate religious ceremony began; awkward farm boys stumbling forward, girls proudly swishing new dresses, with long prayers and solemn adjurations one by one were accepted into the Church and returned proudly to take their places beside their beaming parents. Then came the weddings; shy stammering bridegrooms, blushing tremulous brides, all dressed in the finest clothes that their families provided, stepped forward in pairs, and with a few solemn words were bound together for life, for the Boers did not recognise divorce.

After the last couple had been married the tension relaxed; the women hurried away to prepare the great feast which was almost the most important part of a Nagmaal; the men went back to resume bargaining.

There was no honeymoon for the newly married couples. Their marriage hardly marked a change in their manner of living; when the feast was over, and the oxen once more harnessed to their wagons, the young bride, instead of climbing up beside her mother and father, was hoisted into her husband's wagon, and rumbled off beside him to his homestead, instead of returning to the farm on which she had been born and raised.

Another account of a visit to Kruger was written rather later in his period of rule by the American author Poultney Bigelow, and appeared in *Harper's New Monthly Magazine*:

Opposite the five army tents stood a long low house, all the rooms of which were on the ground floor. A veranda ran along the front, and perhaps six feet of shrubbery separated the stoep from the sidewalk. It was a typical farmhouse, such as a prosperous Boer farmer would be inclined to build, and was almost concealed by lofty shade trees. There was no driveway to the front door, no sign that the house contained any but an average citizen of Pretoria. But at the wicket-gate were two soldiers with rifles, who challenged us as we attempted to pass. My friend the legislator said who he was and that sufficed, for no further questions were asked. The front door was wide open; we rang no bell, but walked into the small and rather feebly lighted hallway, and looked about us in the hope of attracting the attention of a servant. But no servant was to be seen, though we walked through to the back of the house and made as diligent a search as the circumstances warranted.

Then we returned to the front door. To the right of the hall was a reception-room, occupied by a few ladies, who were, I presume, calling upon Mrs Kruger. To the left was a corresponding room, but the door was closed. Gruff voices I could distinctly hear, and my friend said, in a relieved voice, "He's there; it's all right!"

I thought, "On the contrary, it's all wrong." For I had no mind to intrude myself upon Paul Kruger when he was talking gruffly with his fellow-burghers. I had also just learned that the liberated prisoners had come from jail directly to Kruger's house, and there thanked him for his clemency. I felt that this must have been a hard official day for the aged statesman, and that he was having at that moment another of the many political tussles through which he has had to make his way in order to rule with effect amongst people like himself.

In an armchair beside a round table sat Paul Kruger. The rest of the room was occupied by as many swarthy burghers as could find seats. They wore long beards, and gave to the assembly a solemnity, not to say sternness, suggestive of a Russian monastery. My friend led me at once through the circle of councillors, and said a few words to the President, who rose, shook hands with me, and pointed, with a grunt, to a chair at his side. He then took his seat and commenced to puff at a huge pipe. He smoked some moments in silence, and I watched with interest the strong features of his remarkable face. I had made up my mind that I should not say the first word, for I knew him to be a man given to silence. He smoked, and I watched him – we watched one another, in fact. I felt that I had interrupted a council of state, and that I was an object of suspicion, if not ill-will, to the twenty broad-shouldered farmers whose presence I felt, though I saw only Kruger.

And, indeed, his is a remarkable face and form. I have seen him often since, during church service, on the street, and in his office, but that first impression in his own home will outlive all the others. I should like to have known him in the field, dressed in the fashion of the prairie – a broad-brimmed hat upon his head, a shirt well opened at the throat, his rifle across his shoulder. There he would have shown to advantage in the elements that gave him birth, and lifted him to be the arbiter of his country, if not of all South Africa. Kruger in a frock-coat high up under his ears, with a stove-pipe hat unsuited to his head, with trousers made without reference to shape, with a theatrical sash across his breast after the manner of a St Patrick's day parade – all that is the Kruger which furnishes stuff to ungenerous journalists who find caricature easier than portrait-painting. That is the Kruger whom some call un-graceful, if not ugly. But that is not the real Kruger.

His features, like those of most good men, are of striking size and form, and, moreover, harmonious. The mouth appears set by an act of will, and not by natural disposition. It parts willingly into a smile, and that smile lights his whole face into an expression wholly benevolent. All those who know Kruger have noticed this feature – this beautifying effect of his cheery smile. The photographs of him give only his expression when ready for an official speech – not his happy mood when chatting with his familiars.

Contemporary descriptions of Kruger's appearance varied widely according to the tastes and prejudice of the writer. Thus Mrs Lionel Phillips, wife of one of the Jameson Raid conspirators, noted the "clumsy features, and small cunning eyes set high on the face with great puffy rings beneath them, his lank straight locks worn longer than usual". His features, she thought, showed strength of will, cunning and the dullness of expression one sees in peasants' faces.

Dr Engelenburg, Editor of *Die Volkstem* and confidant of Kruger, noted his strong harsh voice and abrupt gestures which he said were like those of a man who owes his success to swift action after mature consideration. Kruger, according to Dr Engelenburg, was not readily affable to strangers nor did he bedeck his normal gruff style of address with artificial courtesies. His manner remained that of a farmer – though in fact he had little time to be one. He was fond of company and hospitable.

Natalie Hammond, wife of John Hays Hammond, Rhodes's Yale-educated consultant engineer, who went to see President Kruger in the days following the Jameson Raid in order to procure the release of her husband, saw Kruger somewhat differently:

The home of the President of the South African Republic is an unpretentious dwelling, built of wood and on one floor. There is a little plaza running across the front, on which he is frequently seen sitting, smoking his pipe of strong Boer tobacco, with a couple of his trusted burghers beside him. Two armed sentinels stood at the latch gate. I hurried through the entrance.

A Negro nurse was scurrying across the hall with a plump baby in her arms. A young man with a pleasant face met me at the sitting room door and invited me to enter. It was an old-fashioned parlour, furnished with black horsehair, glass globes, and artificial flowers. A marble-topped center table supported volumes bound in pressed leather with large gilt titles. There were several men already in the room, all Boers . . . At the further end of the long room sat a large sallow-skinned man with long, grizzled hair swept abruptly from his forehead. His eyes, which were keen, were partly obscured by heavy swollen lids. The nose was massive, but quite handsome. The thin-lipped mouth was large and flexible, and showed both sweetness and firmness. A fine mouth! He wore a beard. It was President Kruger.

As she left, after a non-committal discussion, the President rose, "removed his pipe from between his teeth and, coughing wildly, gave me his hand. Mr Grobler* escorted me to the gate."

The President was, indeed, a heavy smoker and was known to have drawn so hard on his pipe that he set the bowl alight. His doctors told him to give it up and he did so for a few days. Then he took to smoking harder than ever and persuaded himself that he was a better healer than his physicians.

The President usually woke at first light and was dressed before sunrise. He invariably wore black, though sometimes the cloth looked rusty with wear. His first act after dressing was to unlock the front door, after which he would go to his private study to read a chapter from the Bible by the light of a paraffin lamp or tallow candle in the days before electric light had been installed. Next came his first cup of early morning coffee. In summer he then went out of doors and sat on the stoep to receive his first callers. In winter he sat indoors beside a large Bible. There was nothing formal about his audiences – which might be with friends or strangers. To each of them the President extended his massive hand as a sign that he was ready to listen. A cloud of tobacco smoke quickly followed.

Breakfast, preceded by a prayer and a reading from the Bible in High Dutch, was served at 8 a.m. Women and girls sat at table with covered heads as if in church, and since the President ate quickly he was soon ready to put on his Presidential robes and set off for the office. He seldom read the morning papers and preferred to rely on a summary prepared for him by Dr Leyds. He took no regular exercise, which could hardly have been good for a man so accustomed to outdoor life.

In the early days of his Presidency he travelled in an ordinary landau carriage. The State Coach that carried him to the Volksraad building in later years was a more impressive vehicle with dark blue body work, bordered with the colours of the Vierkleur and lined with pale blue watered silk. On State occasions it was accompanied by a mounted guard provided by the State Artillery – ten riding in front, ten behind and two on either side of the carriage. On these occasions the President wore the medals given him by foreign governments as well as his sash of office and his top-hat with the enormous crêpe band round it.

At the Volksraad his first appointment was with his Executive Council with whom he discussed the affairs of state in far greater

---

* Piet Grobler, Kruger's nephew, by this time Under-Secretary for Foreign Affairs.

detail than should have been necessary if he had had a properly organised Cabinet Office and enough reliable officials. For example, the President himself had to point out that the new coins so carefully minted for the Republic were unusable as they showed the symbolic trek wagon as having two shafts instead of a single central one. (He had taken a big risk in allowing a graven image of himself to appear on the reverse side.)

Hundreds of requests had to be personally investigated and assessed by the President; and thousands of documents signed. Here Kruger's remarkable memory helped him. He could recall the wording of documents unseen by him for several years, and until well into his seventies could also remember the date and the full circumstances in which this or that decision had been taken.

As soon as his business with the Executive Council was finished, generally before 10 a.m., Kruger entered the Volksraad and took his seat to the right of the "Speaker" to listen to (and frequently to intervene in) the debates. No smoking there, alas, but Kruger was known to have taken an orange with him and occupied his spare moments peeling and eating it at high speed.

At midday the President returned home for lunch and had a rest from politics, while hearing Mrs Kruger's account of her morning. From 2 p.m. to 4 p.m. he was back again in the Government building, after which he received committees dealing with particular problems. Then he came home again for a cup of coffee. Next it was time to receive visitors and offer round his otter-skin tobacco pouch either on the stoep outside or in his reception-room.

Dinner was taken early because the President preferred to be in bed by nine o'clock.

Mrs Kruger, known in the family as Tante Sanna, played a large part in the President's life, though she tried as far as possible to avoid being involved in politics. It was generally conceded that she was short, stout and dignified. It was Tante Sanna who saw that enough coffee for 40 people was always ready (though on Kruger's birthday in 1896, when he was at the height of his popularity, 1,000 cups were served to callers in a single day). She seldom left the house except to go to church and never, of course, used the State Coach. A photograph of her taken when she was 68 shows her with an almost unlined face and hair that shows no signs of turning grey. She had a plump "motherly" countenance and a near snub nose but a firm mouth and determined chin. Lady Greene, wife of the British Agent in Pretoria, found her peeling peaches when she called. It is also said that she milked the President's cows, which were stalled at the back of the house, and was prepared to sell the milk. She helped to prepare the biltong – dried and salted meat which was stored under the roof of the back balcony.

Her business it was to keep the children quiet at meals – and the other adults too, if the President had something on his mind.

Meat of some kind garnished with sweet and ordinary potatoes was usually served three times a day in the Kruger household. The President was not averse to fat mutton and was particularly partial to "Kop en portgis" (sheep's head and trotters). Dried peaches or raisins or peaches and cream formed the dessert and coffee followed. Bread and milk were served during the meal and the President sometimes combined the two by soaking his bread in the milk. He ate hastily and untidily. Kruger was not a professed teetotaller but held off strong drink.

Tante Sanna saw further into his mind than most people.

She was present in the room one day when Mr Joseph Benjamin Taylor, a diamond- and gold-fields' pioneer and confidant of Rhodes, came to see the President about one of his mine managers who was in danger of prosecution for having allowed rock crushing to take place on a Sunday. With him came Mr Nellmapius (a close friend) who had a permanent entrée to the Kruger house.

After Taylor had explained the purpose of the visit, the President gave no direct reply. Instead he recalled how, many years before, he had taken part in a trek in search of a new land of milk and honey. His party had explored a large desert area where food and water was scarce, and had had to turn back. One Sunday they left the desert and found themselves on a fine grassy plateau well stocked with game. They had not tasted fresh meat for months and when they came near to a herd of gnu, Kruger's wife said, "Paul, take your gun and shoot one of those beasts. Our people are in desperate need of food, and though it is the Sabbath, it would be the Lord's will." She took the gun and handed it to him. He raised the ancient weapon and aimed at the herd. There was a flash in the pan and the weapon refused to fire. "You see," he said turning to his wife, "it is not the Lord's will," but, just as he was handing her the gun, the charge exploded and brought down the biggest and fattest animal in the herd.

Taylor and Nellmapius were mystified by the Presidential anecdote and when Tante Sanna went back into the kitchen they followed her and asked what the President could have meant.

"You must be dense," she replied. "Can't you see that the President is an Elder of the Church. He cannot officially sanction Sunday working."

No prosecution was brought, and, in the end, Sunday working

was authorised, if it could be shown to be necessary for the proper functioning of the mine.

Kruger was far less intolerant than might have been supposed, and when Dr Leyds hesitated to accept office under him because he was not of the same religious faith as the President – and had not had his sons baptised – Kruger replied, "If you are an honourable and able public servant I shall never ask you what your religious views are."

He allowed "deserving Catholics" to hold minor positions and was not deterred from friendships with Jewish "randlords", as for example Sammy Marks and Barney Barnato. When called on to open a synagogue he did *not* however say, as sometimes reported, "I declare this synagogue open in the name of Jesus Christ, Our Lord, Amen."

What he did say was, "I call those my people who obey the laws of the land. The Jews are God's ancient people. I respect the Jewish and other faiths without distinction."

In his speech of acceptance as candidate in his first Presidential election, he made a plea for religious toleration. "We find nowhere in the Bible that Christ has given His people command to persecute others by reason of their belief," he declared.

In later years Kruger allowed himself to give up wearing the special Dopper clothes which Kotze had noticed on their first meeting.

His own religion, however, came before politics and he clove to the Vrije Gereformeerde Gemeente Church, although its rival, the Hervormde Kerk, was the original State Church to which holders of important offices – including the Presidency – were, at one time, obliged to belong.

He attended no public entertainments, and when one of his Cabinet suggested that they should go to the races, his reply was that he was now 60 and had long ago learnt that one horse could run faster than another and it did not matter to him which it was.

He could not understand why people organised prize-fights. Murder he could understand even if he did not approve of it. But not boxing, and in July 1889 he threatened to ban a match between Woolf Bendoff, an Englishman, and the South African boxer, J. R. Cooper, until Barney Barnato put it to him that this would look like cowardice on the part of the Republic.

Undoubtedly Kruger had a highly developed sense of humour. Judge Carl Jeppe, a member of the first Johannesburg Town Council, for example, relates how an uitlander once badgered the President to tell him some stories of the narrow escapes he had had while hunting as a young man. After much urging Kruger recalled how he had once wounded an elephant, a cow with very fine tusks. Soon after firing he noticed that she had a calf with her, and somewhat regretted having begun hostilities as, under such circumstances, the ladies of that species are not to be trifled with. Sure enough the elephant charged. The bush was so dense that Kruger could not leave the elephant path in which he found himself and, having no time to reload, he ran down it at his best speed. Luckily the path was curved and the elephant had some difficulty in following. Presently it straightened out, and Kruger saw to his consternation a lion facing him 20 or 30 yards ahead. There was no time to think. Against the elephant he would have no chance, but the lion might possibly give way; so Kruger kept on running.

Perhaps because of this determined attitude, or because the elephant's head now appeared above the bushes, shrilly trumpeting, the lion turned tail and fled. Kruger had the advantage of a flying start and passed the lion; the latter got up pace and forged ahead; a spurt by Kruger and he was leading; another trumpet blast by the elephant and the lion was in front. Kruger said it was the best ding-dong race he had ever run. All the time the elephant was rapidly gaining on both, the President said. But just at that moment Dr Leyds came in to say that the President was expected in the Volksraad. And notwithstanding all his efforts the uitlander was never able to persuade the President to finish the story.

Kruger was not averse to an occasional practical joke and would hoax the more credulous visitors to his house by pretending to blow out the electric light while covertly operating the switch behind his back. He sometimes gave the sentries on duty outside his house a smart pinch on the behind as he passed them, particularly if they were in favour with him. And though he seldom spoke English, he would from time to time call Mrs Kruger "My dear" in an affected English drawl.

Now and then, it was said, he would find it irresistible to give one or two members of the choir the wrong tuning note to chime in with at choir practice.

Then there was the story of one of his friends who undertook a special journey to Pretoria to find out from Kruger whether the State really had a Secret Service and what it was doing. The President told him that this matter was a State secret. But the friend persisted. At last the President in a confidential manner asked, "Can you keep a secret?" His friend, drawing up his chair closer said, "Yes, President, of course I can." "Then," said Kruger "so can I."

He was fond of children – in their right place.

At home, when the children got too much under his feet, or made too much noise, the President reminded them, "The Bible says 'The meek shall inherit the earth'."

And if they showed an unseemly interest by crowding round their elders and betters the President would sometimes say, "Now then, why so close? Do you really want to count our teeth?"

His deportment was not that of an English vicar and there were those who objected to the spectacle of him paring his nails in public with the end of a sharp knife, or spitting on the floor.

Yet he observed good manners as he understood them, and would never, as a guest, have dreamt of lighting up his pipe until his host had invited him to do so. Nor did he light up when in the presence of Dr Leyds, whose throat he knew was affected by tobacco smoke.

What else did people find likeable – as distinct from admirable – about Kruger? Well, he remembered and tried to repay past kindnesses as Harry Pauling, a railway engineer, discovered after he had given Kruger and two companions a shakedown for the night in his office while they were waiting for the coach to take them on their way to London. When Pauling called on Kruger ten years later to seek work, Kruger told his staff to give him any contracts that might be currently available.

Kruger inspired loyalty in his staff because although he might criticise them in private at home, or in his room at the Volksraad, he defended them stoutly in public debate. Dr Leyds was particularly touched by Kruger's willingness to confess when he had been in the wrong. He once appeared on horseback in the middle of the night to knock up the doctor and apologise for having wronged him.

There was also the time when the President came to the station to meet Leyds on his return from Europe, an honour he usually reserved for Mrs Kruger alone. He told Leyds that he had missed him very much and prayed for him every day, adding in a classically mixed metaphor on the question of their periodical quarrels, "You know, your blood is hot, and so is mine, and when they touch then the sparks fly." Kruger inspired respect because he refused to use information to the discredit of his opponents which he had acquired at a time when they had been friends of his.

He was probably at his worst where he was most often visible – in the public arena.

Chapter 12

---◆◆◆◆►---

Kruger in Politics

The Raadzaal, to which Kruger directed himself after his early morning meeting with the Executive Council, occupied the whole of a city block in Pretoria. Anyone could go in. There was no doorman or guard, and the strangers' gallery was free for all, except during a secret session. All members had to appear in black clothes and white tie; some brought their top-hats, but even they joined with the rest in spitting, according to their desires, on the floor.

Kruger, who was compelled to speak in High Dutch because the Afrikaans vernacular was not yet recognised as an official language, did not find it easy to express himself. "He claps his hands together as he speaks and discharges sentences like a Maxim gun," wrote Neville Edwards. "Every now and then they draw a response of approbation from his listeners in the form of a deep-voiced 'Hoor, hoor'. And then your eye wanders to the old man, with the green sash of office across his chest, standing on a dais hammering hard-sounding sentences into his stolid listeners. You presume they are hard facts, for the voice is harsh enough for anything, and sounds as if he were trying to speak with cinders in his mouth."

Captain Francis Younghusband, who had travelled to South Africa as Special Correspondent for *The Times*, wrote of the Raad in his book *South Africa of Today*:

Seated in concentric, semicircular rows round the raised dais upon which sat the Chairman and President Kruger, the latter dressed in an old frock-coat with a broad vivid green sash bound over his shoulder, were some 40 or 50 rough-bearded men, sombrely dressed in black, and of very much the same type as one would see at a country vestry meeting at home. One after the other would get up and speak very volubly and excitedly for five or ten minutes, each stating his opinion of the matter under debate, with great vehemence and much gesticulation and thumping of the table, but with little attempt at reasoning. At frequent intervals during the debate the Chairman himself would join in and speak equally excitedly, and still more frequently would President Kruger do so. On the first occasion upon which I visited the Raad I saw

Mr Kruger, almost before the original speaker had finished, rise and roar in his deep big voice at the meeting, and almost break the table with his violent thumps upon it. I thought that something very important must be under debate, but was told that they were merely debating whether some minor official's salary should be cut down or increased! Mr Kruger is always emphatic upon whatever subject he speaks. But when he wishes to really enforce a point he comes round to his great stock argument that the independence of the country would be endangered if what he wishes is not agreed to. This is unfailing, but must surely now be getting a little thread-bare.

But bellowing and table-thumping seemed to work, and Kruger was able to speak almost invariably of "my officials, my burghers, my country and my Volksraad". The insecure and dangerous circumstances in which his country found itself must have helped to consolidate his power.

Only once was he known to have been really nonplussed in the Volksraad. That, according to F. W. Reitz, was when one of his house-boys arrived with a message, "Baas, Baas, the old Missus says you must come at once. Someone has stolen all the biltong from the clothes-line in the back yard."

Kruger jammed on his stove-pipe hat and went out without a word. He was not seen again until the following morning.

He had supporters in the Volksraad who could be counted on to vote with him and who were consequently known as "Ja-Broers" (Yes-brethren). And occasionally it was said that he told his supporters, "Never mind what I say in the Raad, vote against me." He was thus able to claim that he had done his best to pass a measure that was defeated.

Only someone with Kruger's immense qualities could have afforded to lose his temper so often in public and keep his people guessing whether he was doing so deliberately. There was the occasion when a Kruger appointee, V. R. Bok, was deposed from his post as Minute Taker to the Volksraad and Kruger stormed out of the Chamber muttering to himself and throwing his sash over an un-offending member. At other times he merely walked out, showing every sign of anger.

Joubert spoke of Kruger's "Buffalo rushes" and "bellowing".

A particular instance of attempted intimidation occurred when Kruger, then Vice-President, tried to appoint a puisne judge whom Kotze considered unsuitable:

It so happened [Chief Justice Kotze wrote] that, while there could be no objection to the legal qualifications of the gentleman proposed as Judge, there was considerable public ill feeling against him on account of the attitude he had taken up during the late [Majuba] war. Mr Kruger urged that the party in question had rendered meritorious services in the Boer cause and was a properly qualified lawyer. While admitting the legal qualifications of the person proposed, I pointed out that other suitable qualifications were likewise necessary and emphasised that the real value and use of the judiciary consist in the respect and confidence the public entertained for its members and their administration of justice, and that however proper it may be to add another judge to the Court, care should be taken not to impair this respect and confidence.

I further suggested that some other suitable and substantial way might be found of rewarding the candidate proposed for his services. In this view Commandant-General Joubert, a member of the Triumvirate supported me, but Mr Kruger was stubborn and continued to press his point with the others while the others remained silent. I was then forced either to acquiesce or play my last card. I resolved on the latter course, and calmly and seriously intimated to Mr Kruger that I much feared that the contemplated appointment, if made, would mean my resignation as Chief Justice. Mr Kruger, quick as a flash of lightning, jumped up from his chair and said in a thundering voice: "Now you are threatening me, and I never allow any man to do that." I was certainly surprised at this unexpected outburst from the Vice-President; however, I quietly yet gravely replied, "I have too much respect for you Mr Vice-President, and for the Fathers of the People, whom I see sitting round this table, as well as for myself, to indulge in threats when discussing so important a matter as the administration of justice; and I much regret that you should for a single moment entertain such a thought." Mr Kruger thereupon resumed his seat and said, "I am sorry that I was a little hasty."

Another office was eventually found for the gentleman in question.

It has been fashionable in some quarters to represent Kruger as someone who would have been a progressive if he had not been held back by his supporters from the outback. Certainly he was in favour of economic expansion, and endeavoured to disabuse the burghers of "the absurd impression that prevails among the farmers that debts contracted by the State lowered its prestige in the eyes of the other nations".

Also, he tried unsuccessfully in March 1890 to persuade the

burghers to agree to a Department of Agriculture, and he successfully supported the abolition of public executions, but he was cautious.
"I can't take too much hay on my fork," he would say to anyone who
reproached him for not moving fast enough.

It is not easy to come to a definite conclusion on how much
Kruger's acceptance of the literal truth of the Bible spilled over into
his political life. Did he believe, for instance, that the texts which he
quoted in his political arguments were really applicable to the case he
was discussing?

When he opposed holding a census on the grounds that the Lord
had punished David for numbering the people, did he really believe
that it was wrong for man to enumerate the works of the Lord? Did
he believe it was for vanity rather than for inquisitiveness that David
had been punished? Or did he think that the census would be unpopular in the Transvaal and that he would have no answer if the
burghers who opposed it cited the fate of David in their objections –
or the example of Herod?

And when he opposed the erection of pillar-boxes in Pretoria in
September 1894, was it really because – as he represented – city-
dwellers ought not to have conveniences denied to the rural population? Or the modernisation of farms on the ground that this would
"take the bread out of the mouths of my poor burghers"?

Did he really believe that the earth was flat or did he prefer to
maintain the authority of the Book from which he so often quoted?
Almost certainly there were times when the Good Book was invoked
to justify policies towards which Kruger was directed by sentiment,
prejudice, or a desire to play safe.

Probably the consideration uppermost in his mind was how to
promote the interests of the Afrikaner nation and to hold together
its discordant elements.

Kruger's techniques outside the Raadzaal were many and varied.
When talking to the Executive Council he often kept them guessing,
and at times they believed he was about to reject their arguments
when, really, he was getting them to answer the kind of objections
he might be expected to meet with in the Chamber.

With individuals he varied his approach.

Nicholas Smit, the hero of the battle of Ingogo, complained that
Kruger used four different techniques. First he argued, then he
stormed, then he got out the Bible and quoted from it, and, if all
else failed, he besought Smit with tears in his eyes. Smit found the
four-pronged attack irresistible.

To those who questioned him he was sometimes sharp. A Rustenburg farmer decided to heckle Kruger on the liquor concession which

he had granted to his friend Alois Nellmapius, and arrived at the meeting well fortified. When question time came he raised his voice to ask, "What good is the concession that you have given to Nellmapius?" The President stared intently at his interrogator and replied, "Can't you feel the good in your own body?"

Kruger's style when refusing favours was not perhaps Chamberlain's but it was effective. A young Hollander who fancied himself to be qualified for a high-ranking job in the South African Republic once asked the President for help in getting it. But Kruger was somewhat nettled by his condescending manner.

"How much do you know?" he asked.

The young man reeled off a list of languages he could speak and added that he had studied half a dozen scientific subjects as well.

"Tell me," said the President. "Do they need clever people in your country?"

The young man gave his assurance that indeed they did.

"Then why did you leave it to come here?" the President wanted to know.

The interview was concluded on the spot.

He was no less effective in dealing with matters of protocol. On one occasion there was a dispute between two diplomats and their wives as to which should go in first to a State banquet in Pretoria. As no one else could resolve the difficulty, the matter was laid before the President himself. His solution was simple. "You should give precedence," he said, "to the man with the elder wife." The problem quickly vanished.

Sometimes Kruger got back as good as he gave, and Carl Jeppe related how a member of the Volksraad Executive Committee, whose meetings were often held at the President's house to the accompaniment of Presidential coffee and cigars, expressed his sympathy on one occasion to the President on his recent severe financial losses. Kruger was astonished and asked what his guest could mean. "I was referring to your unfortunate losses on the Stock Exchange," replied the guest. The President became angry. "You know I never gamble," he declared.

"Well, but there must be something in it," persisted the guest. "How dare you say that," the President roared. "I tell you I haven't lost a penny in that or any other speculation!"

"Then how is it we get no cigars today?" asked the guest plaintively.

"I beg your pardon, gentlemen," chuckled the President as he hurried off to get fresh supplies.

"His great power lies in preaching the word," said John Xavier Merriman, the Cape politician, adding that a large proportion of the

Boer population believed that the President was divinely inspired. John Kotze in his memoirs was less impressed. Kruger would occupy the pulpit of the church at Rustenburg when no Minister was available, Kotze noted, but "his sermons were after the old style and method, somewhat rigorous at times", and they generally took more than an hour to deliver.

There were three political elements in Kruger's Republic. The first consisted of the Hollanders whom he had imported as advisers because of the lack of local expertise in the Transvaal. They were despised because they were poor horsemen and because they had a weakness for highbrow classical music. They were feared as constituting a barrier between the President and his loyal burghers. The proportion of Hollanders in the Transvaal administration probably did not amount to more than one-sixth of the total staff, and many of them had already lived in the Transvaal for years. Nevertheless they were highly unpopular.

Dr Leyds was especially distrusted because he had not attained the age at which Boers began to respect each other, because he spoke foreign languages, and because he was thought to have a near-monopoly of the private ear of Kruger. He was a particularly un-Boerlike individual with soulful eyes, a romantic moustache and a city-slicker taste in apparel.

Kruger's difficulties become clear when we consider some of the speeches made in the Volksraad by "his" burghers who formed the second side of the political triangle. For example, Mr G. P. Roos, member for Pretoria, opposed a plan for the Government to take action against the plague of locusts on the ground that this would be a defiance of the hand of the Lord. The best measure to take, in Mr Roos' view, would be repentance of one's sins. As a special concession, however, it was agreed by 12 votes to 11 that the South African Republic should be allowed to correspond with other countries about the problem of locusts, provided that neighbouring states co-operated in a day of prayer and intercession with God.

Education was none too favourably regarded by the true Boers, and at a meeting addressed by Chief Justice Kotze on 1 October 1892 Mr O. J. Coetzee, ex-member of the Volksraad for Lydenburg, pointed out that the Transvaal had formerly had an educated President, Mr T. F. Burgers, for whom he himself had voted. And what was the result? He had handed the keys of the State to Shepstone and the English.

Parks were opposed as providing needless pleasure when the ground could be split up and handed over to needy burghers.

P. C. Greyling, the member for Heidelberg, declared in August

1893 that he did not see any necessity for railways and that the country was prosperous enough without them, and A. A. Stoop, the member for Wakkerstroom, supported him by saying that trams were not needed and could "easily hit and kill people in the dark".

J. du P. De Beer opposed spending money on a museum on the ground that "every schoolboy had seen a scorpion, a chameleon, and other nonsense of that kind". He was also disturbed over the expenditure of £100 on foreign newspapers of the public budget, and went on to say that this was shameful and disgusting.

So, according to Jeppe, was an attempt to supplement Johannesburg's water supply by exploding dynamite beneath promising-looking clouds:

> This action aroused a storm of indignation in the Backveld country, and hundreds of petitions were presented to the Volksraad protesting against so impious a proceeding [he wrote]. Several of the retrogressive members of the Raad strongly supported the request that a law be passed to prevent any repetition of the experiment, on the grounds that it amounted to a defiance of the Almighty, who would send rain when He deemed it well, and that to compel the clouds to perform services for man before it was God's will, could be regarded as nothing short of sacrilege.
>
> To the consternation of the Progressive Party, one of their number actually supported the petitioners, but when he gave his reasons for doing so, their surprise was mitigated. Mr Maré said that he, too, held that the conduct of the water company was an affront to Providence but not on the same grounds as the previous speakers. He did not think that the Power above would take much notice of the explosions. He would think them beneath Him in every way. But there was a serious aspect of the question. For what purpose, he asked, had Providence given us dynamite. Surely it was to rend the rocks and compel them to yield up their gold so that the rich might prosper and the poor might find the wherewithal to live. But not – surely not – for the purpose of wasting it on fruitless explosions on the clouds? Such action was one of base ingratitude, and should be stopped by every means at our disposal.

The third element in the Kruger Government was the so-called Progressive Party, made up of the richer more sophisticated and better-educated Afrikaners. Most of their attacks were mounted against the more ignorant and short-sighted burghers, but they were not averse to criticising the Hollanders or even the President himself if opportunity served.

It was, however, as we shall see, not too difficult for Kruger, by one means or another, to defeat all efforts to oust him from power.

Kruger summed up his position very well when he explained to Viscount Bryce why there was no opposition party in the Transvaal such as existed in Britain. "When we have found an ox who makes a good leader of the team, we keep him there instead of shifting the cattle about in the hope of finding a better one."

Many problems remained with Kruger throughout the whole of his "reign". One was that of the monopolies which he granted to private individuals on such items as leather, soap, matches, bricks, cyanide, jam and even water and electric light. Those lucky enough to be selected as recipients of the Presidential favours had, of course, to pay something for them, and Kruger no doubt saw this as a convenient way of raising ready money quickly from a people not noted for their willingness to submit to the more normal forms of taxation. For example the right to levy tolls at certain points on the main roads was put up for public auction and the buyer received permission to levy a charge of 30 shillings on any ox-wagon carrying loads of 6,000lb and upwards.

In some cases, concessions were a convenient way of establishing new industries in the infant State. But the small scale of production meant high prices, which could be sustained only by protectionist tariff walls raised against the cheaper products of the Cape and elsewhere, and this led to complaints about increases in the cost of living.

A typical case was the monopoly which Kruger granted for the manufacture of dynamite. The President clearly believed that it was desirable to have his own sources of supply for this commodity as part of the national armament. But the mine-owners who needed it for gold production also had some cause for complaint.

The Transvaal Government showed its first real interest in dynamite in December 1887 when it granted Edouard Lippert, an enterprising red-bearded German, the sole right of manufacturing dynamite, gunpowder, ammunition and other explosives, for a period of 16 years, provided that he built and equipped a factory for this purpose within a year. He was allowed to import machinery and raw materials (but not finished dynamite) duty free, and all imports of dynamite were to cease as soon as the factory was able to meet the requirements of the Republic.

Lippert, in turn, sold the control of the concession to a French-financed firm, and the factory began production in January 1889, though under none too favourable terms, since the rival Anglo-German Trust had taken the precaution, while still free to do so, to import enough dynamite to last the Republic for the next two years.

Meanwhile Lippert and the Frenchmen had been saving themselves much trouble and had also scored a considerable profit by importing duty-free material which they described as "impregnated cellulose", a raw material for the manufacture of dynamite, but which was in fact the dynamite itself. An investigation was launched.

The President warmly defended Lippert and claimed that it would be grossly unfair and quite needless to test the material imported by him by exploding it since he (Kruger) and everyone else knew that it was explosive. The question was: was it dynamite? But even when this was shown to be the case, Kruger opposed cancelling the contract on the ground that this would damage the prestige of the State and give aid and comfort to her enemies. There was no point in giving to England what had been taken away from France, the President said.

The result was that the Government itself felt called on to take over the factory and handed the management of it back to Lippert who on this occasion split the new concession between the French and Anglo-German companies.

Under the new agreement Lippert, among others, received a substantial royalty per case of dynamite, the French company was indemnified for the loss of the original concession and the result was that the dynamite cost 40 shillings a case more than it need have. Practically no local raw materials were used and the profit, or most of it, went overseas.

The liquor monopoly aroused almost as much controversy. Originally the sole right of making "spirituous liquor" was granted to Kruger's friend Alois Nellmapius for an annual payment of £1,000. Soon afterwards Nellmapius formed a partnership with Samuel Marks, Isaac Lewis and Barnet Lewis and eventually sold the monopoly to a company for £120,000. But it was not this aspect of the liquor concession which drew most criticism. The more censorious declared that it debauched the native mine-workers, and were only half satisfied by Kruger's reply that although the factory did unfortunately produce liquor, it provided a ready market for large quantities of the burgher's grain.

Once when Kruger came under pressure about the cyanide concession, he went so far as to say that he was opposed to concessions in general but that if something could be made in the Transvaal that would compete with an imported article, then a monopoly could be beneficial: "If we have to buy everything in the cheapest market, everything will have to come from overseas and in that case how will the country ever become self-supporting?" On another occasion he pointed out that, ten years earlier, the burghers had opposed granting concessions for a sugar factory and a wool factory and the result was that they still had neither in the Republic. No one would set up a new factory unless they had protection at least for some years.

But as time rolled by, the President became more and more touchy about criticisms of the system (as he often was when he had a weak case). For example, when Mr Paul Maré, the member for Zoutpansberg, described the concession system as the country's "financial cancer", Kruger demanded the withdrawal of these words which constituted, he said, "a direct insult to the Government".

Not long after Kruger told the Volksraad that where concessions were concerned, its members must trust the Government or choose another Government that it could trust. The President said that he would never dream of granting any major concession without the agreement of the Raad, but he had to draw the line somewhere. He could not ask for competitive tenders to be submitted every time someone broke a window pane in the Parliament building. But the President must have had a fairly elastic idea of what amounted to "a major concession" because only the day before, without informing the Raad, he had signed away concessions for road repairs, bridges, the Pretoria tramway and the Johannesburg water supply.

When one member of the Raad, Mr E. P. Meintjes, more persistent than the rest, asked for a list of concessions, three officials entered the Chamber each weighed down with books. The President added with satisfaction that there were many more books to come. An official inquiry did nevertheless take place and Kruger was compelled from then on to be more sparing with his favours.

He evidently considered that he had the right to be fairly casual about money matters although no one went so far as to say that he profited personally from this laxity.

Some corruption was probably inevitable in a Government without a trained civil service and composed of men who, for the first time in their lives, were being called on to handle very large sums of money. Nevertheless in 1898 it was disclosed that during the previous 16 years no less than £2,400,000 had been advanced to officials without a proper account having been kept. Order forms signed by the President were sent automatically to the Treasury which did not consider that it was called on to inquire whether the amounts signed for by the President were backed by the endorsement of the Volksraad. But the Volksraad itself sturdily resisted all attempts to appoint a public watchdog.

One of the worst scandals arose out of the Government's decision to allow officials to buy the mining rights of plots, or "stands", originally allotted to the mining companies for storing water and the mining residues, instead of putting them up to properly advertised public auction.

Kruger's argument that the expense of advertising the auction would have put up the price beyond the reach of the poorer classes must have been one of the weakest ever advanced, and his alternative explanation that some private people as well as officials had been granted stands was not much better. In the end he was reduced to challenging people to point him out any law decreeing that stands must be sold at public auction. There was none.

Nor was Kruger more convincing when he set out to defend the 11 members of the Raad who were presented with "spiders" (light high-wheeled carriages) as an inducement to vote in favour of the Selati railway project. He said that he saw no harm in anyone receiving a present as long as it did not amount to bribery. As for officials, they should not speculate in matters concerning their own work but it would be unfair to say that an official could not properly act in his own interests in other respects.

Another charge that was levelled against Kruger was that of nepotism. It would have been surprising indeed if a man who had produced 15 or so children and 120 or so grandchildren resolutely excluded all of them from employment in the service of the State of which he was President.

Certainly there were instances of Kruger relations in positions of strength. Piet Grobler, his grandson, was Under-Secretary of State. Piet Kruger, another grandson, became Master of the High Court. Hans Malan, another grandson, was appointed Chief Inspector of Roads . . . and so on, although Kruger claimed that he had kept his dependants at home on the farm rather than let them draw State money.

Kruger's handling of the concession for supplying Johannesburg with water from the Vaal river was also open to criticism, for no one seriously challenged accusations in the opposition paper *Land en Volk* (*Land and People*) according to which F. C. (Frikkie) Eloff, the President's son-in-law and private secretary, used his influence to obtain the water company concession thereby making £30,000 for himself.

Every five years the President had to submit himself to the ordeal of re-election, the first occasion being in 1888 when his rival was Commandant-General Joubert. Joubert, with his high-piping voice and lack of self-confidence, was no real threat to Kruger either inside or outside the Volksraad, and he got only 834 votes against Kruger's 4,483.

The 1893 election, however, was a different affair. By the time this contest took place a fairly strong Progressive Party had formed up behind Joubert. It included capable men like Lukas Meyer and Koos de la Rey who resented the influence of the Hollanders like Leyds (whose appointment as State Secretary had been renewed in 1892 for four years), and who deplored Kruger's methods and the fact that the country despite its wealth remained so backward. The reformers wished to see the country ruled by men of ability rather than by Boer backwoodsmen.

Kruger was attacked during the 1893 campaign on the issues of corruption, financial maladministration, nepotism and concessions and the scandals arising out of them. He was criticised for his bad temper, his autocratic ways, his love of Hollanders, and his – at times – unctuous manner. The President's salary (£8,000 a year) also came in for criticism and a proposal that it should be reduced to £5,000 came before the Volksraad in 1892. Even Louis Botha, who was afterwards to become the first Prime Minister of the Union of South Africa, turned against Kruger. *Land en Volk*, the opposition paper, supported Joubert, and Joubert Committees sprang up. The election results were a shock. Joubert received 7009 votes to Kruger's 7881.

Even if we discount the accusations of the Opposition that many of Joubert's supporters had been wrongly prevented from voting, the result was a warning to Kruger, and it must have been clear that his power and influence over the voters was waning.

Yet as the President grew older he became more rather than less dictatorial. Two cases are enough to illustrate the extreme obstinacy and wilfulness of the President.

The first – a good example of the President's judicial style – occurred in 1886 when his good friend Mr Nellmapius was arrested, charged with embezzlement, found guilty by a jury, and sentenced by Mr Justice Brand to 18 months' imprisonment with hard labour. His Counsel appealed for six points of law to be referred to the High Court.

But while the case was still *sub judice*, a petition for his release was forwarded to Brand by State Secretary Bok who asked the judge to report on it. Brand replied that the case was already in the hands of the Court of Appeal. Bok then sent a second note saying that the matter was being considered that afternoon by the Executive Council who were expecting the judge's immediate ruling on the issue. This looked to Brand like political interference with the course of justice, and he went to complain to the President – who of course had been the moving spirit in the whole affair. Indeed, Kruger during the course of the interview asked Brand to release Nellmapius on bail. Brand told the President that this was not possible. He repeated this the next day in a letter to Bok explaining that the matter was outside his own jurisdiction and in the hands of the Court of Appeal. Later the same day Bok sent a further message to Brand telling him that Nellmapius' Counsel had now withdrawn the appeal. He added that the Executive Council had been waiting to hear from the judge since ten o'clock that morning about the question of Nellmapius' release and asked that a reply should be sent by the bearer immediately.

Brand however took his time and sent a reply the next day. It amounted to a rebuke to the Executive for trying to interfere with the course of justice. He pointed out that an appeal, once lodged, could not be withdrawn without the permission of the judge concerned.

Bok's answer was a note to Brand informing him that the Executive had decided to grant a pardon to Nellmapius and that he was being freed. In view of the fact that the case was still *sub judice*, Brand felt called upon to resign.

Chief Justice Kotze, who had been informed while on circuit of these deplorable events, hurried back to Pretoria. He took Brand's part and the unfortunate Nellmapius was then re-arrested. In justifying his action, Kotze explained to the President that the Executive Council had acted illegally in awarding a pardon in a case where the trial of the prisoner had not yet been concluded. In its reply "the Government and Executive Council" disagreed with the rulings of both Kotze and Brand, and said that Nellmapius would receive a pardon whatever the decision of the Court.

The conviction was duly squashed by the Court and Nellmapius was freed by Court Order.

The second example of Kruger's methods concerned the Constitution of the South African Republic and the President's determination to overrule it when convenient.

The Constitution which was drawn up over the years 1855–1858 in the days when the Republic was completely pastoral, without main roads or railways, provided that three months' public notice had to be given of any law before it was introduced into the Volksraad "except in the case of laws which could suffer no delay". Only laws duly passed after such public notice could be officially described as such. Other regulations, approved by the votes of the Volksraad, were known as besluiten (decisions), and on a number of occasions the question was raised as to whether such "decisions which were frequently hasty and ill-considered and sometimes inconsistent with each other" had the full force of laws as provided under the Constitution.

Chief Justice Kotze, in a highly controversial ruling delivered in 1884, declared that the Volksraad, as the supreme authority, was free to decide in what form its laws should be promulgated, and that the Courts had no authority to question the legality of its actions. Decisions taken by the Volksraad had therefore full legal validity. Kotze re-affirmed this decision in a case decided three years later.

But on this occasion Mr Justice S. G. Jorissen (son of Dr E. J. P. Jorissen) took a different view. He reckoned that the Volksraad had been established by the Constitution and not the Constitution by the Volksraad. It followed that the Volksraad could not consider itself to be above the law, but must legislate according to the Constitution. This minority verdict was however overruled and the Volksraad continued as before to go its own way.

In 1895, however, the problem arose in a new and much more controversial form. The trouble blew up when the Government issued a Proclamation declaring the farm known as Witfontein to be a public digging and open to prospectors from 19 July. One of them, named Brown, pegged out 1,200 claims for himself that day and applied under the Gold Law of 1894 to the Mining Commissioner for licences to hold them. In the meantime, however, armed bands of prospectors had arrived on the spot and the Executive Council, not liking the look of things, stepped in on 20 July and suspended the Proclamation. Brown promptly brought an action in the High Court against State Secretary Leyds, but the Volksraad formally approved the action of the Executive Council in a besluit which ruled that no one should have the right to claim damages because he had not been granted a claim licence. In the High Court, Chief Justice Kotze, however, ruled that the Volksraad had no right to pass a resolution overriding an existing law such as the Gold Law which provides for the issue of licences to prospectors.

The Court's finding, which was a reversal of Kotze's previous ruling, was, of course, highly embarrassing to the President. The decision meant that the Government would have to pay out £372,400 in damages to Brown, and that, furthermore, much of the President's future power and freedom of manoeuvre in the Volksraad would vanish since the decision he obtained there could subsequently be contested in the Courts. Volksraad decisions for years back might now be invalid.

The Court's finding might also lead to a demand for Leyds to be dismissed. And that would never do.

Kruger reacted in the only way open to him. He called on the Volksraad to legitimise its own authority by passing a further besluit – naturally without the three months' notice. In the course of an emergency session, a Bill known as the Testing Right Law was introduced. The Bill proclaimed that resolutions of the Volksraad had been recognised and respected as having the force of law ever since the foundation of the Republic; that the Judiciary had no power to set aside the decision of the Volksraad; that the Constitution conferred no power on judges to "test" laws and that the Courts must decide cases according to the law of the land. Moreover, judges and magistrates must now take a new oath disclaiming the right of test or forfeit their offices.

Kruger supported his case with the full force of his authority. He attacked Kotze's loyalty and patriotism and declared that the Testing Right had been invented by the Devil who introduced it into the Garden of Eden when he incited Adam to test God's word by eating forbidden fruit.

Most of the judges, led by Kotze, protested against Kruger's interference with their independence and refused to go on circuit. It seemed as though the deadlock was unbreakable. Eventually, however, a compromise was reached. The judges agreed to refrain from claiming the Testing Right on the understanding that the President would, "as soon as practicable", submit to the Volksraad a Bill providing for a new Constitution to which future decisions of the Volksraad must conform, and guaranteeing their judicial independence. The judges offered their assistance in preparing the Bill.

This compromise agreement was reached in March, and the next ordinary session of the Volksraad in which the President could have submitted his Bill did not begin till 3 May.

But 3 May came and went without Presidential action. So on 6 May Kotze wrote and reminded the President of the assistance offered by the judges, pointing out that their circuit would have finished at the end of May and that they would then be available to help in drafting the Bill. The President, so far from taking any action himself, turned the matter over to a Committee of "three to five people, some or all" of whom might be members of the Volksraad, to consider a Bill to revise the Constitution and to limit the manner in which it could be altered in future.

The Committee would act in consultation with the President and the Executive Council. No time limit was imposed on them. Furthermore, the Committee was asked to revise, amend and clarify the local laws of the Republic and arrange them systematically, a task which would have taken perhaps two or three years. In July, therefore, Kotze wrote to the President to point this out. The President replied that the new Constitution which he planned would certainly provide for the independence of the High Court and that he had then fulfilled his undertaking to the judges. They would of course be consulted in due course but he had not bound himself to call them in, or to rely on them exclusively. On 10 September Kotze wrote again to Leyds, who was conducting the correspondence on Kruger's behalf, and yet again on 15 December, pointing out that Kruger had still failed to carry out his agreement to introduce the promised Bill personally in the Volksraad, a matter which could have been accomplished quickly enough if the judges had, as contemplated, been consulted. No reply was received. Kotze sent a further note in early February pointing out that the Government Testing Law had not been repealed and that he, Kotze, regarded himself as released from his undertaking not to exercise his right to test decisions of the Volksraad. Kruger replied on 16 February 1896 that in that case he felt free to dismiss Kotze with immediate effect.

And so the original Constitution, as interpreted by Kruger, remained in force until it was destroyed by the British.

It could even have been effective but for the fact that Kruger had not one opposition in the Transvaal but two – the Progressives and the uitlanders, drawn to the Republic by its new wealth.

Chapter 13

The Uitlanders

Gold had been found at Lydenburg in the Transvaal as far back as 1870 and President Burgers had visited the miners there.

But it was not until 1885 that Hendrik Struben, a former diamond prospector, and his brother, Frederick, were able to show President Kruger and members of the Volksraad samples of rich gold quartz taken from the Witwatersrand, not far from Pretoria.

Contrary to legend, Kruger did not, on this occasion, deplore the discovery, and prophesy, as he might well have done, that gold would prove to be a disaster for the country. Instead he thanked the Strubens for disclosing the discovery, and promised that the Government would assist and protect those who endeavoured to develop the nation's mineral wealth.

At first the workings were shallow, and the gold lode could be followed fairly easily along shafts of limited gradient. Later, however, the shafts had to be sunk more deeply into the ground and expensive machinery for drilling, transporting and crushing the rock had to be imported. After crushing, the dust, mixed with water to form a pulp, had to be treated first with cyanide, then with zinc dust and finally with acid before being filtered, smelted and refined.

All this called for experienced geologists, mining engineers, analytical chemists, physicists and, above all, industrialists and financiers able and willing to risk capital.

The development of the mines was certainly as rapid as the most sanguine President could have desired. In 1887 the Transvaal produced 35,000oz of gold bullion worth about $600,000. In the following year, however, the yield was 10,000oz for the single month of February.

Within seven years the population of the Rand had risen to 30,000. The leaders of this community were as eccentric in origin and character as the veins of gold they hoped to exploit.

"Sammy" Marks, who came closer than most to becoming Kruger's financial adviser, was born in Tsarist Russia in 1843 in the pretty town of Neustadt-Sugind in Lithuania. His father, Mordecai Marks, was a travelling tailor in a fairly prosperous way (to judge by the father-and-son photograph in which Mordecai wears a rakishly

Edwardian trilby, and young shoulder-high Sammy a black silk top-hat). At the age of 16 Sammy was sent to relatives in Sheffield, Yorkshire, to study steel production, and before he left there he had met and married a young widow, Bertha Guttman. He arrived in South Africa as a young man of 25, and the Jewish community at the Cape lent him the money to buy a horse and cart and a stock of cheap jewellery which he used for trading with the farmers. When news from the diamond-fields reached the Cape, Sammy went into partnership with his cousin and lifelong associate Isaac Lewis and set off for Kimberley with a cartload of digger's equipment and stores. Lewis and Marks soon had enough money to set up their own store and young Marks turned to the diamond business itself, and bought stones for re-sale and setting in the Cape.

By 1881 he controlled several farms, and supplied firewood from them to the diggers. He converted one of his farms, Hatherley, into an industrial estate to be known as Eerste Fabrieken, which did indeed provide the Transvaal with its first factories. The estate eventually included a tannery, a boot factory, a brick and tile works and a fruit and meat cannery. Marks was granted the sole right to produce jam and spirits and made his own jars and bottles for both products. He raised a pedigree herd, and grew the Transvaal's first commercial crop of grapefruit. Here was an uitlander who saw how to build up the industrial and agricultural potential of the Transvaal, a man who could not fail to win the approval of the President. Later, Marks turned his attention to coal and steel and founded a company known as the Zuid Afrikaansche en Orange Vrij Staatche Kolen en Mineralen Mijn Vereeniging.

Another "Randlord", but a contrast to Marks, was the egregious Barnett Isaacs, better known as Barney Barnato. He was a talkative Cockney from Cobbs Court, near Petticoat Lane, East London. Barney was an ex-variety artist and looked the part. He had tow-coloured hair, blue eyes, chubby cheeks and a waxed moustache. He arrived in Cape Town with a stock of 40 boxes of cigars of doubtful quality. He set off across the Karroo as the voortrekkers had done before him, but paid for a "ticket" which allowed him to walk along-side the carrier's wagon when it moved, and to sleep under it when it stopped. The menu was mealie porridge and biltong. When Barney reached the diamond-fields he bought and sold stones like Sammy Marks had and used the profits to buy up claims. Soon he became a millionaire – so much so that even Rhodes had the greatest difficulty in raising the money to buy him out. Barney then moved on from the diamond-fields to the gold-fields, and was equally successful there, both in shares and real estate. Though he never hid his weakness for the boxing-ring, the card-table, or the music-hall, Barney got on well with Kruger. The explanation, again, was a simple one. Barney saw the Transvaal as a business proposition rather than as a political arena. He once said:

The Transvaal Government is like no other Government in the world. It is indeed not a government at all but an unlimited company of some 20,000 shareholders which has been formed to exploit a large territory, and, after being unable, for 30 years, to pay any dividends or even pay the clerks, suddenly struck it rich. There was neither capital nor skill in the company itself for development and so it leased its ground to those who had both. Kruger the President – and I am glad that there has been no other President in my time – is simply Chairman and Managing Director, with his Executive Council as the Board, and the State Secretary as General Manager. Of course Kruger always tries to do the best he can for his shareholders, the burghers. They had a hard time in the early years and he thinks they are entitled to all they can get now. That is all right, and quite in my line. Through my companies and those I am interested in, I have often to see the Managing Director of the parent company and we always get on all right.

When Barney called on Kruger he avoided talking politics as far as possible and, instead, gossiped with the President on a man-to-man basis over cups of coffee. Leo Weinthal, Editor of the pro-government bi-weekly the *Press*, did the interpreting and left out the worst of Barney's indiscretions. Sometimes Tante Sanna was called in to hear Barney's latest jokes.

J. B. Robinson, a former wool-trader who later turned to diamonds and gold, was another uitlander who kept clear of politics.

But these, as we shall see, were exceptions.

They were surrounded by many less important and less desirable characters: horse-copers, saloon-keepers, gamblers and women of doubtful character, by no means all white. The atmosphere was not conducive to the refinements of civilised society. Water was drawn from wells, a dangerous practice in an area where there was no proper drainage system. Men slept wherever they could find a place – possibly on a mattress below the billiard-table, surrounded perhaps by broken bottles, or sharing a room with three others. There was dust everywhere: in the hair, the clothes and on the food.

The thirsty could choose from nearly 300 different bars, and 17,000 customers voted in a referendum held to find "the most popular lady assistant in any bar, café or restaurant in Johannesburg".

Perhaps it was not surprising that Kruger looked with some

distrust on the newcomers and was not over-eager to see much of them.

His first chance came in February 1887 when Johannesburg was about six months old. The city had been decked with arches and placards reading "Welcome" and "Long live the President" in Afrikaans, and 200 men rode out to meet him. The Mining Commissioner read an address of welcome from a stand erected in front of the Government offices.

But there were also a number of petitions from the inhabitants of a somewhat querulous nature. The diggers asked to be provided with a daily post, they wanted their own concession-licensing court and their own town council. They called for a system which would allow freehold of staked claims. They also wanted a reduction of customs duties and mining dues.

They apologised for bothering him at such an early period in their history but pointed out that this was because they were not represented in his Volksraad and so had no other chance of making known their problems.

The President was surprised, but he agreed to receive a deputation in the afternoon to discuss the grievances. He told them that he wished to make the laws acceptable to all. But the laws must be obeyed. "I have secret agents in Johannesburg," he said, "and here, as elsewhere there are scabby sheep among the flock who want to break the law. I would like everyone, of whatever nationality, to know that if there are any disturbances I will first call on you diggers to catch the diggers, but if this fails I will call out my burghers and treat you as rebels . . ."

Perhaps it was just as well that soon afterwards a sharp shower put an end to the proceedings.

The next morning the President was more conciliatory. He would see that improvements in the Gold Law were discussed by the Volksraad; he had already given orders for a telegraph line to be brought to Johannesburg.

That evening Rhodes himself proposed the President's health in an informal conversational style, and took the opportunity to appeal to Kruger to make friends with the newcomers and to extend the privileges of the older inhabitants to "his young burghers – like myself".

The President replied with a short and non-committal word of thanks. This was to have been followed by some words from J. B. Robinson, but before Robinson could begin the President rose to his feet, saying, "My time is up; I must be off," and abruptly left the banqueting room. Once again the uitlanders were disconcerted.

Kruger visited Johannesburg again in September 1887 and attended a sumptuous banquet given in his honour on the occasion of Johannesburg's first birthday.

Replying to the toast which had been drunk to his health, the President assured his audience that he did not wish to make any distinction between the old inhabitants of the Transvaal and the new, except in respect of the right of representation in the Volksraad. In other matters he was willing to meet the needs of the uitlanders as far as he could, and would have no objection to their having their own railway to connect Johannesburg with the Cape or with Durban, provided that his own line to Lourenço Marques was completed first.

In December 1888 he was again in Johannesburg, and although he rejected the demand for a separate town council for the city – it would, he thought, turn out to be a state within a state – he could point to the fact that the citizens now had a Sanitary Board charged with the duty of caring for public health, and the meeting passed off peacefully.

Three months later Kruger again passed through Johannesburg on his way to meet Sir Henry Loch, with whom he was to discuss the future of Swaziland, and on 4 March he addressed a large meeting on the Wanderers' ground. On this occasion however, the circumstances were less propitious. Many of the uitlanders had gambled unwisely in gold-mines that either did not exist or that needed time and capital for their development, and were suffering accordingly. But although he was soon to become Honorary President of the Witwatersrand Chamber of Mines, the speculators' disappointment commanded but little of the President's sympathy, and his speech dealt with the railway, still non-existent, and went on to justify the compulsory use of Afrikaans for official business. His words were not well received and the President, for his part, resented the murmurs and interjections with which his words were greeted.

A delegation led by a petitioner of the name of Leebman accused him with some brusqueness of treating the people of Johannesburg with contempt. "No," shouted the President, "I do not treat the people with contempt, but you." After this, even the President's roar of "Blij stil" failed to silence the crowd, which now began to sing "Rule Britannia" and "God Save the Queen". Kruger stamped off the platform in disgust and returned to the house of Carl von Brandis, the magistrate with whom he was staying. But this was not the end of the matter. The crowd tried to swarm into von Brandis' house, tearing down the garden railings and even part of the garden wall, and when von Brandis, with tact and good humour, persuaded them to leave, they gathered on the steps of the Post Office. There, inspired by a series of inflammatory speeches, they tore down and trampled on the Vierkleur flag.

It was hardly a good reason for giving the uitlanders the vote. As Kruger said afterwards to Sir Henry Loch: "Yes, Sir Henry; these people remind me of a baboon I once had, which was so fond of me that he would not let anyone touch me. But one day we were sitting round the fire and unfortunately the beast's tail got caught in the flames. He turned round and flew at me, furiously thinking that I was the cause of the accident. The Johannesburgers are just like that. They have burnt their fingers in speculations and now they want to revenge themselves on Paul Kruger."

This version of the affair did not find much favour with the citizens of Johannesburg when it was related to them.

Nor did they appreciate Kruger's description of their city as Duivelstad, or Devil's Town. Moreover, shortly afterwards Kruger made another error of judgement in a speech at Paardekraal. "People of the Lord," he began. "You old people of the country, you foreigners, you newcomers, yes, even you thieves and murderers!" The President afterwards said in explanation that he wished to call upon everybody, even thieves and murderers, if there were any such at the meeting, to humble themselves before God and to acknowledge the wonders in God's dealing with the people of the Republic, and that his words applied just as much to the old as to the new population. But the uitlanders were not ready to accept this explanation, and the incident cast a blight over the important concession which Kruger made when he created a second Volksraad in which the uitlanders could voice their grievances and propose solutions for them. It was an attempt by the President to wean the uitlanders from their foreign allegiance – to cure them of continually looking over their shoulder for help from Westminster. Kruger, when introducing his proposal to the Volksraad, explained that there was a risk of disturbances occurring if the unjust policy of giving the newcomers, already more numerous than the older inhabitants, no rights was pursued.

On the other hand, the Republic would lose its independence if thousands of strangers were to get the vote. Many of the newcomers meant well by the State and were prepared to throw in their lot with it. It would be wrong to reject them, and that was why he sought the compromise solution of establishing a second chamber.

There was, however, very little danger for the honest burghers. The main Volksraad remained the sole authority for passing measures for which the Government was obliged to find the finance, and the discontent of the uitlanders remained unallayed.

Already their resentment, following the authorities' refusal to grant wider powers to the Johannesburg's Sanitary Board, had led to the formation of the "Transvaal National Union", whose object was to "obtain by all constitutional means equal rights for all citizens of this Republic and the redress of all grievances".

At a public meeting held in Johannesburg's Amphitheatre in August 1892 Charles Leonard, a prominent Johannesburg solicitor, expounded the philosophy behind the Union:

Who made the Transvaal? We came here and found the original burghers settled upon farms; they had no market; no means; their only means of living was to contract their wants . . . Who enabled them to live, who made markets for them? We! Yet we are told that we are mere birds of passage, and that, because they were here before us, we have no rights. We send our best men to Pretoria and let them plead their best – only to be snubbed. Memorials are sent to the Volksraad, and referred to a Committee, and thereafter they are never heard of again. Unless we rise as one man and tell our feelings we shall never be understood and listened to. It has never been done yet, but I hope this meeting will do it.

Nevertheless, Kruger did not abandon his attempts to reach a compromise. Speaking at Boksburg near Johannesburg in October 1892, he told the uitlanders that while still maintaining that new-comers must show their loyalty to the State before they could be regarded as trustworthy, he was prepared to offer further significant concessions:

I stand between two fires: the old population and the new. Now as regards the franchise, it would be absurd to insist on a residence period of 20 years before a man could vote. It would be just as absurd to grant the vote to anyone arriving for the first time in this country. This would endanger the independence of the State, and the Volksraad, in refusing it, speaks for the majority of the people. However I am determined to see that the uitlander is not deprived of his rights. I will do my best when the Volksraad next meets to reduce the minimum period of residence required before a man can vote from its present length of five years to one or two years. The residence qualification for eligibility to sit in the Second Chamber (in which the uitlanders' interests are most accurately represented) is now 15 years. I will try to get it reduced to four and the qualifying period to sit in the First Chamber will be ten years.

It was a courageous speech for the President to make in an election year, and it would have done the uitlanders no harm to have recognised the fact.

They had other things to be thankful for as well. The Railway from the Cape to Johannesburg was completed the same year and electric light appeared for the first time in the city.

Nevertheless, relations continued to be strained. There were strong feelings on both sides on the question of whether the uitlanders were liable for the same compulsory military service as the burghers, who might be called on at any time to provide their own horse and rations for commando expeditions against recalcitrant natives, and Kruger believed, along with the majority of judges in his Supreme Court, that all male residents aged between 16 and 60 were liable for such service unless they were resident foreigners exempt by treaty, or had applied for and been granted personal exemption. The judges ruled that it was not contrary to international law for a State to call on foreigners to perform services of a military kind in order to maintain law and order, provided that this did not involve fighting against a power at peace with their own country or in a civil war in the host country.

Now Britain, unlike Belgium and Portugal, had not signed a blanket treaty of exemption, and only British nationals who had registered with the British Consul within a year of 8 August 1881 were automatically exempt.

Kruger evidently felt strongly about Englishmen. They owned so much of the country that they should be willing to defend their assets, he thought. And so three of those who refused to obey the call-up were arrested and sent off under guard in June 1894 to join the fight against Chief Malaboch on the Blouberg mountains of the Northern Transvaal. In the end the Volksraad did agree to a blanket exemption for the British but the incident did not add to their popularity with the burghers.

Then at the time when the conscription wrangle was at its height there took place the famous visit to Pretoria of Sir Henry Loch, still High Commissioner in South Africa. Unwisely perhaps, the authorities, fearing a demonstration, tried to conceal the time of arrival of their honoured guest. But the uitlanders were equally determined not only to see Sir Henry but also to present him with a petition setting out their grievances. Some, already in their places on the platform of Pretoria station as early as 6 a.m., were astonished to observe that the President, perhaps to avoid being accused of kow-towing to the British, had not put up a single Union Jack as a sign of welcome. Someone found a Union Jack, fixed it to a long carriage whip and put it in the hands of a sturdy six-footer to hold above the crowd.

When Sir Henry arrived, the crowd, to the obvious displeasure of the President, greeted the visitor with a spirited rendering of "God Save the Queen" and went so far as to take the horses out of the President's carriage in order to do honour to their own High Commissioner. Furthermore, a Mr Horner, described by one contemporary as a quiet man who had never taken any part in politics, "seized the Union Jack and sprung onto the box of the carriage with it".

From time to time the flag draped itself round the shoulders of His Honour The President, and although he struck at it repeatedly with his stick he was unable to free himself from its attentions. In due course the procession arrived at the Transvaal Hotel where Sir Henry was to stay, and the volunteers then abandoned the shafts of the Presidential carriage and presented a further petition to Sir Henry recounting their grievances. They sang further patriotic songs, while the President waited unattended and in discomfort.

Sir Henry, it is true, tried to make amends. He pointed out to the assembly that he was the President's guest and asked them, if they respected the Queen, to respect also his own position as her representative. "By complying with my request you will assist me in looking after your interests," Sir Henry added. He even called for three cheers for the President.

Inside the hotel Sir Henry endeavoured again to soothe the President, and a delegation of solid citizens led by Sammy Marks called on Dr Leyds, the State Secretary, to register their strong disapproval of the demonstration and to assure the President that he could count on their firm support.

But by this time Kruger's hopes that the uitlanders and the burghers might be united into a single law-abiding people had vanished for good.

He had to take account of those who in his own Volksraad felt like Mr C. B. Otto, the member for Marico, who asked one day in August 1895 in the Volksraad, "Who are these people who have come to enrich themselves? I fear no threats from them. If they want to fight, let them come – and the sooner the better."

Chapter 14

The Jameson Raid

The Jameson Raid gave Kruger the first unmistakable warning that he might once more have to defend his infant Republic against a full-scale British invasion. It was an attempted coup, amateurishly prepared, inexpertly carried out and ingloriously concluded. However it involved not only Jameson but the Colonial Secretary, Joseph Chamberlain, and, in a remote degree, the Prime Minister, Lord Salisbury.

Also there was Rhodes, who conceived the idea that the Transvaal should be brought once more under British rule, preferably his own. "I do not like the idea of British subjects becoming burghers," he said, "that is why I prefer that the burghers should become British subjects." He had been disappointed in his new wonderland, Rhodesia, which had yielded no rich gold-fields. He had been delighted by reports from John Hammond, the ex-Yale American mining engineer, who declared that untold wealth lay waiting in the Transvaal ready to be unlocked by new deep-mining methods. He sensed that he had not got long to live. He must strike quickly.

Then there was Britain and her ambitious Colonial Secretary with his eyeglass and orchid buttonholes. Joseph Chamberlain had joined a Conservative Government now, one whose ministers were only too eager to add jewels to the Crown of their imperious Queen. They were anxious, too, to forestall their rivals in the scramble for Africa, especially the Germans under Kaiser Wilhelm II. They naturally regretted Gladstone's error in restoring independence to the sturdy Boers. And to this extent their hopes ran in tandem with those of Rhodes. But the hard core of British civil servants preferred to promote the interests of Whitehall's own authority and had no desire to see the Transvaal become the booty of that swashbuckler Rhodes.

Rhodes' first task therefore was to transform, or at least modify, this unfriendly attitude on the part of the establishment towards himself and his empire-building. On 4 December 1894 Queen Victoria in her diary credited Rhodes as having expressed, as a Privy Councillor, the opinion that the Transvaal "which we should never have given up" should eventually come once more under British control.

Thus, in the Queen's mind, Rhodes was indelibly linked with the possibility of recovering her "lost" possessions. He had already felt able to ask even the Liberal Government under Lord Rosebery for favours. To Chamberlain he proposed that Bechuanaland, which was then under direct imperial rule, should be divided between the Chartered Company* of which he was Managing Director, and the Cape Colony of which he was Prime Minister. The Prime Minister demurred at this; so did the missionaries, and so did some of the Chiefs who would have been affected by the transfer. They even undertook a special mission at their own expense to London to ask to be allowed to continue to be ruled only by "their mother" the Queen. In consequence, Rhodes was allowed to acquire from the natives only a strip of land down that part of Bechuanaland that flanks the Transvaal border, which he needed, he said, in order to build a railway from Mafeking in the Bechuanaland Protectorate up to Bulawayo in Rhodesia.

But just when things looked so unpromising, Rhodes received help from a totally unexpected source – Kruger. For, in October 1895, the Transvaal President, in an effort to drum up trade for his own expensive railways, unwisely closed the drifts or fords across the Vaal river which carters had been using to bring up goods from the Cape by road. Lord Salisbury's Government, alarmed at the possibility that the links between the Cape and the mines might be interrupted, decided to give Rhodes more scope. His company was granted not only the railway strip but also an area amounting to about 100,000 square miles – in fact the Protectorate, less some land reserved for the natives. He was allowed to raise a force to protect this new territory, and Dr Jameson, the man with the fawn-like eyes and double-bass voice, who, as Administrator of Rhodesia, was already closer to Rhodes than his own brother, was appointed Resident Commissioner at Pitsani, the capital of Rhodes' new territory.

The Protectorate remained under the British flag: a disadvantage for Rhodes who saw it as an obstacle in the path of the agreement he hoped to make with the Transvalers. But, for the time being, there was nothing else to be done. Co-operation between Chamberlain and Rhodes was essential – for Rhodes.

Dr Jameson, who had already increased the strength of the Mashonaland (Northern Rhodesia) Mounted Police, now brought part of this force – "in the interests of health and economy" – down to Pitsani, disbanded the old Bechuanaland Border Police and arranged for the Company to buy its equipment. About 200 of its

* The British-South Africa Company, was usually known as the Chartered Company because of the Charter which Queen Victoria had granted it in October 1889.

men were then merged with the Rhodesian contingent under a single command – Jameson's. Thus the essential preparations for the invasion of the Transvaal had been made.

It remained to prepare the inhabitants of Johannesburg for the part they were to play.

Some of the uitlanders were averse to political activities which might interfere with "progress". Others were not against having a finger in the political pie, but believed they could do better by working through the liberals who opposed Kruger in the Volksraad. The Americans in Johannesburg said they did not want either a revolution or "English interference". Other uitlanders, including Barney Barnato, claimed to be on good terms with Kruger himself and in a position to ask for favours. Accordingly, Dr Jameson forebore from telling the majority of the uitlanders of the preparations he had been making at Pitsani. But undoubtedly the uitlanders were hampered in their economic activities: over-taxed, under-represented and condemned to exist in primitive and insanitary surroundings. The water supply was deplorable and the post office declined to distribute letters except by calling out publicly to those waiting outside the post office the names of those for whom mail had arrived.

It was upon these grievances that Rhodes decided to play. In May 1895 he invited Alfred Beit, one of the most influential of the "Randlords" in Johannesburg, to stay with him at the Cape. Beit allowed himself to be persuaded that if Kruger did not help the uitlanders, the uitlanders must help themselves.

Beit in turn allowed Rhodes to approach other leading figures including Lionel Phillips, Chairman of the Johannesburg Chamber of Mines, Wernher Beit, the Senior Resident Partner in Johannesburg of the Consolidated Goldfields Eckstein group, a firm which was linked with Rhodes' interests, and Charles Leonard, Chairman of the Transvaal National Union. John Hays Hammond was also brought into the conspiracy.

That autumn Rhodes invited Phillips, Leonard and Hammond to a meeting at the Cape. He told them that in an effort to protect his investments he was ready to protect the uitlanders with armed men if Kruger's Government failed to introduce reforms – good government, better administration, fewer restrictive practices, better schools, improved sanitation, equitable taxation, political rights, etc. The great man emphasised – and this appealed to his audience – that he was not campaigning on behalf of his Chartered Company nor yet on behalf of British imperialism. There was no plan to force the Transvaal to join a federation. Indeed there need be no fighting at all, and Rhodes would guarantee that his old friend Sir Hercules

Robinson, Britain's High Commissioner in South Africa, would intervene if there was the slightest sign of trouble.

The only favour which Rhodes asked in return was that, if the uitlanders were successful in getting the reforms they wanted, they would use their influence to promote free trade between the states and colonies of South Africa.

According to Leonard's account:

We read to him [Rhodes] the draft of our declaration of rights. He was leaning against the mantel-piece smoking a cigarette, and when it came to that part of the document in which we refer to Free Trade in South African products he turned round suddenly and said: "That is what I want. That is all I ask of you. The rest will come in time. We must have a beginning and that will be the beginning. If you people get your rights, the Customs Union, Railway Convention and other things will all come in time."

Reassured by this the conspirators returned to Johannesburg, and formed a secret cabal which later blossomed out into the Reform Committee. Only those in whom complete confidence could be placed were invited to join, and the Transvaal National Union, whose programme did not include military training, were kept in the dark. The reformers were financed by the Chartered Company and through the New Concessions Account opened in Johannesburg by Frank Rhodes.

The money was needed to pay for three Maxim guns and rounds of ammunition which were to be smuggled into Johannesburg. Jameson undertook to do the moving, and said that he would be able to bring an extra 1,500 rifles with him to Johannesburg. Others would be seized from the Arsenal at Pretoria which was believed to hold 10,000 rifles, a battery of field-guns and millions of rounds of ammunition.

At a meeting with the secret committee in Johannesburg on 19 November Jameson asked for something in return – a letter to show that any action he might take would be the result of a call for help from the uitlanders.

The text was apparently dictated by Jameson himself and was then signed and handed to Jameson by the four chief conspirators. It was undated and could therefore be used by Jameson at any time – a somewhat disconcerting possibility. Furthermore, it occurred to the conspirators that the letter could even fall into the wrong hands. The Reform Committee therefore made it clear to Jameson that the letter was intended for him personally, to justify his actions to the Chartered Company or the British authorities, and it was not to be acted on without a definite request from the Committee.

But, once he had it, Jameson held the master card which implicated the reformers in the military adventure. Leonard, for one, realised this and asked Jameson next day to return it. Too late! The original had already been sent off to Rhodes for safe-keeping. It read:

The position of matters in this State has become so critical that we are assured that at no distant period there will be conflict between the Government and the uitlander population. It is scarcely necessary for us to recapitulate what is now a matter of history. Suffice it to say, that the position of thousands of Englishmen and others is rapidly becoming intolerable. Not satisfied with making the uitlander population pay virtually the whole of the revenue of the country, while denying them representation, the policy of the Government has been steadily to encroach upon the liberty of the subject, and to undermine the security for property to such an extent, as to cause a very deep-seated sense of discontent and danger.

A foreign corporation of Hollanders is to a considerable extent controlling our destinies, and, in conjunction with the Boer leaders, endeavouring to cast them in a mould which is wholly foreign to the genius of the people. Every public act betrays the most positive hostility, not only to everything English, but to the neighbouring States as well. In short, the internal policy of the Government is such as to have roused into antagonism to it not only, practically, the whole body of uitlanders, but a large number of the Boers, while its external policy has exasperated the neighbouring States, causing the possibility of great danger to the peace and independence of this Republic.

Public feeling is in a condition of smouldering discontent. All the petitions of the people have been refused with a greater or less degree of contempt, and, in the debate on the franchise petition, signed by nearly 40,000 people, one member challenged the uitlanders to fight for the rights they asked for and not a single member spoke against him.

Not to go into detail, we may say that the Government has called into existence all the elements necessary for armed conflict. The one desire of the people here is for fair play, the maintenance of their independence, and the preservation of those public liberties without which life is not worth having. The Government denies these things and violates the national sense of the Englishmen at every turn.

What we have to consider is, what will be the condition of things here in the event of conflict?

Thousands of unarmed men, women, and children of our race will be at the mercy of well-armed Boers; while property of enormous value will be in the greatest peril. We cannot contemplate the future without the gravest apprehension, and feel that we are justified in taking any steps to prevent the shedding of blood, and to ensure the protection of our rights.

It is under these circumstances that we feel constrained to call upon you to come to our aid should disturbance arise here.

The circumstances are so extreme, that we cannot avoid this step, and we cannot believe that you, and the men under you, will not fail to come to the rescue of people who would be so situated. We guarantee any expense that may reasonably be incurred by you in helping us, and ask you to believe that nothing but the sternest necessity has prompted this appeal.

Gardner Williams, General Manager of the De Beers company in Kimberley, was made responsible for receiving and storing the arms which were smuggled over the Transvaal border into Johannesburg and hidden in disused mineshafts. Andrew Trimble, an Irishman whose appointment as Chief Detective for the Transvaal Republic Kruger had recently refused to confirm, was recruited and told to organise a police force whose task would be to keep order after the coup. There were those who believed that Jameson should postpone his arrival until after the rising had begun – though in view of the letter which Jameson already possessed this was hardly a practical proposition.

Once the military arrangements had been planned, a campaign was launched to whip up pressure on Kruger for reforms. Lionel Phillips took the lead on 20 November on the occasion of the opening of the new Chamber of Mines Building to which – exceptionally – women had been invited. Phillips' speech made clear for the first time that the big capitalists were at last behind the reform movement. He attacked the Government on its weakest point, the cost of living, which had been raised artificially by tariffs imposed to safeguard Kruger's local monopolies, and said that his community would not consent indefinitely to remain subordinate to an oligarchy dominated by Hollanders. Its tone was such as to alarm even the moderates who had been opposing Kruger in the Volksraad. The following month he declared in another speech that the time of hoping patiently for some solution to appear to the problem of the uitlander was now at an end. A manifesto was issued on Boxing Day setting out the uitlander's "rights" which, Kruger said, would be granted over his dead body.

But the conspirators were by no means professional revolutionaries;

it was impossible for them to remain in the shadows. Indeed some of them were personally ambitious, and were by no means anxious to oblige Rhodes.

Neither did they command a disciplined movement poised to strike at the appropriate moment. At first the raid was fixed for 28 December. But by Christmas it had become clear that the ordinary citizens were not of one mind. Most of them had been kept in ignorance of the fact that they were now implicated in preparations for a full-scale revolt, and when this became semi-public knowledge some of the Americans began to back out. Mr J. B. Robinson, one of the more prominent English mining magnates, was one among several Randlords who were positively opposed to it.

Also, it began to become obvious that the attack on the State Arsenal at Pretoria might not be as easy as it had seemed. For one thing, many Boers from the countryside would be in Pretoria for the Christmas Communion Service and could turn the balance of numbers against the reformers.

In addition no one was happy about the prospect of Jameson crossing the Transvaal border not merely to safeguard Rhodes' investments but to hoist the Union Jack over them. Their immediate reaction was to send Captain Younghusband to Rhodes as their representative to find out whether the Union Jack now formed an indispensable part of the plan. Rhodes appears to have assured the Captain that he need have no fear about Jameson intervening prematurely but was less than reassuring about the flag. The Transvaal would be maintained. But the rumours continued to circulate, and on Christmas Day a second mission headed by Charles Leonard was sent southwards.

They too were reassured, but not completely, and in their report to the reformers in Johannesburg they suggested that there was no immediate hurry. Time was needed if they were to get their supporters solidly behind them.

Jameson had been ready to leave for Johannesburg with his troops as early as the first week of December. The rising would start two days later to coincide with his arrival. But on 7 December Frank Rhodes, who was supposed to be kindling the emotions that would lead to the uprising, telegraphed to Jameson that the "polo tournament" (one of the many code words used to denote the rising) would have to be postponed from 28 December for one week "or it would clash with race week".

Rhodes on the other hand was under pressure from Jameson not to delay for fear that news of the conspiracy would leak to Kruger and his advisers. The Managing Director of the London *Times*, Moberly

Bell, and his Correspondent on Colonial Affairs, Miss Flora Shaw, both of whom were privy to the British Government's thinking on the matter, urged that any postponement might be fatal to the success of the project. On 10 December Miss Shaw cabled directly to Rhodes asking when "plans" would commence and Bell cabled two days later: "Delay dangerous sympathy now complete but will depend very much upon action before the European powers given time to enter protest which as European situation considered serious might paralyse Government; general feeling in the Stock Market very suspicious." *The Times* knew that Dr Leyds, Kruger's special envoy, was about to launch a "Stop Rhodes" campaign in the Chancelleries of Europe.

On 17 December Rhodes received an even more urgent cable from Flora Shaw which she sent after having interviewed Dr Leyds: "Held an interview with Secretary Transvaal, left here on Saturday for Hague, Berlin, Paris, fear in negotiation with these parties. Chamberlain sound in case of interference European powers but have special reason to believe wishes you must do it immediately." The meaning here was that Chamberlain would be prepared to shrug off the protests of European powers if the plan was carried out promptly. Chamberlain himself wrote a letter to Sir Robert Meade, Permanent Secretary at the Colonial Office, saying that if the Transvaal crisis could not be postponed indefinitely for a year or two (and there would be no point in intervening to arrange a postponement unless we could be certain of success), then it would be better for the crisis to come at once since "the longer it is delayed the more chance there is of foreign intervention".

The result was that Rochfort Maguire, Rhodes "alternate" on the Board of the Chartered Company, sent a fateful cable to Rhodes in Cape Town. We do not know to this day exactly what it said, but its effect was to cause Cecil Rhodes to wire Jameson that the "flotation" would begin on Saturday 28 December 1895.

From then on, neither telegrams nor messengers from the reformers could sway Jameson from his resolve to push ahead with the expedition.

So it was unfortunate, to say the least, when Rhodes, alarmed by the firmness with which the second mission from the reformers stated their case against accepting a rising under the Union Jack, began in turn to have his doubts.

Perhaps if Rhodes had cabled clearly to Jameson that the whole idea had now to be postponed, Jameson might have held off. But Rhodes put off sending any definite instructions to Jameson until it was too late for them to be effective. Afterwards, but only afterwards, he published the text of the message that he had planned to send, but there is no certainty that this was the true text as the message was never left with the telegraph staff.

Next there is the part played in the affair by the various British officials. Lord Loch perhaps flew the first kite in June 1894 when, in answer to complaints from the uitlanders of his day, he asked how many rifles they possessed. It seems clear that Chamberlain was in the know, though did not want to hear anything officially. As far back as 2 October, however, he had written to the High Commissioner, Sir Hercules Robinson, to ask for the High Commissioner's views on a rising at Johannesburg "with or without assistance from outside". Robinson consulted his old friend Rhodes on the reply. His views and recommendations were: (1) a revolt would take place "sooner or later and an accident might bring it about any day"; (2) most of the Englishmen would prefer to live within a liberalised and Anglicised Republic than as a British Colony; (3) if they rose and set up a Provisional Government "the High Commissioner as representative of the paramount Power in South Africa should issue a proclamation directing both parties to desist from hostilities and to submit to his arbitration"; (4) HM Government should announce their intention of supporting this attitude with force and take action to prevent the Hollanders around Kruger from encouraging German intervention; (5) the High Commissioner should order an election for a Constitution-making assembly to be held at once on the basis of equal voting rights for all white male adults; (6) if this procedure were followed, the coup might take place without loss of life or a shot being fired, in which case the Cape Dutch would be likely to acquiesce; (7) once elected, the Constitution-making assembly might conceivably be influenced into declaring themselves a British Colony.

Thus Sir Hercules was already apprised of Rhodes' and Chamberlain's thoughts about the affair.

In reply to Robinson, Chamberlain said he hoped that no movement would take place unless success was certain. If the Johannesburgers would accept the British flag they would be allowed to choose their own Governor.

Meantime, in mid-October, Robinson had been approached by Rhodes through Sir Graham Bower, who, as Imperial Secretary, was Robinson's deputy. Rhodes swore Bower to secrecy and then told him of the plans. Bower advised Rhodes to give Robinson the same information, also in confidence, and although Robinson never admitted having known anything of plans for a raid, he co-operated almost at once with Rhodes in giving orders which made it possible for Rhodes to concentrate the Chartered Company Police and the

Rhodesia Horse Volunteers at Pitsani ready to strike. Robinson gave the orders authorising the contractor to place the forage stores belonging to the Post Office at the troops' disposal along the route.

Then on 26 December Chamberlain, a little late it might be thought, informed the Prime Minister, Lord Salisbury, that he had received "private information" that a rising in Johannesburg was imminent and would probably take place in the course of the next few days, and that he had given previous instructions to the High Commissioner as to how to deal with it. He added that he had done nothing to provoke it but that it could nevertheless turn out to be "to our advantage".

This, then, was the state of the conspiracy when Jameson crossed the border. The story of the disaster that followed is soon told.

No advance rising took place in Johannesburg. Some uitlanders had panicked in advance of the crisis, and as Mark Twain, who was touring the area about this time, put it:

> As soon as it was known in Johannesburg that Jameson was on his way to rescue the women and children, the grateful people put the women and children on a train and rushed them for Australia. In fact the approach of Johannesburg's saviour created panic and consternation there, and a multitude of males of peaceable disposition swept to the trains like a sand storm. The early ones fared best; they secured the seats – by sitting on them – eight hours before the first train was due to leave.

(Of Rhodes he added, "I admire him, I frankly confess it; and when his time comes, I shall buy a piece of the rope for a keepsake.")

Other accounts, however, speak of women and children hastening to the railway coaches standing in the shunting yard at Braamfontein a mere five hours before the engine arrived to pull them.

There was heavy competition for the seats, and cries of "Get the men out" were raised when it was observed that a large proportion of the travellers were masculine. In the city, shopkeepers put up the shutters, warehousemen hired armed guards to protect their stocks and there was a run on both the banks and the grocery stores.

The use of the telephone was forbidden.

Viewed in this light, the advance was no longer a rescue operation but a stark invasion. An invasion which, in addition, was unsuccessful since Jameson's forces were first shadowed, then ambushed by Boer cavalry, and forced on 2 January 1896 into unconditional surrender. Not a single armed man was sent to his aid by the Johannesburgers.

Meanwhile, Chamberlain believed on 29 December, the day on which Jameson crossed the border, that all bets were off and that the operation had been postponed. "I think the Transvaal business is going to fizzle out," he had written to Salisbury. "Rhodes has miscalculated the feeling of the Johannesburg capitalists, and it is now quite possible that Kruger will make some concessions, in which case the affair would be terminated, for the present at any rate."

But Chamberlain had also been warned by Edward Fairfield, Assistant Under-Secretary at the Colonial Office, that Rhodes or Jameson might nevertheless press on regardless with his plans, and, for safety's sake, the Colonial Secretary thought it wise, on the evening of 29 December, to send a confidential warning to Robinson on this subject:

> It has been suggested, although I do not think it probable, that an endeavour may be made to force matters at Johannesburg to a head by someone in the service of the Company advancing from the Bechuanaland Protectorate with police. Were this to be done I should have to take action under Articles 22 and 8 of the Charter [i.e., cancel the Charter]. Therefore, if necessary, but not otherwise, remind Rhodes of these Articles and intimate to him that, in your opinion, he would not have my support, and point out the consequences that would follow.

Chamberlain's warning came too late to stop Jameson but it enabled Sir Hercules to behave with conscious rectitude at an early stage in the crisis. He ordered a horseman to be sent from Bechuanaland in pursuit of Jameson with a declaration disavowing Jameson's actions. He sent a letter to Rhodes repeating Chamberlain's threat to cancel the Chartered Company's concession, and he telegraphed to Sir Jacobus de Wet, the British Agent in Pretoria, instructing him to declare that Her Majesty's Government completely disapproved of Dr Jameson's action and was ordering him to retire at once.

He was also able to reassure Kruger that the British Government deplored Jameson's action.

Meanwhile, how had Kruger been dealing with this threat to his security? He had not been caught unprepared.

Mr Montagu White, who acted as Consul-General in London for the Transvaal Government, stated in a letter to *The Times* that on 16 December he received information about the preparations being made for the Jameson Raid, and eight days later the German Consul in Pretoria reported to the German Foreign Office that "news from Johannesburg points to the preparation of disturbances by the English party there, and the Government is taking precautionary measures".

Baron von Marschall in turn drew the attention of the British Ambassador in Berlin, Sir Frank Lascelles, to the report and, after pointing out the possible consequences of bloodshed, emphasised once again the necessity for maintaining the status quo. The German Secretary of State cabled a copy of the Johannesburg report to the German Consul in Pretoria adding: "Impress energetically on the Transvaal Government that it must most scrupulously avoid any provocation if it wishes to retain German sympathy."

But it was not only in the Chancelleries of Europe that trouble was expected.

As President Kruger was returning from his annual tour of some outlying districts of the Transvaal, he was met at Bronkhorstspruit by a number of burghers, one of whom, Hans Botha, told the President that he had heard that there was some talk of a rising in Johannesburg and added that although he had many bullets in him (it was currently believed that five still remained), he could find room for more if it was a question of tackling the Britishers. The President replied that he had heard of the threatened rising, and did not believe it: he could not say what was likely to happen, but they must re-member this – if they wanted to kill a tortoise, they must wait until he put his head out of the shell.

Kruger had been taking protective measures ever since Chamber-lain had threatened to go to war over the Drifts question. On Christmas Eve Commandant-General Joubert had been recalled from Wakkerstroom to Pretoria, and he in turn summoned Com-mandant Erasmus and Field Cornet Uys to join him.

On 27 December the strength of the Mounted Police was increased by eight officers and 75 men.

But Kruger withdrew all police from the streets of Johannesburg and confined them to barracks. "While I am beating out the fire on the frontier, on no account let it burst out in Johannesburg," the President said. And on Monday 30th he received a deputation led by representatives of the Mercantile Association and undertook, subject to confirmation by the Volksraad, to remove the special duties on foodstuffs immediately. He promised to give equal subsidies to British and Dutch schools and said he would approach the Nether-lands Railway Company about lowering their charges.

That night he signed a proclamation warning the inhabitants of Johannesburg to obey the law, but added that "the Government is still prepared to take into consideration all grievances that may be laid before it in a proper manner and to submit the same to the people of the land without delay for treatment."

On Monday, 30 December the Government sent two "scouts" – Abraham Malan, General Joubert's son-in-law, and Eugene Marais, Editor of *Land en Volk* – to Johannesburg to discover, if they could, the strength of the resistance movement and the numbers that it commanded. They were told that anything from 30,000 to 45,000 men could be put into action.

On hearing their report Kruger decided to play for time while he made sure of catching Jameson. He would deal with the uitlanders later.

No doubt he had learnt something from the two deputations of American citizens who came to see him about this time. To one of them he put the question, "If a crisis should occur on which side shall I find the Americans?" "On the side of liberty and good government," replied their spokesman. "You are all alike," answered Kruger, "tarred with the same brush; you are British in your hearts."

Then there was Mr J. C. Bodenstein, Field Cornet of the Krugersdorp district, who stated earlier in the Johannesburg Government organ *Standard and Diggers' News* that he had heard of a young lady whose fiancé was serving in the Bechuanaland Border Police who had sent her a letter saying that he intended paying her a visit around New Year and that he would not be alone as the whole force was coming to Johannesburg. When interviewed she confirmed the story.

On the previous Friday, 27 December, a German from the Free State had told Bodenstein that Dr Jameson's men might be expected at any time.

"On hearing the confirmation of the report in the letter, I went at once to Pretoria," said Mr Bodenstein. "I got there at eleven o'clock at night, and early next morning I saw the President, and informed him about the letter and about what I had been told. He remarked quietly, 'Yes, I have heard all about it.' General Joubert then added: 'All right: I will send you the necessary ammunition.'"

Nor was secrecy maintained about Jameson's exact movements, for although the main telegraph lines to Cape Town and Pretoria had been duly severed, a branch line running from Zeerust to Pretoria had been overlooked, and when Marais, the Commissioner of Mines at Ottoshoop, reported that the invaders had passed through the township at 5 a.m. on 30 December the defences swung into action. Commandant-General Joubert no doubt deserved most of the credit for the speed with which Jameson's troops were traced and captured.

But even more masterly was the way in which Kruger dealt with the reformers in Johannesburg without giving a pretext for any kind of intervention. Certainly the position of the uitlanders was unenviable.

The leaders believed that they had been successful in persuading Jameson to abandon his plans. Even a telegram sent by Jameson on 29 December saying that he would cross the frontier that evening failed to disillusion them. They were certain in their own minds that he had sent it off before either of the two messengers who had been sent to stop him, had reached him.

They were soon proved wrong. On Monday, 30 December, Dr H. A. Wolff, who had been made responsible for setting up the supply depots along the route, received a telegram, sent that day, telling him to carry out the "distant cutting" operation, and Abe Bailey also received information soon after midday on the same Monday that the "veterinary surgeon", the code word for Jameson, had left the previous evening and would be in Johannesburg on Wednesday.

The news was confirmed in a further telegram received later that afternoon by Mr A. L. Lawley.

The Reform Committee was hastily formed that night. Its leaders hoped to put the city in a good defensive position with a view to negotiations with Kruger. Obviously they could not publicly repudiate Jameson because of their impulsive letter asking him to save them from oppression. But the Transvaal National Union, having ostensibly been kept in the dark, had no hesitation in doing so, and later John Hays Hammond, one of those who had signed the Jameson letter, insisted on the Reform Committee swearing allegiance to the Transvaal Government and on having the Vierkleur hoisted over the Goldfields Building.

J. W. Leonard, brother of Charles, and also a lawyer, declared in a public speech that the Reform Committee had constituted itself a Provisional Government under the flag of the Transvaal Republic.

Sub-committees were formed to deal with such matters as police patrols, control of natives, medical services. Volunteers distributed arms and began throwing up earthworks and setting up gun positions for the Maxim machine-guns to put the town in a state of defence. A Bicycle Corps was recruited and held its foundation meeting in the skating rink. Sir Drummond Dunbar, a Scottish baronet, formed a Ladies' Revolver Club and was unlucky enough to lose the top of his finger during a practice session. The mines were closed, the bars too. Windows were covered with boards or sheets of corrugated iron. The population were advised not to commit any acts of hostility against the Government. An urgent wire was sent to Sir Hercules Robinson pointing out the peril in which they stood following Jameson's action and calling on them to make good Rhodes' promise that he would intervene to prevent bloodshed.

The next day, Tuesday, Marais telegraphed from Pretoria to Lionel Phillips in Johannesburg asking if the Johannesburg leaders would receive an unofficial deputation from the Government. On receiving a favourable reply, both Marais and Malan were called in to see Kruger who coached them in what they were to say.

The two men addressed a meeting of the Reform Committee at their headquarters in the Goldfields Building. They made it clear that while the Government wanted peace it would not shrink from armed conflict, and that if the reformers wanted any concessions they would have to send representatives to Pretoria to ask for them. This the Committee decided by unanimous vote to do.

The next day Lionel Phillips, who had been sleeping on the linoleum floor of the Goldfields Building, went with three other uitlanders to meet three Government representatives, headed by Chief Justice Kotze, in Pretoria. While there, they were authorised by telegram from the Reform Committee in Johannesburg to tell Kotze that, if the Government allowed Jameson to reach Johannesburg uninjured, the members of the Reform Committee would guarantee with their lives that he would leave the country peacefully. In the discussions that followed Phillips could not, of course, deny his connection with Jameson. All he could do was to say that the reformers had not ordered the raid.

Judge Ameshoff, another of the Kruger negotiators, asked whether, in that case, the uitlanders would lay down their arms; and Phillips said that they would. But Jan Kock, the third negotiator, asked how the Government could be sure that the Reform Committee, for whom Phillips was speaking, was representing Johannesburg as a whole and was not just a rebel group. Phillips fell right into the trap and undertook to send the Government representatives a list of names of those he represented.

At the same time Kruger, who had spent New Year with his white horse ready saddled, agreed to "Herklars" Robinson coming up to Johannesburg "to assist me to prevent further bloodshed", i.e. in order to cow the Johannesburgers into submission. In the meantime the Government would hold its hand provided that the Johannesburgers also kept the peace.

Sir Hercules, who from the very start had wanted to have nothing to do with Rhodes' schemes, would have preferred to stay in Cape Town away from the reformers and their troubles where he could act as a post office for any messages which Chamberlain might want to send to Kruger. He suffered from heart trouble and dropsy. He already had a crisis on his hands with Rhodes in the Cape and realised that he could not enter the Transvaal on the summons of the uitlanders alone, but must wait for an invitation from President Kruger.

When he arrived in Johannesburg on the night of Saturday, 4 January – two days after Jameson's surrender – it was with a nurse in attendance. His foot was troublesome. No business could of course be transacted with the Boers on the following day – Sunday – and when he met them on the Monday he had to remain lying on a couch, while they sat literally over him at a table.

With Jameson as a hostage for the reformers' good behaviour, Robinson had no cards in his hand and, in the meantime, the Boers had been able to make elaborate preparations for subduing Johannesburg. The inhabitants were already running short of coal and water.

There was nothing that Robinson could do – even though he was under pressure from Chamberlain.

The Colonial Secretary had heard of the raid as he dressed to go to the annual servants' ball at Highbury. A special messenger brought him the news of the raid, and after consulting his brother Arthur he decided to leave at once for London. A cab took him to the station so that the coachmen should not miss the ball and he just caught the 12.50 a.m. "milk" train. He arrived at his empty London house at 4 a.m.

He did indeed denounce the raid, but in the meantime the public in Britain had heard both about the uitlanders' appeal to Jameson and about the telegram of felicitation sent to Kruger by Kaiser Wilhelm (who, it should be added, enjoyed the rank of Admiral of the British Navy). This telegram read:

Berlin 3 January 1896
I express to you my sincere congratulations that without calling on the aid of friendly Powers you and your people by your own energy against the armed bands which have broken into your country as disturbers of the peace have succeeded in re-establishing peace and defending the independence of the country against attacks from without.

William I.R.

Bismarck afterwards said that he could see nothing wrong in the telegram. "Indeed," he said, "the Emperor's telegram might with especial fitness and decency have been sent to President Kruger by the British Government itself."

Nevertheless, the effect upon public opinion in Britain was sharp and immediate. The Queen wrote from Osborne to Kaiser Wilhelm:

As your grandmother, to whom you have always shown so much affection and of whose example you have always spoken with so much respect, I cannot refrain from expressing my deep regret at the telegram you sent President Kruger. It is considered very unfriendly towards this country, which I feel it is not intended to be, and has, I grieve to say, made a very painful impression here.

Because the Kaiser had criticised him Jameson became a hero, and on 11 January *The Times* published verses by the newly appointed Poet Laureate, Alfred Austin, in praise of his exploit. Later these were recited nightly at the Alhambra Theatre by a performer dressed as one of the Chartered Company's police on a stage decorated with tropical palms intended to represent the Transvaal. Soon after, Chamberlain felt able to send a telegram asking when Kruger was going to honour the promises he had made a few days earlier to a mercantile delegation from Johannesburg to whom he had granted an interview.

However Kruger himself had demands to make. He had collected some 8,000 Boers and could not keep them hanging about doing nothing indefinitely. He said that the Johannesburgers must surrender their arms unconditionally before negotiations could begin on their grievances or Jameson's future be considered. Moreover, there was no time to waste. He must therefore ask for a definite "Yes" or "No" to this demand within 24 hours from Monday, 6 January, at 4 p.m. It was Sir Hercules' painful duty to convey this news to Her Majesty's subjects in Johannesburg.

The reformers hesitated but Sir Hercules was inexorable. He sent the British Agent in Pretoria, Sir Jacobus de Wet, to tell them that Jameson's life was in their hands, and that if they did not comply by laying down their arms, they would forfeit all sympathy of Her Majesty's Government. Sir Jacobus led the reformers, or some of them at least, to believe that if they took his advice and surrendered they would not be victimised, and that the High Commissioner would co-operate in negotiating with the Transvaal Government about their grievances.

On 7 January Robinson was able to confirm that Kruger had decided not to try Jameson and the other prisoners on the spot but to hand them over to the British to be dealt with. But when he raised the question of grievances with Kruger, the old President reminded him that he had been invited to the Transvaal to prevent further bloodshed and not to discuss its internal administration.

There was indeed a moment when it seemed likely that Robinson might, after all, have to intervene. The crisis arose on Wednesday, the 8th, when he received a message from Kruger's Executive Council to the effect that since only 1,814 rifles and three Maxim guns had been handed over, the Government did not consider that the terms of the ultimatum had been carried out and that a commando attack had been ordered on Johannesburg.

Robinson's reply was that the ultimatum required the surrender of guns and ammunition for which no import permit had been granted and that it was up to the Transvaal Government to show that guns and ammunition were still concealed for which no permit existed. If any hostile steps were taken against Johannesburg before this investigation had been made, Robinson said he would consider this as a violation of the undertaking for which he had made himself responsible to the people of Johannesburg and he would "leave the issue in the hands of Her Majesty's Government". This brought the Executive Committee up short, and after the period of grace had been extended to 6 p.m. on Friday, 10 January, and another 800 or so rifles collected the Government declared itself satisfied in a "forgive and forget" declaration which nevertheless made clear that in present circumstances it would be impossible to grant Johannesburg an elected Municipal Council.

Kruger had now accomplished almost all that was necessary. Jameson had been defeated. Rhodes had been discredited – he was eventually compelled to resign his office as Prime Minister of the Cape. The Johannesburgers had been disarmed. He had used Jameson as a bargaining counter to subdue the uitlanders. By releasing Jameson and the other prisoners Kruger had avoided making martyrs of them, he had saddled the British with the dilemma of either condoning the invasion or punishing those who carried it out. He had safeguarded his independence by declining offers of military and political help from the Germans.* The leaders of the Reform Movement had been discredited by their failure to support Jameson to whom they had appealed for help. He had given the British no excuse to intervene and had obliged Chamberlain not only to disown Jameson, but also, as Kruger put it in his memoirs, "to telegraph to me to thank me in the name of Her Majesty for my magnanimous act".

All that remained was to satisfy his own burghers, who had baulked at the release of Jameson and were clamouring for "holes to be drilled" in the members of the Reform Committee, that it had all been worth while.

So, soon after the leaders had finished using their influence to collect the rifles Kruger wanted, the police were sent to arrest them; 64 were rounded up on 9 and 10 January.

They were excellent material for public humiliation: rich, prominent and incapable of martyrdom. Dependent on creature comforts,

---

* The Kaiser had suggested sending up 50 marines from the cruiser *See Adler* in Delagoa Bay "to guard the German consulate". But Kruger unhesitatingly replied that if the Emperor was really concerned he would spare 50 of his own burghers to do the job. The incident was said to have rankled with the Emperor.

they should be publicly deprived of them. They should be made to beg for mercy in petitions to which maximum publicity would be given. In retaliation for their treasonable activities they should be frightened by the shadow of death.

The jail, of course, was not the kind of accommodation to which its latest prisoners had been accustomed. They found that the cells had mud floors on which were spread straw mattresses that had been used by former occupants. The cells were insanitary and the stench in the height of a Pretoria summer was almost unbearable.

One prisoner was so incautious as to remark, "Awful place this jail of yours." "Yes," said the jailor. "You are right; it is the only place the English built when they were in occupation here, and it is a disgrace to any town."

But in less than a fortnight after their arrest, all the prisoners except the five ring-leaders (Lionel Phillips, George Farrar, a later signatory of the Jameson letter, Frank Rhodes, J. H. Hammond and Percy Fitzpatrick, who had been closely associated with Rhodes' interests and who was Secretary of the Reform Committee) were released on bail.

The preliminary examination of the prisoners with a view to bringing them to justice was begun by the State Attorney, Dr Coster, on 8 February in the second chamber of the Volksraad. It lasted about a month.

Then in the latter half of April came the indictment which accused the prisoners on four counts. The first was the treasonable offence of conspiring to endanger the safety of the Republic. The second charge referred to the preparations made to assist Jameson and the third to the distribution of arms. The fourth charge referred to the usurpation of authority by the Reform Committee.

By arrangement between the parties the prosecution agreed to drop charges one and two in the case of the rank and file, and charges two, three and four in the case of the leaders, provided that the leaders would plead guilty to the more serious charge of High Treason contained in the first charge. And since the prosecution now possessed a certified copy of the Jameson letter, there seemed little else to be done.

The President was understood to have expressed his satisfaction at the outcome.

On 18 February four of the leaders were allowed to leave prison and live under armed guard in a private house in return for a deposit of £10,000 each; Hammond who was suffering from dysentery was allowed to return home a day later on condition he reappeared for the trial.

The formal committal and hearing of pleas took place on 24 April. The trial started three days later on 27 April in the covered market in Pretoria. Judge Reinhold Gregorowski, who normally sat in the Orange Free State, had been brought specially to Pretoria for the occasion and appointed "Acting Judge". Spectators described him as balding, with sideburns and a heavy moustache covering the lower half of his hawk-like features. He wore pince-nez spectacles attached to his person by a string.

The Counsel for the prosecution and the defence sat in front of the judge's box, the prisoners to one side. The court-room was said to be stuffy and the acoustics indifferent.

Since the prisoners had pleaded guilty, the task of the prosecution was far from exacting. The incriminating documents, including a number of telegrams exchanged between the conspirators, were handed in without being read and the State Prosecutor then closed his case and asked for the maximum penalty to be imposed.

The defence argued that the Reform Committee had done their best to prevent Jameson from entering Johannesburg and could not without his help have endangered the safety of the State. Their letter to him was not a direct invitation and was not intended for use in the circumstances that existed. The reformers had also done their best to discourage the population from committing acts against the Government. Counsel suggested that the penalties imposed should be those of the Transvaal Statute Law which provided a maximum fine of 500 rix dollars and banishment – although there remained the possibility that all their property could have been forfeited for rebellion within the boundaries of a gold-field.

Dr Coster, however, rejected this submission and insisted that their offence should be tried under Roman–Dutch Law under which the penalty for treason was death. The Court then adjourned for the day.

By next morning it was clear that something unusual was afoot. It had become known, for instance, that Commandant Henning Pretorius had paid a visit to the Cape shortly after the Jameson Raid and had bought, from the owner of a farm at Cookhouse Drift, the beam from which five Boers had been hanged in 1816 at Slagter's Nek for rebellious conduct against the British. Pretorius had removed the beam from the house into which it had been built and had it transported to Pretoria. And there were reports that some Boers had gone to the President and said that now that the beam was handy there was no need for a trial.

The prisoners were not entirely reassured by reports (which in fact were quite true) that the President had rebuked the deputation of Boers and asked them whether they themselves approved of what had happened after Slagter's Nek, and that when they said "No" he had retorted, "Well why do you want me to copy it?"

However there were other more ominous signs of trouble ahead. On the morning when sentence was to be pronounced, the Court was surrounded by mounted burghers, State Artillery, and mounted and foot police. The doors of the Court were guarded and the streets surrounding it regularly patrolled. The inhabitants of Pretoria besieged the entrance, waiting for the climax.

When the Court opened the rank-and-file prisoners took their places in the railed-off enclosure of the Court, but four of the ringleaders (Phillips, Farrar, Rhodes and Hammond) were ushered into a portable dock which had been passed up over the heads of the spectators.

Judge Gregorowski appeared genial enough, but his first order was for ladies to leave the Court. He then stated that Roman–Dutch Law must be applied to the case and that death was the only penalty that could be imposed. He commended the prisoners to the magnanimity of the President and his Executive Council. The other prisoners were condemned to fines of £2,000, two years in prison and banishment for three years.

The trial had ended.

The President did not have much difficulty in securing the approval of the Executive Council to the death sentences being commuted to fine and imprisonment, but felt that he could not consider further reductions in the sentences unless the prisoners themselves were prepared to make a formal request through the judge. It was suggested that in these petitions they should express regret for their conduct and undertake to behave better in the future.

Some of the prisoners, however, thought that this might be a device to break their spirit or even to extract some further form of admission from them. They did not appreciate that the President could hardly risk acting without the advice of a judge and that the judge could hardly be expected to move without having received a petition from the prisoners.

Once he had received the petitions the judge did, indeed, exercise his discretion in favour of some at least of the prisoners. He distinguished between those who had pleaded guilty merely because their names were on the list of the Reform Committee, and those who had taken a more active part in the rising.

The Government was further spurred to action on 16 May when Frederick Gray, father of six children, borrowed a razor and committed suicide in the prison lavatory, and on 20 May Kruger announced that sentence on the four leaders would be commuted to a term of 15 years. Ten prisoners were released at once on payment of their fines and the remainder had their sentences cut provisionally to less than a year and could renew their petition for release at the end of their term.

Once the first ten men had been released, a campaign was started to procure the release of the remainder, and on 30 May Judge Gregorowski suggested grounds for further mitigation of the sentences of the remaining captives. That day the Executive Council agreed to free all the remaining prisoners, except two who had refused to sign petitions for clemency and, of course, the four leaders. In return those freed had to agree not to engage in politics for three years.

But this concession only led to further demands for the release of the ringleaders. A deputation of some 200 mayors from various parts of South Africa was organised and gathered in Pretoria on 11 June to ask for clemency to be shown, and the Executive Council, on Gregorowski's advice, announced that each of the ringleaders must pay a fine of £25,000 and undertake to stay out of politics for 15 years or submit to banishment. Frank Rhodes alone refused to give his word and was deported the same night.

The remaining two prisoners were released by a Presidential gesture made in honour of Queen Victoria's Diamond Jubilee.

Certain other considerations no doubt helped to guide the President towards leniency. He wanted good relations with the Chamberlain Government if only to secure a revision of the restrictions under which his foreign policy still operated. And Barney Barnato had threatened to close down the mines if nothing was done for the prisoners. There were petitions, too, from American citizens, including Mark Twain and Natalie Hammond who, as we saw earlier, called with Mrs Phillips to see the President.

In due course Kruger submitted a claim for £1 million for "moral and intellectual damage" and £677,983 3s 3d for the cost of suppressing the rising. His reasoning, as he himself said, was, "If a poor man's dog comes into my garden, I shoot it. If a rich man's dog comes, I tie it up and make his master pay."

But as far as individuals were concerned he felt that he had been, if anything, too magnanimous.

It was one of the issues on which Kruger felt most deeply. It was not so much the fact that the raid had taken place – although that was bad enough – it was the attitude of the British public and Government towards the perpetrators. Dr Jameson, Kruger noted in his memoirs, "was released from prison on account of illness and recovered his health immediately afterwards".

No judicial commission was set up to try Rhodes, but only a

committee of politicians (which included Chamberlain, the underwriter if not the sponsor, of the raid). Missing telegrams which could have implicated Rhodes and Chamberlain had been conveniently burnt. And Rhodes was not even in disgrace. He remained a member of the Privy Council and a Director of the Chartered Company; and Kruger drew the inference that Rhodes and Chamberlain had been accomplices in the raid, and that in the inquiries that followed each shielded the other.

It was a lesson he never forgot.

Chapter 15

The Resurgence

It could hardly be expected, after the Jameson Raid, that relations between Kruger's Government and that of Her Majesty Queen Victoria would become more cordial. But for some time it appeared that efforts were being made to render them so, and Kruger himself visited the Witwatersrand Agricultural Show in 1896, a fête organised by the British element.

On 17 January 1896 Sammy Marks in Pretoria cabled to Isaac Lewis in London telling him to suggest that Chamberlain ask the Transvaal Government, through Robinson, to send a Commission, with Kruger as a member, to London to discuss outstanding problems. "If it can be arranged it is anticipated that the results will be favourable," Marks' cable said. "Keep this strictly private," it added.

Lewis discovered that Chamberlain was ready to invite the Commission, provided it was understood in advance that the invitation would be accepted and that there could be no alteration to Article IV of the Pretoria Convention of 1884, under which the South African Republic undertook not to conclude a treaty or engagement with any state or nation other than the Orange Free State, or with any native tribe to the eastward or westward of the Republic until the same had been approved by Her Majesty the Queen. "Such approval," the Article stated, "shall be considered to have been granted if Her Majesty's Government shall not, within six months after receiving a copy of such Treaty (which shall be delivered to them immediately upon its completion) have notified that the conclusion of such treaty is in conflict with the interests of Great Britain or any of Her Majesty's possessions in South Africa."

As an inducement to come to Britain, Kruger was offered a free passage in a naval vessel and "suitable entertainment" when he got there. Furthermore, in order to enable him to get a mandate from the Volksraad, it was stated that no limits would be placed on the discussions in London which would cover "all questions involving the general welfare of South Africa and the security of the South African Republic".

No doubt the flexibility of the British Government was due in part to reports sent by Robinson from the Cape warning Chamberlain not to take a "hard-line" policy. Robinson maintained that the Cape Dutch would oppose any new attempt to redress the uitlanders' grievances other than by negotiation; that Kruger would rather fight than discuss the internal management of his Republic with Chamberlain, and that the Orange Free State and the Dutch in Natal would support Kruger in the event of hostilities, which, even if they were successful, would involve Britain thereafter in the maintenance of a costly permanent garrison.

Be this as it may, the British Government appeared to be so anxious to receive Kruger as their honoured guest that they suggested he should not wait to consult the Volksraad at its normal session in May, but should at once call a special session for the purpose.

If this were not done, Chamberlain alleged, then it might be difficult to arrange the visit before the end of July when the Queen would be preparing to set off for Balmoral, and would therefore be unable to receive the President.

For Kruger, however, the offer was a disappointment for, in addition to discussing Article IV, Kruger wished to revive his claim for a way to the sea and he was not prepared to negotiate about either the "grievances" of the uitlanders or the way in which the South African Republic should commit itself to remedying them.

And how could he, at his age, undergo the rigours of a journey to London unless there was really something to be gained there?

Before the end of March the honeymoon was over. Later that year the uitlanders founded a new pressure group, the South African League, which was ready to look to the British Government rather than to the Republic for the redress of their grievances.

Part of the trouble was Kruger himself. When a deputation called on him during the post-Jameson Raid period to thank him for the release of some of the prisoners and to ask for clemency to be extended to others, he was reported to have said: "I sometimes have to punish my dogs, and I find that there are two kinds of dog. Some of them who are good come back and lick my boots. Others keep their distance and snarl at me. I see that some are still snarling, I am glad that you are not like them."

The story lost nothing in the telling in the bars of Johannesburg and the story was revived that after Majuba Kruger had gloated: "Then shall it be from the Zambesi to Simon's Bay, Africa for the Afrikander." Moreover, the President refused to entertain Barney Barnato's suggestion, that the railways and the dynamite monopoly would prove less costly if they were nationalised. There was also the suspicion that had been in the air ever since Kruger's speech in January 1895 at the dinner for the Kaiser's birthday that the President had been, as Robinson put it "coquetting with a foreign power". In that speech the President recalled how well he had been received in Germany, and how well the Germans behaved in the Transvaal. He hinted that "if one nation tries to entrap us, the other will try to prevent this", and added: "The time will come when our friendship will be closer than ever."

And now – in mid-February – there were rumours that Leyds, Kruger's State Secretary, who, much to the indignation of British diplomats, was soon to be appointed Kruger's "Ambassador", had written from Berlin to advise the President not to enter into any new arrangement with Britain but to maintain an armed neutrality. Leyds had, indeed, been making contacts in Germany. He interviewed Prince Hohenlohe, then Chancellor, and visited Bismarck at his estate, Friedrichsrühe, wondering, while there, at the "high-pitched small tenor voice" coming from such a bulky figure. It is true that Bismarck had told Leyds that no territory left in the world was worth the bones of a single Prussian soldier, and that Leyds had rejected the idea of the Transvaal becoming a German Protectorate. But that was not how things looked to Chamberlain, and when Leyds, an invited guest, insisted on watching the Diamond Jubilee Naval Review at Spithead from the deck of a Dutch warship, the suspicion that Kruger was engaged in subversive intrigue grew.

Furthermore Leyds, with Kruger's permission but on his own responsibility, had been looking into the possibility of holding an international conference to establish the legal status of the Transvaal and to pledge to protect its independence.

All this made the question of Article IV more ticklish. The sentence in Article IV which caused the most trouble was the one which called on the South African Republic to deliver to Her Majesty's Government a copy of any proposed treaty "immediately on its completion". Kruger argued that a treaty was not "completed" until it had been ratified according to the constitutional procedures of the parties concerned. On this interpretation, therefore, it was not necessary to give Her Majesty's Government a chance to disapprove of any treaty until it had already come into force. And this indeed is what happened, for instance, when the Republic signed a Treaty of Extradition with the Netherlands Government.

There was also some doubt as to whether the Republic would be entitled to sign a Treaty with the Orange Free State if this involved new relationships between the Republic and third states with whom Kruger would not have been otherwise entitled to conclude an agreement. It was obvious that this nebulous situation would, in the interests of all, have to be more clearly defined.

To Kruger, the argument involved the whole question of the independence of the South African Republic.

The Convention signed in Pretoria in 1881, after Majuba, between Britain and the Transvaal had dropped all claim to complete British sovereignty by Britain over the Transvaal. Instead, the British had retained only "suzerainty", a term indicating that certain undefined aspects of sovereignty had been retained to the Crown, despite the fact that those concerned were not strictly speaking British subjects. In the Preamble to the 1881 agreement, the word "suzerainty" occurred without any further definition of what it was intended to mean.

But the word "suzerainty" was nowhere to be seen in the text of the later 1884 London Convention which Kruger had signed in the British capital with Lord Derby, and Kruger argued that the word had been intentionally omitted from this later agreement. He pointed to the fact that the draft of the London Convention showed those parts of the earlier Convention which it was intended to omit in the later text, ringed in black ink, and that the Preamble containing the reference to suzerainty was among these ringed portions. Furthermore, the London agreement had a new Preamble which replaced the former one, and went on to say that what followed this new Preamble was a new Convention.

Accordingly Kruger, on his return from London after the Derby talks, had felt justified in telling his people that under the London Convention they had recovered their sovereignty.

His view, namely that Britain in signing the 1884 Convention had abandoned all claim to sovereignty, had been supported by the Law Officers of Britain's Liberal Government. As recently as 1894 they had given it as their opinion that, taking into account the negotiations which preceded the London Convention, the construction of the document, and the attitude of Her Majesty's Government towards the Republic, "We are of opinion that suzerainty has been abandoned." And the Law Officers of the Unionist Government to which Chamberlain belonged likewise held that the assertion of suzerainty by the use of that word had been given up in 1884.

Chamberlain, however, was in no way disconcerted by these opinions. At various times he maintained that the London Convention was not a treaty between two States of equal standing, but amounted to a declaration or grant by a paramount power (Britain) to its dependency (the Transvaal) and that only the paramount power could determine the meaning of the grant. He argued that the

Preamble and paragraphs in the draft to which Kruger referred had been ringed with black ink merely to show that it was not necessary to repeat them in the new agreement and not because they were to be annulled. In support of this the British pointed out that the second Convention read, "The following articles shall be substituted for the articles" (and not for the Preamble) of the earlier agreement. Furthermore, the earlier Pretoria Convention had both given self-government to the Republic and reserved suzerainty to Britain. If, therefore, as Kruger now argued, the Preamble to the Pretoria Convention was no longer in effect, then the grant of independence associated with it had also lapsed.

As for Kruger's accusation that if Chamberlain took up the cause of the uitlanders he would be interfering in the internal affairs of the Republic, Her Majesty's Government could argue that under accepted international law Britain had the right to protect British subjects against ill treatment in any foreign state, and all Kruger's protests could not cancel this right.

But in any case it might not be too difficult to show that several of Kruger's laws operated in such a way as to amount to a breach of the London Convention, in which case the whole agreement would fall to the ground.

For instance there was the Bill passed by the Volksraad on 28 September 1896 authorising the expulsion of any alien considered by the President and Executive Council to be a danger to public peace and order. This could be seen as a breach of Article XIV (a) of the Convention which said that "All persons other than natives conforming themselves to the laws of the South African Republic will have full liberty, with their families to enter, travel or reside in any part of the South African Republic."

The question was, "Could these aliens be said to have failed to conform to the laws of the South African Republic merely because the President and Executive Council, without submitting the matter to a Court of Law, had declared the person concerned to be a danger to the public peace and order?" Obviously not.

But to assert himself publicly Chamberlain needed a man on the spot to replace Robinson. He believed that Sir Hercules had shown incompetence and weakness at the time of the Jameson Raid. Earlier he had heard with relief that Robinson's doctors had advised him not to return to South Africa, and had been disappointed when Robinson, ennobled as Lord Rosmead, unexpectedly recovered and had insisted on resuming his post in the late summer of 1896. However, Chamberlain had a second chance when Rosmead retired, after all, less than a year later. His replacement was of a very different type.

Alfred Milner, son of Charles Milner, a doctor, was born at Giessen, a small university city in West Germany, and was one-quarter German through his father's mother, Sophie von Rappard. After a brilliant career at Oxford, and a spell as Assistant Editor of the Liberal *Pall Mall Gazette*, he stood unsuccessfully in the general election of 1885 as Liberal candidate for Harrow. He afterwards became Private Secretary to George Goschen and followed him, with Chamberlain, into the Liberal–Unionist camp. Through Goschen's influence, Milner was appointed Under-Secretary to the Egyptian Ministry of Finance at a time when Egypt was a British-controlled territory, and later was promoted Chairman of the Board of Inland Revenue in the UK Treasury.

Thus he was an administrator rather than a politician, and Chamberlain's first thought was to offer him the post of Permanent Under-Secretary at the Colonial Office as successor to Sir Robert Meade. Milner, however, preferred a post overseas, and was delighted to be appointed Robinson's successor. "I feel it is a great privilege to be allowed to fill any position in the character of what I may, perhaps, be allowed to call a civilian soldier of the Empire. To succeed in it, to render any substantial service to any part of our world-wide State, would be all that, in my most audacious dreams, I ever ventured to aspire to."

Britannia was indeed Milner's only mistress, and he did not marry until three weeks after his retirement, when he was nearly 70. He remained a lonely figure – sincere, morally impeccable, inflexible when once he had made up his mind, a man who found it difficult to satisfy himself with compromises or half measures. He did not communicate easily with his fellow-men except on paper; he found it hard to understand those who had grown up in a background different from his own and, like Rhodes, had the disadvantage of a feeble voice. But he possessed none of Rhodes' geniality or charm. No one could wish of him, as Chamberlain wished of Robinson, that he should be more spirited and "should show his teeth occasionally".

Milner was, as might have been expected, cautious for some time after he arrived at the Cape on 5 May 1897. He distrusted Rhodes, whom he considered to be too self-willed, too violent, too sanguine and in too great a hurry. "He is much the same man as he always was," Milner concluded, "undaunted and unbroken by his former failure, but also untaught by it."

Milner hoped that the passage of time and the efforts of the uitlanders, if not of the more progressive Boers, would force Kruger to introduce reforms; and he was glad to see that the old man had lost some of the popularity he had achieved at the time of the Jameson

Raid. But no reforms followed. Milner was affronted when Leyds proposed that the Republic, like any other Government, should appoint a Consul-General in Cape Town to deal with the Transvaal Republic's affairs.

The uitlanders continued to complain of exorbitant taxation, corrupt administration and denial of their (particularly by the inspectors of mines) own personal rights.

So far from introducing reforms Kruger had apparently to battle with the Volksraad to prevent burgher rights that had already been granted to newcomers from being taken away. In September 1896 the Volksraad had passed the Press Law which allowed the authorities to forbid the distribution of printed publications which it considered harmful to public morals or the good order of the Republic. On 9 December of that year the President suppressed a Johannesburg weekly, the *Critic* (which had indeed been critical of the Government), for a period of six months and, in March 1897, the *Johannesburg Star* was also suppressed mainly on account, it was believed, of a leading article attacking the President for talking "pious patter" and "unmitigated twaddle". Although this was not stated in Court, the Republic's own Court took the view that suppression of a paper for six months, i.e. in respect of material not yet distributed, was illegal.

Even before the Jameson Raid the Public Meeting Act of 1894 allowed the police to be present at any meeting of more than seven people and to disperse it if in their opinion it threatened law and order, the authorities, or the private rights of individuals.

Litigants at Court suffered from the fact that every document used had to be accompanied by a sworn translation in Dutch.

Shortly before Milner arrived Kruger had appointed an Industrial Commission under Schalk Burger, one of the Progressives, to look into the economic grievances of the uitlanders, and as long as this investigation continued the complaints of the Rand population received the same answer, "Wait for the findings of the Commission." But when these came the President sought to ignore the verdict. The Commission's report was turned over to a Committee of the Volksraad which debated the report, and under the President's influence virtually rejected it. Some railway freight charges were cut but not nearly to the extent the uitlanders had hoped for; the tariffs on some foods were also cut, but other duties were increased so that the Government took in more than it had done before. Another recommendation that a local board should be created to prevent desertion by the natives from the gold-mines, thefts of gold from the mines, and the illegal supply of liquor to native labourers, was rejected, and the cancellation of the dynamite monopoly, which had also been recommended by the Report, was referred, after a debate in the Volksraad lasting nine days, by a majority of one vote to Kruger's own Executive Council, Kruger arguing in effect: " 'They' have cut me off from the sea, so we must build up our own industries."

A new tax of five per cent on mining profits served to bring the rebel mine-owners who had broken away from the Chamber of Mines as a protest against the Jameson Raid back into the fold. Nor were the prospects more encouraging for parents who wished that more of the money they contributed to the State education fund should be used for classes in English.

For example A. D. W. Wolmarans, member for Pretoria and at one time Chairman of the First Volksraad, spoke of children "being poisoned by English ideas", and believed that: "If a girl spoke half a dozen words of English correctly she despised her own nationality..."

But it was clear that neither the British Government nor Chamberlain could reasonably intervene on behalf of the British subjects unless they had asked him to do so in a clearer manner than they had asked Jameson.

In Britain the South African Association had been founded in May 1896 with Kipling, Rider Haggard and some keen supporters of Rhodes among the members "to educate British public opinion on South African affairs".

An incident which happened on the Sunday before Christmas 1898 spurred them to do so. A British subject, Tom Jackson Edgar, returning after midnight to his home in a building known as Florries Tenement, overheard a remark made by one of a group of three uitlanders standing near by and, considering it to be insulting, knocked the offender senseless. One of his friends, thinking that the man had been killed, summoned help. Four policemen arrived and gathered outside Edgar's house calling on him to open up. When he failed to unbar the door – thinking perhaps that they were civilians taking the law into their own hands – one of the policemen, Bert Stephanus Jones, broke down the door and forced his way in. Edgar, it was said, then hit the policeman on the side of the head with a stick tipped with a large iron nut, and Jones then fired on Edgar who fell dead into the arms of his wife.

Jones was arrested on a charge of murder, but the Public Prosecutor soon reduced it to one of culpable homicide and released the prisoner on bail. After pressure by Edmund Fraser, Acting British Agent, Jones was re-arrested and charged again with murder. But once again the charge was reduced and he was acquitted. Uitlanders drew the conclusion that they could not expect to get justice under their present rulers. Edgar's friends and workmates then decided to send a petition to the Queen asking for protection. Several thousand Britishers met – there were no inflammatory speeches since these were already forbidden under the Public Meetings Act – and took the petition along to the house of John Emrys Evans, the British Vice-Consul, where it was read to the crowd. It later achieved publication in the *Cape Times*. Evans, in accordance with protocol, then forwarded it to the office of the High Commissioner in Cape Town.

Milner was still on leave at the time, and Sir William Butler, the Commander-in-Chief and Acting High Commissioner, dealt with the petition in a very simple way. He refused to send it on, giving as his excuse that the contents of the petition had already been published before the Queen had been apprised of its existence, and that it would therefore have been improper for him to forward it to her. He even wrote to Pretoria reprimanding Evans for having allowed himself to get mixed up in a political affair.

On 14 January 1899, while Milner was still away, a second meeting was held in Johannesburg in a large hall, known as the Amphitheatre, to endorse the previous petition of 24 December. The meeting was broken up, allegedly at the instigation of certain Government officials, and it was rumoured that the police had received orders not to interfere with the raiders. Edmund Fraser, the British Agent in Pretoria, made a formal complaint to the Government, giving affidavits, naming the Government officials concerned, and, when no action followed, Chamberlain published the affidavits in a Blue Book accusing the officials of complicity.

Also, in January 1899, Chamberlain inquired discreetly whether the mine-owners were going to take any strong or concerted action against the proposal to extend the hated dynamite monopoly concession for another 15 years. He was told that any appeal by the owners to the British Government would be regarded as treason and would be ineffectual unless they received a promise of support from London. Chamberlain then let it be known that he would not object if they made a moderately worded protest to the Government of the Republic on this matter.

This protest was duly made and, at the same time, the mine-owners offered to guarantee a loan of £600,000 to enable Kruger to buy out the monopoly. It was thought unlikely that the President would accept, but on the other hand rejection would put him in the wrong and would at the same time deprive him of his habitual complaint that he never got any help from the capitalists who made so much profit out of the Transvaal.

In mid-February Chamberlain himself forwarded a protest against the extension of the monopoly claiming that it was a breach of the London Convention in as much as it prevented liberty of trade within the Republic.

Kruger did indeed reject both the protests and the buy-out deal but countered with a hint that there might be room for negotiations between the authorities and the mine-owners.

Lippert, on behalf of the Dynamite Monopoly (and Kruger), proposed that the mine-owners should resign themselves to the continuation of the dynamite monopoly, should support the efforts of the Republic to raise money abroad (which was proving difficult because of efforts by the City to obstruct the plan), should discourage press agitation in overseas countries, and dissociate themselves from the South African League; the Government, in return, would grant the vote after seven years' residence and settle the mine-owners' claim to mining rights over the bewaarplaatsen, areas originally granted to them for storing water and the residue of crushed ore.

It was an awkward moment for Chamberlain, for if the negotiations succeeded Kruger would likewise have succeeded in splitting the mine-owners from the remaining uitlanders and thus weakening Chamberlain's hand. Moreover, if Kruger were really ready to back down it would be a pity to confine an agreement with him merely to mining interests. Nor was this the best moment to make an agreement, for if Her Majesty's ministers were really going to assert themselves in the Transvaal, public opinion in the United Kingdom would have to be prepared for the event.

Meanwhile if negotiations were unavoidable one must drive a hard bargain.

Britain was now in a stronger position in the field of international politics than she had been for some time. Germany had withdrawn her support from Kruger's Government and the tension between France and Britain over the Fashoda incident of 1898 had subsided.

Accordingly, the mine-owners were advised to step up their terms and to ask at the second interview for an independent municipality for Johannesburg. If they reached the first objective they could later proceed to the more difficult issue of the franchise. But they must insist on written proposals.

When it came to the point the mine-owners, influenced probably by Milner, gave rather more emphasis to the vote question which was, they said, a vital point on which a settlement must hinge. These terms would almost certainly have been rejected anyway, but the atmosphere of the negotiations was completely wrecked by a letter from State Secretary Reitz making clear that neither the State

Attorney, Jan Smuts, nor Reitz nor Dr Leyds, who took part in the second meeting, had been speaking on behalf of the Government but were acting on their own responsibility.

And at this point the owners, fearing possibly that they might be accused of bartering away the rights of others for their own gain, seem to have lost their nerve just as they did at the time of the Jameson Raid, and someone leaked details of their correspondence with the Government (was this why Chamberlain had insisted on obtaining written proposals?) thus ending the negotiations and making things far more difficult in future for the moderates in the Kruger party.

Meanwhile, even during the negotiations, a second petition to the Queen had been prepared with the greatest circumspection and secrecy. It was supported by 21,000 signatures and claimed that conditions in the Transvaal had now become "well-nigh intolerable" for British subjects. The petition was forwarded at the end of March, but in May the Cabinet was still undecided on whether to support it.

It was at this point that Milner, now back in South Africa, acted in support of the hard line. On 2 May he telegraphed to Chamberlain asking him not to answer the petition until the Cabinet had come to a firm decision about the policy that they were prepared to follow. And, to help them in their decision, on 4 May he sent his famous "helot" telegram. In this he said:

The case for intervention is overwhelming. The only attempted answer is that things will right themselves if left alone. But in fact, the policy of leaving things alone has been tried for years and it has led to their going from bad to worse. They were going from bad to worse before the raid. We were on the verge of war before the raid and the Transvaal was on the verge of revolution. The effect of the raid has been to give the policy of leaving things alone a new lease of life with the old consequences. The spectacle of thousands of British subjects kept permanently in the position of helots, constantly chafing under undoubted grievances, and calling calmly on Her Majesty's Government for redress does steadily undermine the influence and reputation of Great Britain and the respect for the British Government within its own dominions.

Milner called for "some striking proof of the intention, if it is the intention, of Her Majesty's Government not to be ousted from its position in South Africa. And the best proof alike of its power and its justice would be to obtain for the uitlanders in the Transvaal a fair share in the Government of the country which owes everything to their exertions." These letters evidently had their effect.

Even as late as 28 April Chamberlain had proposed that the Cabinet should tread warily. He believed that Kruger might send an offensive reply to any ultimatum "and then we shall have to go to war or accept a humiliating check". A. J. Balfour, who led for the Government in the House of Commons, felt obliged to point out in his paper for the Cabinet that "We ask that the uitlanders should be admitted to the franchise, and we describe this process as one of electoral reform; but the Boers might describe it as a transfer of nationality – and can anyone say that they are wrong?" But on 9 May Chamberlain got Cabinet approval for a very strong note. It would be short of an ultimatum but would make clear that Britain considered her imperial supremacy in South Africa to have been publicly challenged by the South African Republic. Would Kruger buckle under the strain?

When Kruger was re-elected in February 1898 for his final term as President, the campaign, despite the criticism of the Progressives, was no longer the touch-and-go affair that he had experienced five years before.

He was not, perhaps, as universally esteemed as he had been immediately after the Jameson Raid, but he was still the irreplaceable guardian of his country's freedom, and had reminded the electors of this fact earlier in 1898 by asserting, in a note to "Kimberlain" (the pronunciation of Chamberlain's name most generally favoured by Afrikaners) that the London Convention "must be interpreted according to the generally accepted principles of the law of nations", and that any disputed points could be submitted to an independent arbitrator nominated by the Swiss President who could be relied upon to be impartial in such matters.

The suggestion that a minor foreign power should be called in to help pass judgement on the methods by which Her Majesty's Government sought protection for her oppressed subjects in the Transvaal exasperated Chamberlain and had led him to send a near-torrid despatch during the first week of December, in the midst of Kruger's election campaign.

However much this justified Britain's position in the eyes of the world, the despatch could not have failed to win votes for Kruger, though with the opposition split between Piet Joubert and Schalk Burger he hardly needed help. (On election day, 10 February 1898, the two opposition candidates polled only 5,700 votes between them against Kruger's 12,800.)

The result of the election seemed, however, to make Kruger less amenable to compromise, and to have stiffened his resolve. The dismissal of Chief Justice Kotze, which made it possible for the Volksraad to alter at any time by simple majority, without notice, any of the laws of the land, came only six days after the election result. The Progessive wing had thus been smashed, and Milner saw no alternative but for Britain to establish unaided a "good system of government". "The race oligarchy has got to go and I see no signs of it removing itself," Milner concluded.

The President, now nearly 75, had become less fitted to deal with the internal and international problems of his office. His physique had been weakened by malaria and, latterly, by lack of exercise. He was deafer, and relied more on his stick for support on his occasional walks abroad. He was slower at grasping the significance of the unexpected and rambled at times in his speeches and in his writing. He was less accessible to outsiders. He resented being regarded as a tourist attraction – one of the curiosities of Pretoria – and was hurt and displeased when visitors noticed and commented on trivialities such as the stains on the Presidential waistcoat. His ideal Republic had not changed. It should consist mainly of large farms on which practically no work was done – at any rate by the Boers themselves.

Barney Barnato summed him up very well from the mine-owners' viewpoint when he said:

The Pretoria townlands are known to be gold bearing. Their wealth has been proved. For the fourth or fifth time a proposal is made to proclaim them under Gold Law and Kruger goes to the Raad specially. With tears in his eyes and every dramatic effect he implores the members of the Raad not to agree to the proclamation because, mark you, "there is too much gold in the country already". And the Raad, in deference to him, declines the proposal.

Then again we have an unlimited amount of low grade reefs which cannot at present be worked with any satisfactory margin of profit. He knows quite well – I have put it to him more than once – that if our working expenses were lessened by a reduction of the taxes on foodstuffs and better management of the railway, the amount of capital invested at remunerative rates would be trebled and the net revenue of the Republic would be tremendously increased. He says that if the taxes on mealies and forage are reduced his farmers will not get such good food prices, and that it will cost so much more for extra police to keep the new goldfields in order. I wish he would see that the liberal policy would pay him best.

But Kruger continued to believe, probably rightly, that "but for gold Britain would not have lifted a finger to protect her subjects". Hence, the more gold the more interference.

As he grew older, Kruger found that the simple equations that held good in South African tribal politics could not readily be applied to world affairs. Thus the attitudes of Germany, France and Portugal to Kruger's attempts to secure a foothold in Delagoa Bay on the Indian Ocean depended partly on factors outside Africa over which Kruger had no control. Therefore, Germany and Britain combined to seek Portugal's friendship and offered her a loan in the hope of securing concessions in the Far East.

Consequently, early in 1897, Chamberlain felt able to send a naval squadron to Delagoa Bay as a demonstration of his determination to preserve British rights. "The President evidently was greatly startled when I came to the mention of the ships," Greene, the British Agent, reported. "He declared that I was holding a knife to his throat and pressing for an answer." Certainly, as Kruger himself, half in fun, had declared in his speech in Bloemfontein in March 1897, Queen Victoria was a "kwaaie vrouw" – an awkward, difficult woman to handle if you got on the wrong side of her.

But, in the end, it was neither Delagoa Bay nor immigration that brought Kruger into the inevitable clash with Chamberlain and Milner, but the franchise – the right to vote.

Chapter 16

The Confrontation

The franchise was the question on which Kruger was least amenable to reason. At a dinner given in his honour in 1892 by the Jewish community, Kruger had compared the uitlanders to squatters living on a farm whose owner had won the land with blood and toil. How could they have the same rights as the owner, he asked. Perhaps, in time, voting rights could be extended to the uitlander but the original burghers must first be sure that he could be relied on. He must have lived in the land long enough for people to be able to say of him, "Here is a man you can trust. He is not going to be caught stealing tomorrow." Speaking at Krugersdorp the same year Kruger declared that if he handed out voting rights indiscriminately and so lost the country its independence, he would be calling down the curse of Almighty God on his head.

Again in the Great Franchise Debate of August 1895 which discussed a memorial sent by the uitlanders, Kruger took the view that only those who had gone on commando to fight the enemies of the Republic should be granted the vote. Those who showed they loved their country by making such sacrifices were entitled to the franchise, and they should get it, the President said, according to the *Johannesburg Star*. The members of the Volksraad had been threatened every year, he added, about what would happen if they did not open the flood-gates. If the dam was full before the walls had been washed down, some of the water had to be drained off. Well, this had been done in the case of the commando men. They were the clean water which had been drained off and taken into the inner dam which consisted of clean water, but he did not wish to take in the dirty water as well.

Three years later he was equally unyielding. "The discontented people will not be satisfied until they have my country," he said, according to the *Cape Times* of February 1898. "If I give them the franchise they may ask the Chartered people [i.e. Rhodes] to rule over them. Their other grievances, if there are any, are quite easy to redress. I intend making full inquiries into these and other matters. But don't be under the delusion that any concessions I can make will ever satisfy the enemies of my country."

What was the real position and how great was the danger of Kruger losing control of "his" country?

Kruger believed that the uitlanders numbered between 60,000 and 70,000 as against 30,000 of his "old burghers", and a census taken by the Johannesburg Sanitary Board of those living within three miles of the centre of the city credited the United Kingdom with having provided some 16,265 and the Transvalers only 6,205. Some writers, including the scholarly J. S. Marais, estimated that in January 1899 there were probably more Boers, men, women and children, than uitlanders in the Transvaal as a whole although there were fewer women and children and more voters among the foreigners than among the Boers.

Either way – it was not a situation in which, from Kruger's point of view, to take chances.

Up until 1882 anyone who possessed landed property or had resided in the Transvaal for a year had full voting rights. But in that year a new law limited the franchise to those who had lived in the country for five years.

In 1890 when the Second Volksraad was created, mainly to deal with the affairs of the uitlanders, it was decided that the right to elect members of the First Volksraad should be limited to three classes of people: those who either already possessed full voting rights; those who had been born in the Transvaal and had reached the age of 16; and third, those who had lived in the Transvaal for 12 years as naturalised subjects, had reached the age of 40, were members of the Protestant Church and possessed of landed property in the Transvaal. But since the naturalisation process took two years, 14 years had to pass before the newcomer reached a state of political grace.

A new law passed in 1894 was, however, even more restrictive. Only those born in the State of parents who already had full voting rights, or who had established their residence there before 29 May 1876 – that is 18 years earlier, before the Shepstone annexation – were automatically entitled to full political privileges. Anyone who had lived in the Transvaal for 14 years (including 12 as a naturalised subject), and had the necessary property and religious qualifications could still have full voting rights including that of electing members of the First Volksraad, but only if the majority of burghers in his Ward petitioned for this in writing and if the President and his Executive Council raised no objection. Children born in the Transvaal would take the status of their fathers. Hence, a son whose father was not already a full-blown elector might have to wait a further 14 years for his full voting rights, i.e. nearly 28 years in all.

It is true that Barney Barnato, perhaps the most uitlandish of the uitlanders, once said, "Men do not come to the Transvaal to vote, they come to earn money," and that: "It would cost blood and money to obtain the franchise and it would never add sixpence a month to anyone's wages while, even if it was granted not one Englishman in a thousand would give up his birthright to take an oath of allegiance to the Transvaal Republic." But unfortunately Barney had already played the clown so often that neither side was prepared to take him as seriously as he deserved.

On the other hand it was not only Milner and Chamberlain who believed that Kruger was being short-sighted in seeking to preserve the old order in the Transvaal. For example John Merriman, who had served in numerous Governments at the Cape and was later to become its Prime Minister, wrote from the Cape on New Year's Day 1899 to President Steyn in the Orange Free State:

I had the opportunity the other day of a long talk, or rather several talks, with Lippert about the Transvaal. He takes a very sane view of matters there, and is very hopeless [i.e. pessimistic]. He represents Kruger – as others describe him – as more dogged and bigoted than ever, and surrounded by a crew of self-seekers, who prevent him from seeing straight. He has no one to whom he turns for advice, and is so inflated as to have the crazy belief that he [Kruger] is born to bring about peace between Germany and France! If he falls, or dies, who have we to look to? All this plays the game of Rhodes and his brother capitalists.

William Schreiner, Prime Minister of the Cape Colony from 1898 to 1900, also agreed with Milner that Kruger's obstinacy increased the risk of a civil war with some of the four Governments of South Africa on opposing sides.

Lord de Villiers, Chief Justice of the Cape Colony, during his visit to Pretoria towards the end of April 1899, suggested in talks with State Secretary Reitz, Schalk Burger and State Attorney Smuts, that Kruger would be well advised to introduce drastic reforms and to reduce the qualifying period for voting rights to five years (instead of the nine years of which Kruger had spoken in Johannesburg on 1 April). Do not, he said in effect, let the uitlanders look to Rhodes or anyone else outside the Transvaal for the redress of grievances. Eventually he persuaded Kruger's lieutenants to advise the President to offer significant concessions on both the dynamite and franchise questions on the understanding that this settlement would be the final one.

De Villiers, while in Pretoria, had suggested a summit meeting between Milner, Kruger and President Steyn.

In June Jan Hofmeyr, leader of the Afrikaner movement in the Cape, was sent to Pretoria with details of a more liberal franchise offer which, it was suggested, Kruger should put to his Volksraad. Milner wanted to insist on any such measure being submitted first to Her Majesty's Government before it was put to the Volksraad. But this was too much even for Chamberlain who preferred to accept any concessions if they were substantial and complain later if they proved ineffective.

Milner, having persuaded Chamberlain to make the franchise question rather than the non-observance of the Convention the crucial issue, now sketched out his objectives. He believed the uitlanders should have the franchise at once without residential qualification, and wanted them to be allowed to take the oath of allegiance to the Republic of South Africa without having to renounce their British ties. In addition he wanted the seats in the Raad to be redistributed to give Johannesburg its proper representation in the first Volksraad.

Each side believed that the other might be bluffing. Kruger was counting on a weakened and divided Liberal Party in Britain to fight his battles with Chamberlain; he hoped, too, that Queen Victoria would restrain her impetuous Colonial Secretary from provoking another war between Britain and the Transvaal. But her views, even immediately after the Jameson Raid, were that "Dr Jameson is an excellent and able man", and that "the Boers are horrid people, cruel and overbearing". Apart from which her granddaughter, Princess Louise, was married to the Duke of Fife, President of Rhodes' Chartered Company.

The Cape leaders suggested that Steyn should at once sponsor a conference in the neutral city of Bloemfontein. Kruger accepted, provided that the negotiations would not endanger the independence of his Republic. He did not want Steyn, as he put it, to act as the tame elephant that would entice him into the English fold.

Chamberlain would have preferred the conference to have been held later in the summer, by which time he could have set the scene by publishing Milner's "helot" despatch and other material setting out the uitlanders' grievances. But it would look bad if he asked for a postponement.

So the conference opened on 31 May – without even a firm agenda on what subjects were to be discussed and in which order. Kruger had journeyed to the rendezvous by train, through brilliant winter sunshine, and Frederick Rompel, the only newspaperman permitted to travel with him, noted that the President had brought with him his oculist, Dr Heymans, as well as two members of the Executive Council, and State Attorney Smuts. Rompel noticed, too, that the President's eyes seemed more swollen than at any time since Dr Heymans had been treating them. Also the President, who was normally fond of telling jokes and stories during his travels and thereby shortening the journey, was noticeably silent. The train had halted overnight at Kroonstad to give the President a night's rest, but the welcoming party of officials on the platform at Bloemfontein commented on how much Kruger had aged.

On the eve of the conference President Steyn gave a reception at his house – the sort of function, hateful to Kruger, at which the women wore short puff sleeves and low corsages. As Milner arrived Kruger stepped forward and stretched out his hand. But Milner turned first to his hostess in a gesture which, though diplomatically correct, was inept.

The Bloemfontein meetings took place in the Railway Central Bureau on 31 May 1899, in a richly timbered chamber walled with oak panelling and more reminiscent perhaps of the House of Commons, Westminster, than of the age of steam. Abraham Fischer, the first and only Prime Minister of the Orange Free State, acted as interpreter, with Milner on his right and Kruger on his left.

Milner had insisted that the conference should be fully reported – which lowered it from the level of serious negotiations to that of public debate or even public relations, and as Kruger talked to Milner and Milner to Kruger, each was addressing his audience further north.

From the first, Milner sought to confine the discussion to the franchise question. But Kruger asked what he would get in return for giving way on this issue. He needed something to take back home to his burghers and the Volksraad. "If I give something I must be able to tell them that I have got something," he reasoned. But Milner replied that the uitlanders were asking for nothing more than justice and that, in any case, it was in the interests of Kruger's Republic to settle the problem on its own merits. It should not be made part of "a sort of Kaffir bargain". Milner believed Kruger was trying to introduce irrelevant side-issues on which the conference would founder, and was evasive when Kruger asked about such matters as compensation for the Jameson Raid and the future of Swaziland.

On the second day Milner proposed that the franchise should be given at once to uitlanders who had lived in the Republic for five years, and that they should be granted about one-quarter of the seats in the first or leading chamber of the Volksraad. On 2 June, the third afternoon of the conference, Kruger, under pressure as usual from his friends, made a counter-offer which would have guaranteed the uitlanders naturalisation after two years' residence and the franchise after a further five years. Moreover the new subjects would not be called on to swear a special oath of allegiance to the State. Also, the President was prepared to offer them five seats in the Volksraad. In return he asked for the right to withhold voting privileges if the applicant had been dishonourably sentenced or was unable to prove that he had obeyed the laws of the Republic, or had been guilty of acts against the Government or of other special misdemeanours. Kruger asked, too, for discretion to waive the normal property qualification in the case of those who deserved well of the State. He added that his proposal was dependent on the conclusion of successful negotiations on outstanding problems and on agreement to submit future ones to international arbitration.

Milner found the offer "plausible but deceptive". (Certainly Kruger could have manipulated the number of voters by accepting many who did not have the necessary property qualifications but who could be depended to vote for him.) Milner pointed out that under Kruger's offer, no uitlanders would receive the franchise at once, and not very many after two years. Furthermore, new applicants would have to renounce their nationality for five years before receiving full voting rights.

The following day it was already clear that things were not going well. Kruger ordered his train to be ready to leave and then apparently changed his mind.

On Sunday morning, 4 June, the first time that the President had had a chance to sit out on the veranda of his house, Rompel noticed that he was without his habitual pipe. His eyelids appeared still more swollen and the doctor told Rompel that the President had been shedding tears which had inflamed his eyes.

While Kruger was sitting on the balcony, Milner was cabling Chamberlain to say he feared that the conference was going to fail. Chamberlain in reply urged Milner not to break off the negotiations in haste. The Boers, he said, prefer to take their time about coming to decisions and like to haggle over bargains. He was not convinced that Kruger had made his last offer and "you should be very patient and admit a good deal of haggling before you abandon the game". It was of the utmost importance, Chamberlain said, to put the President clearly in the wrong.

But, before Chamberlain's cable arrived, Milner had already declared the negotiations to be over. "The Conference is absolutely at an end, and there is no obligation on either side arising out of it," he announced.

In the final stages of the negotiations Milner had denied that he had any plans which would interfere with the independence of the Republic. But Kruger asked, "If His Excellency wishes me to take advice from someone who has nothing to do with the government of the State, who, then, governs?" Milner suggested that Kruger might set up an advisory Council "who are not burghers of the State but who represent the uitlander community". "How can strangers rule my State?" countered the President. "How is that possible?" Milner insisted that his plan could not affect the government of the State. But Kruger felt the end had come. The tears coursed down his furrowed cheeks as he kept repeating, "It is our country that you want."

The failure of the Bloemfontein conference and the firm stand that he had taken there did not however release Kruger from the rack and he remained under firm pressure from his friends to give peace in our time.

On 12 June, in response to their pleading and to show his good faith, he introduced a Bill into the Volksraad under which newcomers would receive full voting rights seven years after they had applied for naturalisation. Those who had already been registered in the Transvaal for two years could qualify for the franchise in five years, and those who had already been registered with the authorities for nine years, would, provided they fulfilled the not very exacting conditions, qualify at once for full voting rights. Moreover the uitlander would not be obliged to renounce his own nationality while waiting for his new voting rights. Sons of foreigners born in the Transvaal would get full voting rights on attaining their majority.

Kruger resisted all attempts by the British Government to interfere in the passage of the Bill, though its details were made available to the British Agent in Pretoria. On 18 July, at the time it was passed, Chamberlain complained that the measure had been hurried through in order to prevent discussions on how it would work. But it seems more likely that Kruger's haste was made in the hopes of heading off a war.

At any rate, about the same time as Kruger introduced the Bill, Chamberlain published an official Blue Book containing among other features Milner's "helot" despatch. Chamberlain made a speech on the subject of the Transvaal in which he said: "Having undertaken this business, we will see it through. We have tried waiting, patience and trusting to promises which were never kept. We can wait no longer." On 1 August he suggested that a joint Commission appointed by the two Governments should examine the whole franchise question, and on 15 August the British Agent hinted that if this was not conceded voluntarily, it might be necessary to use force.

On 5 August de Villiers wrote from the Cape to tell Kruger:

At the risk of being considered interfering I should like, as your friend and as a wellwisher of South Africa, to advise you most earnestly to do everything in your power to ward off war from the country. I know the strong views which you hold as to your duty to preserve the independence of your Republic, but a patriot should also be prudent and he should even be prepared to surrender part of his independence if by that means alone he can prevent the loss of the whole.

I am perfectly convinced that, unless the Transvaal Government yields more than it has shown signs of doing, peace will not be maintained . . . I do not now wish to enter into the merits of the British claims, for the question no longer is: "What right has the British Government to make its demands?" but "What concessions on your part will preserve the peace?" Whether a war should become a war of races or not, it can only end in a destruction of your Republic. The issue of war or peace is in your hands and I earnestly trust that, like a prudent and practical statesman, you will decide in favour of peace.

Kruger's reply was not surprising:

I am sworn to uphold the independence of my country, and I have the very best reasons for believing that Chamberlain and Milner are determined to rob me of that independence. Can you give me the assurance that if I concede all their demands, others will not be sprung upon me which no self-respecting President could for a moment entertain? . . . I am sorry that you think war can end only in destruction of the Republic, but do you not believe that there is a power above greater than that of England which will see that right and justice will prevail?

De Villiers replied in due course in a further letter:

I thank you for your letter and I am glad that you appreciated my motives in writing to you. If you are firmly convinced that it is the object of Mr Chamberlain and Sir Alfred Milner to rob you of your independence, is that not an additional reason why, as the Transvaal is the weaker of the two States, you should not give them the shadow of an excuse for carrying out their design?

De Villiers added: "You say that, in case of war, a Higher Power will see that right and justice prevail, but there are many instances in history where we would consider that wrong and injustice have prevailed."

On 24 August Chamberlain wrote an official Government minute in which he said:

It is clear that we cannot go on negotiating for ever and we must try to bring matters to a head. The next step in military preparations is so important and so costly that I hesitate to incur the expense so long as there seems a fair chance of a satisfactory settlement. But I dread above all the continual whittling away of differences until we have not casus belli left, although the Boers may claim a partial diplomatic victory and be as disagreeable and intractable in the future as in the past.

Two days later in a speech at Birmingham he told his audience:

Mr Kruger procrastinates in his replies. He dribbles out reforms like water from a squeezed orange and he either accompanies his offers with conditions which he knows to be impossible or he refuses to allow us to make a satisfactory investigation of the nature and the character of these reforms . . . the sands are running down in the glass.

Chamberlain added that if Britain were forced to make further preparations she would no longer consider herself limited by offers she had made in the past but would proceed to establish "which is the paramount power in South Africa".

The Uitlander Council in Johannesburg, which had condemned Kruger's new franchise law the day after it had been passed, accepted this new hint, and responded with a manifesto calling on Her Majesty's Government to get them votes at once, and better representation in the Volksraad, as also a thoroughgoing reform of the system of government.

Meanwhile, on 13 August, Kruger had dribbled out another concession: immediate franchise for those who had lived five years in the Transvaal. It was what Milner had asked for at Bloemfontein. There would also be eight new seats for the uitlanders, and the new voters would be allowed to vote in elections of both the President and Commander-in-Chief – a matter which had apparently previously been in doubt.

But the President could not stomach the idea that the joint commission which Chamberlain proposed should discuss the internal arrangements of the Republic on the franchise. "They do not want any franchise under a Republic," he declared to Steyn. "It is in our interest to keep the peace, but if our independence is to go it must be taken from us by force."

A joint inquiry, he told Steyn, would comprise the independence of his country; and Steyn agreed. But how was Kruger to reject Milner's proposals without risking a showdown with Her Majesty's Government? Eventually he sidestepped the joint inquiry by suggesting a government to government meeting to be held subject to three conditions: (1) that it would not constitute a precedent for future interference; (2) that the suzerainty issue be allowed to drop; and (3) that the principle of settling disputes by arbitration should be accepted provided that "the foreign element" should be excluded.

Milner would have preferred to have rejected Kruger's offer on the ground that it excluded a joint inquiry. What he wanted was an acknowledgement of paramountcy: an admission that the Transvaal had no right to settle its own voting arrangements without submitting to a joint inquiry first. He could also argue that the Kruger proposals were less than acceptable. For they called on the British to undertake to drop their suzerainty campaign and submit to independent arbitration in future *before* Kruger introduced into the Volksraad a motion which might or might not be passed.

Chamberlain believed that it would be foolish to be abrupt. It would be better to encourage Kruger to spell out in greater detail just how his proposals would work. So a note of "qualified acceptance" was sent to Pretoria. The concessions were accepted, but the *quid pro quo* asked for by Kruger was also qualified in the British reply. For example, the British Government could not bind itself to abstain in future from intervening to protect its subjects in a foreign country from injustice. Arbitration without a foreign element could be accepted in some cases, but not as regards the interpretation of the London and Pretoria Conventions. Furthermore, the note added, if there was to be no joint commission, the British Government would make its own investigations and an intergovernmental conference between Milner and Kruger would have to be held in Cape Town to settle certain matters that were not susceptible to arbitration, thus making it clear that reforms asked for by the uitlanders would have to be negotiated as well as the franchise question.

Despite all the pressures, Kruger held firm. An English MP had once asked him, "Mr President, if there were a war between your country and England would you have any chance of winning?" He answered with a question: "Suppose that you are going along a road, armed with nothing better than a pocket-knife and you see a lion, would you be so reckless as to attack the lion with your pocket knife?" "No, certainly not!" replied the MP. "But," Kruger pursued, "suppose that the lion attacked you, would you be such a coward as not to defend yourself with your pocket knife?" "I would certainly try." "Well, Sir," concluded the President, "there you have the answer to your question."

More curtly, as he put it on another occasion, "The riem [strap] is round my throat; I have to fight."

At any rate his reply, sent to Chamberlain on 2 September, announced that he now withdrew his five-year offer of 13 August and replaced it by the previous proposal (which Milner had rejected at Bloemfontein), of a seven-year qualifying period for the vote, and only four extra seats for the uitlanders. He did, however, withdraw his objection to a joint inquiry into the franchise law.

But now the British would not play.

Their note of 8 September declared that Her Majesty's Government could not now return to the seven-year franchise proposal, and that unless the Republic agreed to a five-year period as well as to a joint inquiry the British Government would have to reconsider the situation and formulate their own proposals for a final settlement.

And so at last the time for negotiations had passed, and both sides hastened to make their military preparations for the conflict. The British drafted an ultimatum calling for the repeal of all laws passed in the Transvaal since 1881, for political equality for all resident Europeans and for the right to intervene there whenever the welfare of South Africa as a whole was involved. It was never sent off. For the Boers struck first. They had drawn up their own ultimatum calling for the withdrawal of all British troops from the Transvaal borders, and for those on the way to South Africa to be sent back.

The Boer ultimatum was delivered to Sir W. Conynghame Greene on 9 October 1899, and he handed over the British reply two days later. It said that "The conditions demanded by the Government of the South African Republic are such that Her Majesty's Government deem it impossible to discuss."

After offering up a prayer, the President himself signed Greene's safe-conduct.

The Boer War had begun.

Chapter 17

War

"Peasant, millionaire, rebel, autocrat, lay-preacher, filibuster, visionary and statesman, Paul Kruger is easily the most interesting figure of a president now living," wrote Edmund Garrett, a friend of Milner and Rhodes, in *McClure's Magazine* of June 1900. "I have had the good fortune to enjoy more than one talk with him on matters near his heart. The frame of the old athlete was already bowed and unknit by these later sedentary years, which told their tale in sallow face and flaccid droop under the eyes. Charm of manner or dignity there was none. The little, gross peasant ways which have been described, and over-described, at first distracted attention. The voice, down in some growling depths, was grudging, almost morose, till a vein of feeling was struck, when it became voluble and explosive. But I never doubted that in this hard, shrewd old gentleman in rusty broadcloth fiercely gesticulating with his pipe, I had before me one of the few really significant personalities of our time, and that I should look back to these reminiscences one day, if I lived, much as I look back to conversations I was fortunate enough to have with Gladstone or with Parnell. It was a privilege."

Fair enough. We can agree with that today.

But then, at the end of the article Garrett also painted a picture of the old President which summed up why it seemed justifiable – to the uitlanders at least – to turn him out of his country:

> The "land and folk" for which Paul Kruger has lived and for which he would die, means really a few thousands of families of Franco-Dutch extraction, speaking a Dutch patois, all either cattle-keepers or officials, or both, and largely interconnected by ties of marriage, of religious sectarianism, and of political patronage. The groove of such a patriotism may seem strangely narrow – it is intense in proportion.
>
> Paul Kruger is a visionary: what is his vision? It is of a sort of oligarchic theocracy, with Paul Kruger as its Melchizedek, priest and king in one. He sees the faithful sitting each under his own gum-tree, on his own stoep, and as far as his eye ranges that is his farm, and his cattle are on a score of hills. The young men are

stalwart, greater hunters before the Lord, and the young women are grossly built and fruitful. And to each farm there is a made road and a dam, and the stranger in the land pays for the same. The stranger keeps to himself in the city, and is more or less godless, for he is not of the chosen in the Promised Land. But he gives no trouble, for he is "well disposed", and looks to the Raad for his laws in due season. The burgher has his Kaffirs, who do his work, but they are not cruelly used, because they obey. The sons of the soil are not too much educated, because that spoils an Afrikander; but enough so to be able to hold all offices of state, that these may be purged of the Hollander and the German, no less than the accursed English or "English-hearted Afrikander". And the nations of the earth come vying the one with the other for favors, Germany and France and England, all on the one footing.

And above all sits Paul Kruger, father of his people, dwelling in the house that the concessionnaire Nellmapius gave him, wealthy, but thrifty, living as simply as he used to live on the farm, save that sheep's head and trotters comes round somewhat oftener. And the judges come to him to know how they shall judge, and the Raad members to know what laws they shall make; and on Sundays all come to the little chapel near to hear him expound the Word of God and the truth as set forth by the Separatist Reformed Brethren. And there is peace in the earth. And it is flat, and the sun goes round it.

Some untruths here, some half-truths but one undeniable fact: the judges and the Raad were subservient, and the Republic now began to pay the penalty for the President's absolutism. Its leaders had grown up in his giant shadow with their initiative artificially stunted.

Kruger's authority within the Executive Council and the Krygs-raad, or War Council, was still unquestioned. Indeed he was now less amenable to reason, less capable of profiting from a discussion. His increasing deafness was a source of embarrassment to those around him, and the eye troubles brought on by the misfortune of his ingrowing eyelashes made him short-tempered. His increasing abruptness towards those who disagreed with him discouraged independence of thought among his war commanders, most of whom in any case had made their name in the Majuba campaign nearly a generation before and were already set in their ways.

Leyds, in his memoirs, transcribed by M. Kees van Hoek, declared that he had warned Kruger 12 months before war broke out not to expect help from either France, Germany or Russia. France was prepared to look the other way if she could have a free hand in

Algeria and Tunisia, while Russia was planning to concentrate on her Asian interests. Germany drew back from the prospect of a confrontation with the Royal Navy, and the Netherlands, with its colonies scattered across the oceans, was even more vulnerable to sea power.

In the United States opinions on the war were divided. The Irish, German and Dutch minorities were pro-Boer; but the more influential English-speaking circles were flattered by Rhodes' bequest establishing scholarships for Americans and others wishing to go to Oxford. The United States Government was preoccupied with its own adventure in the Philippines.

Of course Kruger had a staunch ally in the Orange Free State. One Treaty of Alliance had been signed in July 1889, and a second in 1897 soon after Steyn became President. These pacts were honoured without question, though in fact a neutral state lying between the Cape and the Transvaal would have been of enormous assistance to Kruger for as long as such neutrality had been honoured.

The President relied as much on the power of the Almighty as on the support of mankind. Perhaps more so. "They aimed thousands of shells and balls at us [during the Jameson Raid]," he told a combined meeting of the two Raads, "while we shot only with rifles; and how wonderfully was the course of the bullets ordered! Three of us fell, while the enemy had hundreds killed and wounded. And who ordered the flight of the bullets? The Lord. He spared us then, to prove to us that He rules all things. The Lord will also protect you now, even if thousands of bullets fly around you." "Fight to the end in the name of God," he would say. "He is our Commander-in-Chief."

In Britain he became a figure as much abhorred as Bonaparte had been a century earlier. And in a way he seemed more deadly, for in Napoleon's time Britain had allies. Now she had none, and her reputation for winning military victories was being seriously eroded by the initial disasters at the beginning of the war inflicted by a handful of farmers.

Kruger himself was too old to fight, but perhaps he could inspire others to do so. And so he became a one-man War Office, rising often at eleven at night after a mere three hours' sleep to read telegrams until four in the morning.

He paid visits to the field too – in January 1900 to urge an attack on Platsrand, the key to Ladysmith, and, after the relief of Ladysmith, to nearby Glencoe where he refused to shake hands with Boers who, he felt, had shown insufficient gallantry when outnumbered three to one. "If I were five years younger I would show you how to fight and win against a force ten times your strength," he complained. To reach Poplar Grove on the western front he travelled by rail from Pretoria to Bloemfontein, and then another 96 miles west by horse wagon. But the horses had scarcely had time to rest before word came that the English had captured nearby Petrusburg and Kruger had to leave. Shells fell close, and at Abrahams Kraal he emerged unscathed from a spectacular cloud of yellow Lyddite smoke as one of Her Majesty's pills, as he called the British shells, burst near by.

Early in March, to avoid capture, Steyn had to leave Bloemfontein, his capital, and move north to Kroonstad. Kruger was there too, and even collaborated in sending a peace offer to Salisbury. But the British wanted surrender rather than negotiations. In May Mafeking was relieved, and a week later the Orange Free State was formally annexed.

On 7 May, as the British drew closer, watched by the Consuls and attachés of eight powers – the United States, the Netherlands, Portugal, France, Russia, Germany, Italy and Belgium – Kruger made his last speech in the Raadsaal. Streamers of black crêpe decked with everlasting flowers had been placed over the chairs of Commandant-General Joubert, who had succumbed to wounds at the age of 66, and of General Johannes Kock, who had died of wounds after the battle of Elandslaagte. Generals Botha and De la Rey were also absent in the field, and so was General Cronje, captured at Paardeberg. Kruger announced that he was sending a mission headed by Abraham Fischer and C. H. Wessels from the Orange Free State, and A. D. Wolmarans from the Transvaal, to tour Europe and America "to petition for the restoration of peace on the basis of the independence of the two Republics".

Kruger had family woes as well as official misfortunes to oppress him. His favourite grandson, Sarel Eloff, had been captured at Mafeking, two of his sons were killed in the war, and another son, Tjaart, died in Pretoria.

Tante Sanna, too, was depressed. As she told a visitor, "You don't know how the war weighs me down in my old age. Many long years ago I came to the Transvaal with my parents in the Great Trek. We were always retreating – as our people have always done from British power and British territory. I could tell you of the hardships we went through, and how we women and children had to crouch night after night in the reeds by the riverside half in the water, to hide ourselves from bloodthirsty Kaffirs who would have committed any kind of atrocity even on white women. When I think now of the constant anxieties and other misfortunes we had, my heart feels sore that this awful, this unnecessary bloodshed between people of our own kinship and race should darken the evening of our life."

But she added that if her husband had been a few years younger he would himself have been Commander-in-Chief at the head of his burghers.

These were almost the same sentiments of dejection and defiance that Queen Victoria knew in the loneliness of her widowhood. Sir Frederick Ponsonby, Keeper of the Privy Purse for 21 years, wrote in his memoirs: "After war had been declared I found the Queen in a bellicose mood after dinner; she seemed all in favour of teaching Kruger a sharp lesson. But later she became lachrymose about the senseless waste of human lives all this might entail." Later still he reported, "The Queen would often break down and cry at the long lists of casualties . . . She seemed impatient of victory and unable to understand why the British Army did not have one great victory and put an end to the war."

But alas it was not going to be that kind of war. It was going to be a guerrilla war of the type that Wellington had encouraged the Spaniards to wage with so much success against Napoleon's generals.

Kruger was not going to be there to see it, for the President could no longer ride and had to keep to the roads. There would be no chance of escape if he met the enemy unexpectedly. And since it would be disastrous if he were to be captured, his presence became a liability as well as an inspiration for those in the field.

The President wrote in his memoirs:

After the relief of Mafeking, when the British troops began to stream into the Republic from every side, it became daily more clear that, in my old age, I should have to leave my wife, my home and all that was dear to me, in order to seek a refuge in the East of the Republic and there commence the struggle anew. The thought of this departure lay heavy upon my heart, the more so as my wife was so old and weak that I could not think of taking her with me. The doctor had declared that such a journey as this would mean death to her; and yet, I felt sure that I should never see her again in this life. The day of our separation after a long and happy marriage came ever closer and closer, and an uncertain future, full of dangers and privations, faced me.

As the British got nearer a special train was prepared for Kruger's escape. It contained a sleeping-car, a dining-car, a conference-car, a bathroom, a kitchen, an office and a communications-room. The day before he left Pretoria, the house was full once more of close friends and relatives who had come to say goodbye. No one outside the inner circle knew that the Government itself was moving from the capital for good.

As the President was preparing to leave, an American schoolboy, Jimmy Smith, and some friends, called to present a Vierkleur woven in the United States and an address signed by hundreds of his schoolfellows in Pennsylvania. In this address the children of Philadelphia, a city which was the first to declare its independence of Great Britain, "sent a message of sympathy to the leader of the people which was now engaged in defending its independence against the same nation". Kruger put the address in his pocket – for he no longer had an office – and took the flag with him. It can be seen to this day in the museum that was once his house. When the deputation had left he called his family into the sitting-room and offered up a prayer. Then he took leave of his wife, alone with her in the bedroom.

In the coach the President and his party drove to Eerste Fabrieken, their most convenient station, and Kruger began his journey into exile, travelling by the line he had worked so hard to construct.

Delagoa Bay was the obvious line of retreat but, for the time being, the Government was established at the mountain village of Machadodorp roughly half-way to the frontier.

On 5 June Pretoria fell, but Kruger sent a message to be read out publicly to each unit in the field. "Flinch not and fall not into unbelief," he said, "for the time is at hand when God's people shall be tried in the fire. And the Beast shall have power to persecute Christ, and those who fall from faith and their Church will know Him not, nor shall they be allowed to enter the kingdom of Heaven. But those who are true to the faith and fight on in the name of the Lord, wearing their glorious crown of victory, they shall be received in the Church of a thousand years, and enter into glory everlasting. Brothers, I beseech you, abandon not your faith, but hold fast by it, and so go forth and fight in the name of the Lord. Look well into your hearts. If cowardice hiding there whispers to you 'Fly' you are blasphemers, for listening to the Tempter you deny your God."

He also pointed out that Lord Roberts, the British Commander, had issued a proclamation that he would now discontinue the concession by which any burgher swearing the oath of allegiance to Queen Victoria would be allowed to return to his farm, as he (Lord Roberts) had found that in some cases they continued to fight in spite of having taken the oath. In future therefore all males over 12 would be taken prisoner and sent to St Helena.

After a month, during which the weather was bitterly cold, Kruger agreed to move to Waterval Onder, a pretty village in a more sheltered site near by on the Eland river. Here he was able to live in the annex of a modest hotel. The official headquarters of the Government remained at Machadodorp and officials travelled over every day to see the President.

After Botha's defeat at Dalmanutha on 13 June in the last set battle of the Boer War, Kruger decided to move further east, to Nelspruit. It was becoming apparent that it would soon no longer be possible to have a permanent headquarters – anywhere.

But Kruger continued to exhort the Boers not to give up. "Some of our burghers who, overpowered by the enemy, were obliged to lay down their arms, I excuse, if they go in again at the first opportunity in order to go on fighting; but, when others go so far as to lay down their arms and take the oath and not return, then that, according to the Scriptures, is a falling away from God, though to be sure, such men will say, even as the Beast, that they believe in the Lord . . . Read this telegram to the officers and burghers at every opportunity."

On 24 July another circular letter from Kruger attacked the spirit of unbelief with quotations from St Matthew, Revelations, and the Apostles Paul and Timothy.

Throughout this time full protocol was maintained, and when Lord Roberts sent two telegrams to Kruger regarding 900 prisoners taken by the Boers who were said by a Norwegian doctor to be in need of medical attention, he was informed that Commandant-General Botha had replied as "the State President does not correspond direct with the British military authorities".

Nelspruit, the new seat of government, was about half-way between Waterval Onder and the frontier, and one of the first acts that Kruger performed after arriving there was to answer the Proclamation which Lord Roberts had made on 1 September annexing the South African Republic (he had long ago annexed the Orange Free State to the south). Kruger argued that the forces of the Republic were still in the field and that therefore the Republic had not been conquered and could not, under the national law, be annexed. He therefore declared the annexation to be "null and void" and added "the people of the South African Republic are now and will remain a free and independent people and refuse to submit to British rule".

On 10 September, a week after having issued this declaration, it was decided to send Kruger on six months' leave to Europe. The news was published in a three-paragraph notice: "Whereas the great age of His Honour the State President renders it impossible for His Honour to continue to accompany the commandos: And whereas the Executive Raad is persuaded that His Honour's invaluable services can still be profitably employed in the interests of the land and people: Now the Executive Raad does hereby resolve to grant His Honour a six months' furlough in order to proceed to Europe and there promote our cause. His place will be filled in accordance with the law by Mr S. W. Burger."

Burger and F. W. Reitz signed the announcement.

President Steyn, who had joined Kruger towards the end of August, agreed to this and he went with Kruger to take a last farewell of him at Hectorspruit, close to the frontier.

On their way they passed just south of a tract of country that stands today as a memorial to the President – the Kruger National Park.

It had been Kruger's idea to set aside some of this Low Veld area, which was fever-country from October to January, in order to save the lion, giraffe, elephant and other game from extinction.

It had not been easy, for the land, though still belonging to the State, had already been surveyed for "farming". True, when Kruger made his proposal in the Raad in May 1897, there was no formal objection, but the next morning Stoffel Tosen, member for the Piet Retief district, thick-set and short-tempered, led a group which buttonholed the President on the stoep of his house.

"Mr President," Tosen began, "we have come to see you about the Wildtuin – the game reserve that you are proposing to declare in the Low Veld." Tosen argued that the voters in his and other con- stituencies would be opposed to it. They used it for winter grazing, and besides, gold and diamonds had been discovered there.

"Gold and diamonds did you say?" the President broke in. "Gold and diamonds are found everywhere it seems. We won't be able to carry on farming, if it goes on like this. And now you want all the game killed off because there is gold?"

"It's not so much that, Mr President. It's our winter grazing that we worry about."

"And your winter shooting," amended the President. "Look here, Stoffel," he said, pointing at him with the stem of his pipe. "You and I and all of us have had our full share of the wild game of South Africa . . . in the Cape, the Free State, Natal, the Transvaal and even beyond. But if, after this latest attack of rinderpeste, we do not close this small portion of the Low Veld, our grandchildren will not know what a kudu, an eland or a lion looks like."

Tosen was prepared to go on arguing; but the President cut him short. "I am surprised at your objection to reserving this little bit of land for the wild animals of our country. True, it has been surveyed for farming and I will give any one of you a freehold farm down there, provided you will go and live on it for just four months of the year – October to January."

But Tosen continued to protest: "Your Honour, where can we go in future with our flocks during the winter?"

"The time will come when you won't be able to go anywhere, so it is just as well to get used to it now. You say that there is gold there, and diamonds. Have we not enough of them? Listen, if you accept my offer you may go along and select your farm and I will postpone the proclamation for a year." But neither Tosen nor any of his supporters accepted, and so the Park that Kruger himself was never to enjoy was founded.

Kruger's departure caused a sensation in faraway Britain. "When the news came that Kruger had bolted," wrote Ponsonby, "I read the telegram to the Queen and she expressed herself freely about his conduct. She said it was disgraceful his going away with all the money that he had squeezed out of the people. I remarked, 'Yes Madam, and leaving Mrs Kruger behind too,' to which she replied, 'I don't know about that. He was probably right.' " So even then the legend of the Kruger millions was already in circulation. And, on 13 September, Roberts was wiring to the Secretary of State for War expressing the hope that Kruger would be stopped from embarking at Lourenço Marques and that any papers and gold that he had would be taken from him.

The rumour probably arose when Smuts, on Roberts' approach to Pretoria, decided that the Government's money would be safer in his own hands than in the vaults of the bank. There was £500,000 in gold bullion and £400 in cash to be realised. Smuts, feeling his way, tried to draw out the cash, and, when the bank refused to part with it, brought along a posse of 50 police, forced the directors to hand over the bullion, took it to the station, loaded it on a special train and in the nick of time sent it on its way. It lasted the Boers for another two years.

Other cash and gold worth rather more than two million was seized from the Post Office and other banks, and from the mines offices which had been providing currency at the rate of nearly £1 million a month, but the bulk of these assets was still in hand after Kruger's departure. The President took only £150,000 with him into exile, the remainder being distributed between creditors, the men in the field and armament manufacturers. Some of these amounts probably went astray, but how much is unlikely ever to be known with certainty.

Nor did Kruger have impressive resources of his own. He had already lent the Government some £40,000 in cash and his main asset – land – was practically unsaleable so that he had to rely on the Government to finance him on what in essence was an official mission. Neither he nor his staff appeared to live in extravagant style. It would have been contrary to his nature to have done so.

In his day the President had been a rich man. His salary (in the days when a suit of clothes cost £2) was £8,000 per year, plus an entertainment (coffee) allowance of £300 per annum.

In 1892 he resisted a salary cut on the ground that if his salary were reduced, then the salaries of officials must also be cut, but in 1893 he reduced the amount voluntarily to £7,000 per annum.

No doubt when a view had to be taken as to whether a given item of expenditure was justifiable, the President was in a fairly strong position. For the Finance Minister was responsible to the Executive Council and not to the Volksraad.

But until 1890 his salary had been only £3,000, and that year he had to ask the Volksraad to lend him £7,000 because he did not wish to borrow from a private bank.

He had many calls on his purse from relatives of his vast family, which included 17 children, and, when he left to go into exile, 156 surviving children, grandchildren and great-grandchildren. He also made substantial contributions to charities and relief funds.

When he died his estate was valued at £35,381 15s 1d plus personal effects worth £100. After debts and administration costs were subtracted, £28,690 8s was left for distribution.

Nor could Kruger look to Leyds for pocket money. Leyds had been appointed Envoy Extraordinary and Minister Plenipotentiary to the Courts of Germany, Russia, Holland, Belgium and Portugal and to the Government of France, but he declared that his total annual budget was no more than £15,000. No money, gold or precious stones were ever sent abroad from South Africa during the war, Leyds averred. Indeed, Leyds had to pay the bill from Creusot, the French armament firm, with South African railway shares (which Chamberlain incidentally claimed had really belonged to the British Government following the re-annexation of the Transvaal).

As Kruger was about to cross into Portuguese territory Commandant Kotze asked him, "Shall I blow up the bridge behind you?"

"No," said the President. "There has been destruction enough already."

They were his last recorded words on the soil of his country.

Chapter 18

Exile

At Ressano Garcia, the first station beyond the frontier, the Portuguese authorities took charge. They were already planning to allow Britain "free and unhampered action" for arms to be imported across Portuguese territory to finish the war in South Africa.

At Lourenço Marques Kruger's train was diverted into a siding, and from there Kruger made his way under cover of darkness to the house of the Transvaal Consul-General, Mr Pott. He had intended to sail to Europe in the next available boat, the *Hertzog*. But the Portuguese were not having that and, next day, the Portuguese Governor, Antonio Machado, arrived and said that he had been instructed to take the President to his own house as guest of the Portuguese Government. "When I showed some hesitation the Governor declared that I must accompany him at once and that if I refused he would have to use force," Kruger recalled. The real Governor of Lourenço Marques, he said, was the British Consul. He it was, according to Kruger, who insisted that Kruger's escort could not set foot in the town unless accompanied by an aide-de-camp, and, even then, they were not to enter into conversation with anyone. Boer friends were not allowed to visit the President nor was he permitted to receive the congratulations of the Boers in the town on the occasion of his 75th birthday.

Not even Magdalena Eloff, wife of Frikkie Eloff the Younger, the President's grandson, was allowed to speak alone with the President.

On 12 October, Kitchener, hoping perhaps to comfort his Sovereign, wrote with unwarranted optimism: "I feel your Majesty will be pleased to hear that the war is almost over, though there are still several bodies of the enemy in the field; they can do very little harm now and are running short of ammunition . . ." (The war continued for a further two years.)

Of Kruger he wrote, "The Governor's nephew told me that he was a most unpleasant guest . . . never appeared except at meal-times." Kitchener added that Kruger recited a long grace before eating and again at the end of the meal, and when the Governor had a musical evening, he sent down word that the noise upset his reading of the Psalms.

Eventually the President's monotonous and frustrating existence was interrupted by the news that the Queen of the Netherlands was sending a warship, the *Gelderland*, to carry him to Europe with freedom to carry out his mission.

He embarked on 21 October even before the vessel had coaled, and was royally received. When the ship arrived at Dar-es-Salaam after a five-day voyage (during which, for the first time in his life, the President was sea-sick), German officials invited him to dinner. But Kruger did not feel like celebrating. Nor did he accept the invitation of French officials at Djibouti where the boat called on 2 November.

The voyage became almost a triumphal procession as ship after ship saluted the *Gelderland*; the passengers of those that came close enough cheered the President. The warship passed through the Suez Canal and into the Mediterranean where it met with a real autumn mistral, with waves breaking over the decks. Kruger's sea-sickness returned, but he was able to be present at a dinner given by the Captain at which the "saloon" was decorated with the Transvaal flag.

Reuters reported that the *Gelderland* had to proceed at half speed as she neared Marseilles, and Dr Leyds, who had planned to board her at sea, was compelled to stay ashore.

The welcome which Kruger received when he landed on French soil was everything that could have been desired. Napoleon could hardly have asked for more.

Houses and cafés on the Canebière, the Quai de la Joliette and the Rue de la République were decked with the Vierkleur. Pleasure yachts were dressed over all and a band paraded in front of the Customs House. The Netherlands Committee for the Independence of the Boers had sent a telegram of greeting. The Prefect of Marseilles called with a message from France's President Loubet.

M. Santarelli, the director of a coalmine, and M. Lanzi, a banker from Ajaccio, offered the ex-President a villa in Corsica. But such entertainments were not for Kruger, and before he had been long ashore, he poured out some of the bitterness in his heart. He spoke to the Marseilles Committee for the Independence of the Boers from underneath an umbrella in his dark coat and black top-hat, which even the friendly *Figaro* noted was far from new, his sore eyes protected behind thick gold-rimmed spectacles. "The war in South Africa has exceeded the limits of barbarism," he said. "I have fought against many barbarous Kaffir tribes in the course of my life; but they are not so barbarous as the English, who have burnt our farms and driven our women and children into destitution, without food or shelter. I hope that God will not abandon the Boer nation. But, if the Transvaal and the Free State are to lose their independence, it shall only happen when both nations have been annihilated with their women and their children.''

His interpreter, Professor van Hamel from Groningen in the Netherlands, found his job far from easy. Kruger's deafness was a handicap and he did not always understand the Professor's Netherlands Dutch. The Professor at one early stage in their acquaintanceship confused Kruger's "die zwart" (the blacks) with "het zwaard" (the sword) with unfortunate results. And it was much easier to follow the President when he was making a speech than when he spoke in private conversation.

The English community in Marseilles tried to detract from the importance of the occasion, Kruger recalled, by throwing coppers into the street from the windows of an hotel, but the crowd reacted by storming the hotel and the management had to call for police protection. The only disappointment for Kruger's supporters was, according to the local press, that the President's lower lip appeared to be very much less prominent than had appeared in cartoons, though to be sure it was partially obscured by his whiskers.

A special train had been provided to bring the President from Marseilles to Paris. At Lyon, where there was a halt, the Mayor presented him with a medal. At Dijon, where he spent the night, the whole city was illuminated and a salute of guns was fired as he drove to his hotel.

In Paris the newspapers noted that the French President, Emile Loubet, had sent M. Crozier, Director of the Protocol Department of the French Foreign Office, to receive the President of the South African Republic, and an armed unit of the Garde Républicaine presented arms for his benefit at the Gare de Lyon. Kruger drove to the Hotel Scribe, on the Boulevard des Capucines near the Opéra, in an open landau drawn by ceremonially decorated horses. The English believed he had chosen the hotel as his residence partly because it was hard by the well-known Old England shop and a number of other British-owned stores. Edmond Rostand, author of *Cyrano de Bergerac*, wrote a poem in Kruger's honour, and a street in north-east Paris was named Rue du Transvaal.

A guard of 20 policemen and ten men of the Garde Républicaine protected the British Embassy in the Rue du Faubourg St-Honoré, which, it was suspected, might receive the attentions of Boer supporters.

That afternoon the French President sent his State carriage to fetch Kruger for a meeting at four o'clock, and came to the top of the stairs both to receive his guest and to say farewell. But their interview lasted for a bare ten minutes.

For while the imagination of the peoples of Europe had been fired by the resistance of a handful of Boers to the might of the British Empire, and while Emile Zola, amongst others, might be prepared to sign the Boer "Appeal to the Nations" in favour of settling the Boer War by international arbitration, the attitude of governments was far more reserved.

Kruger realised this when he went on the same day after his interview with Loubet to the Quai d'Orsay to see Théophile Delcassé, France's Minister for Foreign Affairs. Kruger was already very tired but, as he glanced round the Minister's richly appointed study, he realised from the way the conversation was going that there was very little chance of getting any decisive action out of the French Government. And Leyds described how weariness spread over the President's face as his sturdy hands fumbled feebly for the top-hat which he had put down next to him, as, bent with age, he rose to take his leave.

Kruger was no more fortunate in his approach to Germany.

After visiting Brussels, Namur and Liège, he crossed the Belgian frontier and sent a telegram to the Kaiser which read: "On treading German soil, I hasten to transmit to Your Majesty the sentiments of friendship and great respect which I entertain for Your Majesty."

It was not enough. The Kaiser had already been advising Edward VII how to win the war. Lord Gough reported on 1 December to the Marquis of Salisbury that the German Secretary in Paris had already informed Kruger on 29 November that a visit to Berlin would be inopportune. Kruger had decided nevertheless to come and had reserved a suite of 25 rooms at an hotel. "The German Government," said Gough, "are said to be vexed at his insistence."

So Herr von Tsichirschky, the Imperial Minister at Luxembourg, was sent to the Dom Hotel, Cologne, to head off the Boer delegation and tell them that His Majesty the Emperor regretted that because of arrangements already made, he was not then in a position to receive the President of the South African Republic. Tsichirschky successfully accomplished this mission on 3 December and Kruger then retreated to the Netherlands. A visit would indeed have been inopportune as the German Minister in Peking had just been murdered and Britain and Germany were planning a joint expedition in retaliation.

Leyds himself had been operating under considerable difficulty. The British Ambassador in Paris, Sir Henry Howard, had orders not to receive him, and British ambassadors elsewhere (notably in

Berlin and The Hague) were instructed to do their best to make sure that he was not formally acknowledged anywhere else. In Russia van der Hoeven, the Chargé d'Affaires for the South African Republic, was denied an official invitation to the wedding of the Tsar's sister, Olga, to the Duke of Oldenburg, and was able to attend only because the Tsar when he heard of his exclusion sent him a personal invitation – to which the British Embassy could not object.

From then on Kruger realised that there was little more he could do. He paid his respects to the Dutch Queen at The Hague and thanked her for her kindness in sending the *Gelderland* to Lourenço Marques. He stayed for a while in Amsterdam, suffered and recovered from a severe attack of bronchitis at The Hague, and moved on to Utrecht where both his eyes were operated on by Professor Snellen. He spent the following summer at Hilversum, first at the Villa Casa Cara and later at the Villa Djemnah, 46 Hooge Naarderweg.

We see him at this time through the eyes of a Mrs Emil Luden who wrote a sympathetic article in the *Pall Mall Magazine*:

Almost every child in England will have by this time drawn Kruger on the flyleaf of his atlas. The tall chimneypot hat, the flat "applepie" boots, the short trousers, the Bible, the long pipe, the oyster eyes, the Newgate frill, the flattened hair, are as well known as Mr Chamberlain's eyeglass, Sir William Harcourt's chin [it had several rolls under it], or Bismarck's three hairs [their position reflected his mood], and lend themselves as readily to elementary caricature.

Uncouth of feature, deaf, half blind, ungainly of body, cursed with all the conscious bighanded awkwardness of the uncultured, ineloquent, stumbling in harsh gutturals through a bastard "taal" that would (O ye gods!) murder a seraphic whisper, his personality, his ego, triumphs over the commonplace flesh, the slop-shop clothes, the offending spittoon, and sings a grand song of exultation above their ugliness.

And yet people have met him at dinners and receptions and gone away unimpressed. To the superficial "the President" is a disappointment. He does not dilate on the subject of the day, or "go in" for diplomatic small talk. He takes a polite but absent interest in wreaths, and the choral singing of societies. On his journeys lately he has even appeared perfectly resigned when the provincial eloquence of municipally surrounded mayors was hurled breathlessly from decorated platforms at screaming engines and ruthlessly departing railway carriages.

He has come to Europe to do work – hard, deep work. The need of obtaining arbitration consumes him to the detriment of every other interest. Even the flattering adulation of crowds counts for nothing in his eyes, save as the voice of a frozen river that may in time battle and churn and escape beyond the ice of cautious governments and kings. The justice, the "fair play" principles of arbitration appeal to him so strongly that he cannot understand why England will not realise the harm that she is working for herself by refusing this neutral searchlight.

"Will no one arbitrate?" he cried to me the other day at The Hague. "Will no one give us a fair hearing, a chance of defending ourselves? We may have done wrongly; we have had our faults, our weaknesses; we declared this war, but our hands were forced – we can prove it! Let someone judge between this England and ourselves. Let someone judge!"

"But England will not hear of arbitration, President," I said, "and we don't want a European war!"

"How can justice bring about a war?" he demanded fiercely. "We ask for light! We want the verdict of a neutral judge! We want justice! Justice!"

And that is part of the power of the man: he does not speak to an audience, nor choose his words with a view to effect – they well up in him spontaneously from the depths of his stricken heart. He is the heavy, clanging bell that voices the soul of a people. He will have lied in his time, like the rest of us – perhaps more, perhaps less – but when he pleads for "die Land", when his great rough voice softens and grows like a woman's who mourns for her sick child, he rings true with the heart-throbs of his fellow-countrymen.

Then suddenly he cast his hands from each other as if they were rending earthly difficulties. "But the Lord will help us!" he cried, "the Lord will help us! In the end we shall win! Be sure of it: we shall win! I do not know how or when, but it is a certainty to me we shall win."

Every little advantage or repulse of the Boer commandos is looked upon by him as a necessary link in the chain to victory. He bows humbly before what he considers the chastisements of God (and, poor old fellow! he must have thought that the Boers have been pretty wicked lately), and never gloats over the discomfiture of his enemies. The little scraps of war news that keep our excitement simmering between the morning and evening papers neither exalt nor depress him. The war is in the hands of God. It is the duty of the Boers to fight – as it is his duty now to wander from land to land seeking "justice". All are vessels of God, to be used at

His pleasure. Many yet may have to fall in battle – many more may perish homeless and brokenhearted. He too may die blind and helpless in a land that he knows not. Good – it is God's will, and the triumph of Right and God's victory will come in His own good time.

But he suffers! – Heavens! how he suffers! – caged in gaudy hotel drawing-rooms; doomed to listen to endless speeches which he cannot hear, to receive long strings of useless persons; to "sit up and give paws", as the Dutch say, when his stormy heart is breaking and his old body is longing for "Tante Sanna" and rest. He seeks "justice", and is treated to sugarplums and toastings; promises, deeds, and they send him floral offerings.

"Don't you think it awful," I asked, "to be smothered with flowers and ribbons like an 'Easter ox', when your whole soul is aching with sadness?"

"I care nothing for the flowers!" he blurted out. "Nothing! nothing! nothing! The people who send them mean well, and I am grateful, but I care nothing for them – nothing!" He threw his hands out from him in a kind of horror; one could see how the festive, the tawdry side of his visit to Europe, wearied and depressed him.

Though he fought with lions, battled with natives, struggled fiercely with all the countless dangers of a vast new land, his tempestuous life in Africa has ever rolled on freely, like a storm-cloud, gathering strength and character as it went. Till, at last, his word there became law – a young country grew up at his feet, and the "folk" around him began to change into a nation with an ambitious future of possibilities before them. But here – in Europe! Think of it, and pity him!

His photographs make him older than he really looks. The homely, coarse features and the untidy beard force themselves upon the consideration – and the expression, the essence of the man, has fled before the ordeal of the camera.

Even at first sight the impression one gets of him is not pre-possessing: a large, heavy face and two great hands on a mass of dark clothing. He does not rise from his ponderous chair unless absolutely necessary. One can see easily how irksome bodily movement has become to this valiant old fighter of battles. He looks up sharply when a stranger enters the room, then his head sinks on his chest again. He has never cultivated "company manners", and his thoughts are all-absorbing. His hands are quite motionless, held finger-tips against his big loose body.

A spittoon, munificently constructed for the contributions of the absent-minded, stands by his chair; a bottle of mineral water is generally near him. There is something very kindly in his eyes when he gives you his hand; one feels that happiness and good fortune would soon mellow him into geniality.

He is painfully deaf, yet those who are used to talking to him do not raise their voices greatly. He understands English only fairly well, and does not care to talk it. Still I find that he hears my English better than my Dutch; but that may be because my Dutch is still somewhat broken.

He speaks the "taal" by preference, and it is a most difficult language to understand. In fact, I believe that if true progress is simply a justification of the old theory of "the survival of the fittest", the "taal" must go under, whatever the future of the Republics may be.

His thoughts form slowly, and are born at last in abrupt travail, throes of words and distress of gesture that are eloquent of passion. For his hands are only motionless when his tongue is passive. As he begins to speak the finger-tips part from each other with a wrench. He throws imaginary weights behind him, strikes the arms of his chair, and drops his hands heavily on his knees. Then, when he has cast his thought forth as only a strong man can, his finger-tips seek their fellows again, his eyes close, and the mask of abstraction is drawn down over the inscrutable face.

"Oh! don't you often wish yourself back there?" I asked him, "especially when you get nothing but feasts and fine words in Europe?"

He looked at me for a moment, and a great pain came into his eyes. "I am old," he said sorrowfully. "I could not go with the commandos, as can President Steyn. I may be of some use here."

I had told him a little while before how sorry I was for "Tante Sanna", surrounded as she is by foes and all the dreary ghosts of a younger and a happier time.

"I am sorry for her too," he answered, with the characteristic violent movement of his hands. "I have deep sorrow for her! But I have far, far more sorrow for 'die Land'. My wife has her children – six are with her still – and the English are kind to her, they have left her in her own home. But 'die Land! die Land!'" and then his voice had died down suddenly, and I could not look at him for the tears in my eyes.

"Two of my sons are dead," he continued, flinging his momentary weakness away from him, and speaking spontaneously for the first time, as if to cover his emotion. "They died on the battlefield.

Two are prisoners, one in St Helena, one in Ceylon. I believe that two more are dead also, for I have not heard from them for nearly two months, and I know they were in the thick of the fight. But 31 sons and grandsons of mine are on the field yet. But I could not go with the commandos – I could not."

The long lids fell over the tired sick eyes for a moment, and then he said: "I have not heard from the wife for the last 16 days, but she has six of the children with her, she is not to be pitied – at least, not as 'die Land' is!"

And then the prayer of his heart, the ache that runs through all his musings, burst from him again with an exceeding bitter cry: "A fair hearing! if they would only give us a fair hearing! Will no one take up our cause? Will no one help us! Justice! I ask for justice! We are a little folk, but we have made great steps – we have given much."

But, as I have said, one must see the man – one must hear him speak – to get at the heart of his words, the passionate agony of his sorrow. I have tried to translate literally, repeating all that I remember of his conversation to myself in Dutch, and then writing it down word for word in English. But to my bitter disappointment the translation is often jerky where the original was grand – unfinished and petulant when I would make it impressive. English somehow sounds thin and tinkering after the "taal": not that that hideous mode of speech is in any way equal to good Anglo-Saxon, but I expect that Kruger would make another choice of words if he spoke in English, and I unfortunately am not clever enough to divine what they might be.

There is another side of his character that I have hardly touched upon – the quiet home side. And by "home side" I mean those traits and peculiarities that are best remembered in "the piping times of peace".

Although – except for the snobberies of feminine ambition – he will never have been a coveted guest at a ladies' tea-party, he has a quiet sense of humour that endears him to many, and yet has sometimes cost him the friendship of the hypersensitive; he can say witty and sharp things without moving a muscle of his face, even that tell-tale feature the mouth being almost entirely under his command. I remember a young fellow telling me how at one of the famous Pretoria audiences, where the President and his colleagues sat against the wall in a row and smoked in a heavy collective silence, the old man had suddenly turned to the shrinking young stranger and asked him to find a newspaper and read it aloud to the assembly. But every subject was objected to, and rejected with scorn, before the miserable reader had got through the first lines of it; and at last, when he laid aside the journal with the determination of despair, the President had glanced at him with twinkling eyes and bidden him hurry away home to look up something worth reading about.

The "beautiful" is the "unknown God" to him, at whose altar he has never learned to worship. Amsterdam is an artistic medley of ancient gables, high bridges, old-world corners, and drowsy, tree-shadowed canals. Yet when he visited it a few weeks ago the only record of praise he left behind him that has reached my ears was admiration of a heraldic design cut out of a turnip and placed upon his dinner-table. This must have so delighted the old gentleman that the vandal cook who perpetrated the abomination got a special compliment when he should have been taken out and shot under the shadow of Rembrandt's "Nacht Wacht".

His intimate knowledge of the Scriptures is marvellous. The Bible is his only book of recreation and refreshment. Friends have told me that when translating his speeches into English (at the laying of foundation-stones or other public ceremonies) it is almost impossible even for a "Dominie" to keep pace with his rapid quotations. A friend of mine once undertook to be his interpreter, but stuck hopelessly in a lengthy chapter of Isaiah. So he begged an English clergyman who was standing by to assist him; but the parson plunged into a perfect mire of half-remembered texts, and floundered pitifully, till the President slapped him on the shoulder with a dour shake of his head, a good-natured twitching about his mouth, and a "Man! man! and you fancied that you knew your Bible!"

But Kruger in the future! What is in store for him? Will he grow stone blind and deaf, and linger through years of angry second childhood, clamouring for "justice"? Will he, like Moses, die within sight of the promised land – with the joy-bells of arbitration pealing in his ears, and a "free" purified Transvaal stretching out before him? Will he return to Pretoria, a President again (and he would tell you that with God "all things are possible"), but one who has learned bitter lessons, as he has given hard blows – a President with a terrible past, and a strengthened belief in the earthly punishments of God?

We cannot tell. But when, in after years, the grain still grows in dark blood patches above the fattened African soil, when the plough turns up white bones and dirt-choked guns and buttons, and the children ask, "Why was the war? Who made it?" may the mothers tell his story tenderly to the little ones – may the fathers forgive him his errors and his weaknesses for the sake of the love that he bore for "die Land" and the faith that he had in its strength!

At Hilversum he received the heaviest blow of his life – a telegram telling him that his wife had died on 21 July. Wolmarans (a member of the Boer delegation which had toured Europe in the hope of securing active intervention against Britain) invited him to stay at Scheveningen, where he retired almost completely from the world, searching his Bible for words of hope. "My profound sorrow was consoled by the thought that the separation was only temporary and could not last long," Kruger said in his memoirs. In December 1901 he moved back to Utrecht and the news from South Africa, particularly with the capture of Lord Methuen, was rather better. Kruger's confidence was still unshaken when peace negotiations began. It was up to the generals in the field, he said, to decide whether and how, under the stress of circumstances, they wished to retract their previous resolutions to fight on.

Camille Huysmans, who, more than 40 years later was to become Prime Minister of Belgium, brought Kruger the news that the Boer generals had signed a peace agreement shortly before midnight on 31 May 1902. Kruger broke down at the news, but cast no blame on those responsible: "I applied to the Generals the text in the Bible 2 Corinthians Chapter viii Verse 3: 'For to their power, I bear record, yea, and beyond their power they were willing of themselves.'

"So far as I myself am concerned, I will not consent to lose courage because the peace is not such as the burghers wished it. For quite apart from the fact that the bloodshed and the fearful sufferings of the people of the two Republics are now ended, I am convinced that God does not forsake His people even though it may appear so."

That autumn he saw three of the generals, Louis Botha, Jacobus De la Rey and Christiaan de Wet, both before and after their visit to London, and they dined with him on the evening of his 77th birthday. They too had failed to enlist the Kaiser's sympathy for their appeal "to the civilised world" on behalf of the widows and orphans of the Boer War.

As winter drew on his doctors advised Kruger to seek a warmer climate. He had hesitated to go south before, feeling that he should not seek comfort for himself while so many of his countrymen were suffering the hardships of war. But now he could go with a clear conscience.

His doctors chose the sheltered resort of Menton on the French Côte d'Azur, or Riviera as it was then called.

There Emily Hobhouse, who had done so much to improve the conditions in the concentration camps (to which the women and children of the Boers had been sent as part of Kitchener's "scorched earth" policy) came to see the old man. She wrote, "Our talk was not long. I saw that already his mind was elsewhere and the world had ended for him . . . He wanted so much to know if I had seen his wife, and when I told him that I had not been allowed to visit Pretoria before her death, he seemed too disappointed to make further effort. The little modern French villa was a cheap and incongruous setting to that mediaeval and puritanical figure."

Kruger spent one more summer in the Netherlands, and paid his last visit to Menton in October of that year. In late May of 1904 he settled in Number 17 Villas Prierriers (sometimes known as Villas Dubochet) on the quai at Clarens on the Lake of Geneva.

His strength was failing and his housekeeper, his secretary and his manservant, Happé, slept within call. The Eloff family, Dr Heymans and the Revd Meerburg, his spiritual comforter, stayed nearby. When he first arrived at Clarens Kruger made a short tour of the neighbourhood but afterwards he kept to the house, and the fishermen, as they rowed past in their boats, could sometimes see him wearing a white panama straw hat, sunning himself on the balcony of his bedroom. Then suddenly, though it was July in the height of summer, he contracted pneumonia. In less than a week he was dead.

Before his last illness he sent a letter of reconciliation to Louis Botha, who had written to tell him about the launching of a new political party, Het Volk, which would guide the political future of the Afrikaners.

Perhaps the style of the letter is less trenchant and less Biblical than the President's normal mode of address. Perhaps Dr Leyds helped with a draft. But certainly the President signed the document. It ran:

Dear General

It is a great privilege to be able to acknowledge the receipt of your cablegram and letter of 23 and 24 May respectively conveying to me the greetings of the Congress held from 23 to 25 May in Pretoria.

In all the sorrow and grief that has befallen me, these greetings have made me deeply grateful. And with all my heart I thank those who have spared a thought for the aged State President during their deliberations about the present and the future; by doing so they show that they have not forgotten the past.

For he who desires to build a future dare not neglect the past.

Seek, therefore, all that is good and beautiful in the past, build on it your ideal, and strive to realise that ideal for the future.

It is true much of what has been built is now destroyed, despoiled and ruined; but through singleness of purpose and unity of strength what now lies scattered can still be restored.

I am thankful to see that this unity and this concord prevail amongst you.

Do not forget that grave warning that lies in the words "Divide and rule"; never let these words apply to the South African nation. Then our people and our language will endure and prosper.

What I myself shall live to see of this, rests with God. Born under the British flag, I do not wish to die under it. I have learnt to accept the bitter thought of death as a lone exile in a foreign land, far from my kith and kin, whose faces I am not likely to see again; far from the soil of Africa upon which I am not likely ever to set foot again; far from the country to which I devoted my whole life in an effort to open it up for civilisation and in which I saw my own nation grow.

But this grief will be softened if I may cherish the belief that the work once begun, continues; for then the hope and the expectation that the work will end well will give me strength. So be it.

From the depths of my heart I greet you and my people.

Milner gave permission for the tough old warrior's body to be brought home and buried there in a grave next to Tante Sanna. And so Kruger came south once more, as his family, perhaps, had been carried, a century or more before in a Dutch vessel – only this was a special one lent by the Queen of the Netherlands. Back from the cold grey skies of Europe, for it was November, across the Equator and into the spring sun of the Cape. From there a special train carried the President's body north again – across the burning karroo over which the trekkers had once passed, over battlefields once red with dust, past the diamond-fields and the gold-mines, and so to the peace and shade of Pretoria. The driver had orders to halt during the night whenever he saw a light so that groups who had travelled across the veld and wanted to catch a glimpse of their hero's coffin should not be disappointed.

The world took many different views of Kruger's life and times. Vienna's *Allgemeine Zeitung* said, "His death removes one of the founders and one of the destroyers of the South African Republic." The *Fremdenblatt*, published in the same capital, wrote, "Only a peasant, but a great peasant whose name history will preserve in honour." The *Petit Parisien* wrote: "England has received the news of the death of ex-President Kruger with dignity. She has spoken of her unrelenting foe in correct terms and she has respectfully saluted her vanquished enemy whom she had never ceased to admire. Actuated by sentiments that do him honour, Lord Milner at Johannesburg has placed the British flag above his residence at half-mast, showing thereby that he does reverence to the patriotism of the ex-President of the Transvaal Republic. The spirit of this demonstration was similar to that which dictated President Loubet's telegram to the daughter of the grand old man who has just passed away. Such acts are understood by all those whose hearts beat with high and generous feeling."

The French paper was probably too kind. *Blackwood's Magazine* moralised predictably: "His was not an amiable career. For many years he waged civil war against all those of his countrymen who hindered his policy. He fought Schoeman with as persistent an energy as he afterwards fought the English."

Littell's Living Age commented that death found him not the ruler of his State nor even the citizen: "He has died in exile, leaving his country in subjection to the foreigner and its lonely and silent farms, won from savage nature and savage man at a cost few modern Englishmen would face, slowly emerging from their ruins. His wife had died with the enemy bivouacked in the capital where once he had governed the Republic, and he has died with that enemy in possession." The paper went on to suggest that Kruger should have "trusted the British proletariat on the Rand. It was the object of the financial party (on the Rand) to aggravate a social quarrel. The war meant the capture of a political movement by a financial movement: the success of capitalism in appropriating and directing to its own ends the forces of racial discontent and chagrin. President Kruger ought to have divided this alliance. Nobody pretends that a State is bound to distribute its franchise among immigrants; but it would clearly have been a wise and far-seeing policy to have disarmed the political movement, and thereby prevented the large interests from concentrating in one attack on his State all the restless and exasperated and predatory elements in this shifting and difficult community."

Compared with this, *The Times* obituary seems very unenterprising, although it stretched across four and a half columns of fine print. Its conclusion was that: "The total collapse which characterises the last act in the drama of his life must of necessity prevent his figure from living in the annals of history with that halo of the heroic about it which is readily accorded by a generous posterity to the unfortunate."

The *Cape Times* wrote: "To sit indomitably on the safety valve may be the highest bravery but it inevitably led to disaster."

L'Indépendence Belge wrote: "One would have preferred to see him die full of glory amid the din of battles surrounded by his comrades in arms to have seen him linked with his country's fortunes to the last and conquered with her, instead of seeking oblivion in the old world."

But the era of Queen Victoria and the Boer War had passed away. There were many other projects afoot. The French National Bastille day on 14 July 1904 had, *The Times* noted, been celebrated in Paris this year with more enthusiasm than usual. The presence of the Bey of Tunis might, *The Times* correspondent suggested, have been one reason why Parisians had "spared no pains to adorn their houses".

Then the Viceroy of Canton appeared to be evading his obligations with regard to the recruiting of Chinese labourers for South Africa, by raising technical objections such as his contention that Hong Kong was not a treaty port.

The Dalai Lama of Tibet had recently been recalcitrant, and had shown "gross disrespect to the Government of the King and Emperor" (Edward VII), and an expedition to Lhasa was being organised.

Nevertheless, a French evening paper, *Le Temps*, found space enough to make a prophecy that came close to the truth: "South Africa will never witness the reconstitution of the peasant particularism of the Boer Republics," said the anonymous writer. "The truth is that a mixed nationality is in course of formation – namely, that of the Afrikanders: furthermore, it is for the nationality, and not for the Empire, that Chamberlain, Milner, Roberts and Kitchener have laboured; and finally, sooner or later, that great continent will shake off the yoke of a distant metropolis and will realise the formula of Africa not for the Africans, but for the Afrikanders."

Appendix

Kruger as Negotiator

When Kruger and Dr Leyds met Rhodes and Lord Loch on 6 March 1890 at Blignaut's Port on the Orange river, the future of Kruger's Republic was at stake. Kruger wanted a route across Swaziland to the Indian Ocean. The British were not prepared to agree unless the Transvaal surrendered its commercial independence by joining a customs union devised on British terms.

Here we see Kruger the negotiator, the man who makes most use of poor cards and conceals as far as possible where his real strength will be.

Kruger opened with a statement that could well have perplexed the most experienced British negotiator: "I look upon this meeting as official but also as of a confidential nature. *I have no definite authority from the Volksraad to enter into any agreement*, but I should like to speak openly and freely with you here, as I have done in times past with Sir Hercules Robinson. Our talk will be confidential, and your Excellency *must not be offended at anything I may say* and you will, I hope, talk openly yourself. Our utterances will not, I hope, be considered as strictly official."

Thus, although the meeting was to be "official", Kruger's utterances were not to be strictly official, nor could he be bound to enter into any agreement.

Loch, understandably, wanted at least the prospect of a settlement. He said: "I quite concur in your Honour's view that this meeting should be of a private and confidential nature; at the same time I think it would be desirable that you should freely express your own views on the matters we discuss, so that we may arrive at some understanding which will serve as a foundation for an agreement to be entered into between Her Majesty's Government and that of the South African Republic, as it is desirable that there should be some finality in these matters."

Kruger, as usual, picked up only that part of his opponent's statement which interested him. "I quite agree that there should be a definite expression of views upon all matters of policy which we discuss, but I do not want the open discussion that takes place to appear in the newspapers," he said. To which Loch countered: "I am of the same opinion. The notes that are being taken are not for publication, but only in order that I may have a record of what has passed, and are only for my own information.

"It may now be convenient if I suggest the topics for discussion and the order in which they should be taken."

Here Kruger stepped in quickly: "The chief point is the compromise proposed to me by the English Government." (This was a suggestion for joint control of Swaziland by Britain and the South African Republic.)

But Loch headed Kruger away from this: "I think that what has been causing anxiety to Her Majesty's Government, and also to myself, are the reports which have reached me of a trek into Mashonaland from the South African Republic, and I propose that this should be the first point to be discussed. The next point I would propose for discussion would be the future of Swaziland; then we might discuss the desire, which I understand has been expressed by your Honour, for communication through Swaziland and Amatongaland with the sea." The discussion continued:

KRUGER: I am pleased with the subjects which you have proposed for discussion, but they appear to me to all form part of the same question, and I do not see how they can be discussed separately.

LOCH: We cannot discuss two or three subjects at once. The first point is that upon which all the other questions depend. After these questions are discussed I shall refer to other matters which are of Imperial interest in South Africa and of interest to South Africa generally.

I propose first of all to refer to the rumoured trek into Mashonaland, and relying upon the good faith of the Transvaal Government and the assurances I have received from your Honour, I should be glad to learn whether I may say that the Government of the South African Republic will hold themselves responsible for any trek into Mashonaland from that country.

Kruger replied that he had issued a proclamation forbidding any trek to the north and that there was no organised movement in that direction.

LOCH: The proclamation which was issued by the Government of the South African Republic referred specially to a trek said to be organised by Mr Bowler.

KRUGER: The proclamation in question made special mention of Mr Bowler, because I heard that he was trying to induce my people to join him in an expedition northwards, and I was afraid he might succeed.

LOCH: From information I have received it appears that a certain number of men who were anxious to go on a trek into Mashonaland did not consider that they were bound by the terms of this proclamation. Would it not be better to issue a proclamation in more general terms?

KRUGER: It would be *ridiculous* to issue such a proclamation at present, because I am informed by my officers in the Transvaal that there is not the slightest necessity for it. Should, however, any movement of the nature indicated be brought to my notice I will issue a very strong proclamation on the subject.

LOCH: If any such movement should assume a form likely to lead to an incursion into Matabeleland, would your Honour send a Commissioner into the district where such movement was reported to be taking place, to take means to prevent, by force if necessary, the proposed trek?

KRUGER: I cannot make such a promise today, because I do not know what the time or occasion may be. If the compromise which I proposed to Her Majesty's Government becomes an established fact I would agree; then we would stand together and carry out a definite policy.

LOCH: In pressing this point upon your Honour I wish to establish a good understanding between the two Governments, and to ensure that it may be founded upon a true basis; but your Honour's hesitation in giving the assurance I ask for places difficulties in the way of a good understanding.

KRUGER: I think your Excellency's proposal goes a little too far; it is very little use for a man to struggle when his hands are tied.

LOCH: Yes, but the point is that your Honour must forego all claims to the territory to the north-west of the South African Republic, which has been declared to be within the sphere of British influence, and a charter in respect of that country given to a company. Her Majesty's Government would view it as a very serious breach of good will towards England, if your Honour refused to give the assurance which I ask for.

KRUGER: In the first place I have a treaty with Lobengula, which is of earlier date than that with Her Majesty's Government, and if reason and fairness are to be the test I am prepared to contend that my claims to Matabeleland and Mashonaland are superior to those of Her Majesty's Government. But rather than have any difficulty or dispute with Her Majesty's Government, I would undergo a loss. But I want fairness. I will never be unthankful for what I have received. Your Excellency will remember that the Transvaal was at one time annexed by Her Majesty's Government, owing to certain reports which they had received. Afterwards, finding that there had been a mistake, Her Majesty gave back my land to me, and I am not unthankful for that. Her Majesty's Government has treated me with kindness by extending my border, and has also given me friendly assurances that my policy respecting the Delagoa Bay railway will not be interfered with. Her Majesty's Government has also been ready to make an alteration in the convention with regard to Indians and coolies. And for all these reasons I cannot but feel grateful, and nothing would induce me to have a dispute with Her Majesty's Government; I would rather bear a loss and give up anything. I would rather that any differences should be settled by arbitration. Under these circumstances, and seeing the desire of Her Majesty's Government to have Matabeleland and Mashonaland, and also in view of the concession lately granted to the English by Lobengula, it appeared to me that an opportunity arose for encouraging the prosperity of South Africa – I supporting Her Majesty's Government upon my side, and Her Majesty's Government giving me the rights I ask for in Swaziland, and a sea-border on the east. This policy of mine met with the general approval of my people as soon as I explained it.

LOCH: By the proclamation you issued you desired, I presume, to prevent any trek into Mashonaland.

KRUGER: Certainly, that was my object. Any such trek would prove a great stumbling-block in the way of united action by the two Governments.

LOCH: Therefore, I do not see why your Honour should not go a step further in the way I have suggested to prevent any movement northwards.

KRUGER: The one hand must wash the other. If I wash your hand you must wash mine. I want assurances from your Excellency also.

LOCH: You have already given the assurance by the proclamation which has been published, but you have not gone quite far enough. The proclamation leaves it open for the trek to go on.

Kruger then hinted that he might not be able to stop his burghers going north unless the British strengthened his hand by supporting expansion elsewhere. He also offered to provide Afrikaner volunteers for Rhodes "expeditions".

KRUGER: I think there is a misunderstanding. If the compromise which I proposed to Her Majesty's Government were adopted, I would then be in a position to oppose forcibly any such trek. You already have my assurance that I will give no support to anything of the kind, but my hands will be strengthened if my policy is supported by Her Majesty's Government; if it is not, it may lead to the shedding of many people's blood. Your Excellency would find it difficult to give a guarantee that people from the Cape Colony would not trek to the north; and so in the same way I cannot be responsible for what people in the Transvaal may do in that way.

LOCH: If such a trek from the Cape Colony with hostile feelings to the South African Republic were to be contemplated, I should take good care to stop it, by force if necessary. If your Honour will assure me that you will do your best to prevent a trek into Matabeleland, we can go on to the next point. Supposing a party of ten or 15 men from one part of the country, and another party from another part, were believed to be organising on the frontier, I should consider that the Government of the South African Republic would be bound to put a stop to it, if it were brought to their notice.

KRUGER: I will give this assurance: I will take note of what is going on in my country, and if I see any sign of a movement northwards, I will oppose it; but I think I may say that there need be no apprehension of any such movement. If any of my people were to trek into Matabeleland, they would be interfering with my policy of friendly action with Her Majesty's Government, and I should be the sufferer; if I approved such a thing I should be cutting my own throat.

In the event of my proposed policy becoming an established fact, my position would be this: While I will not allow my burghers to go into Matabeleland, I will tell them that they are at liberty to volunteer to help Mr Rhodes to carry out any expedition he may wish to make into that country.

MR RHODES: In the one case, for instance, if I were drowning in a river your Honour would hold a stick out to me from the bank; but, in the other case, you would jump into the river at the risk of your life to help me.

KRUGER: I now go further than I did in my first letter on the subject. I now say that I will support Her Majesty's Government in Matabeleland with all the influence I have.

Secondly, in case it should be necessary to resort to arms in Matabeleland, I could offer inducements to my burghers to go in and help Mr Rhodes if he wants them. My men are not better soldiers than other men, but they would be useful in a bushy country like Matabeleland. Mr Rhodes must not think that my policy is to stand aside; it is to help him as much as I can.

Having gained nothing much so far Governor Loch turned to what Kruger had originally wanted to debate.

"I would now propose to discuss the question of Swaziland," Loch began. "Before we enter upon the subject, I think it right to state that Her Majesty's Government feel it would be impossible to submit to Parliament, with any chance of success, a proposal which involved the Government of the *whites in Swaziland* by any form of government not supported by the *joint Governments* interested in the administration of that country." (This was because *both* Governments had guaranteed Swazi independence.)

But Kruger argued that one authority over Swaziland was enough. He insisted that if a "civilised" government were to be established in Swaziland it should be provided by the South African Republic.

KRUGER: With regard to the independence of the Swazis, I do not recede from the position I have always held. But I do not see how it will be possible to have a dual government over the whites. So long as Swaziland is able to govern itself, the independence of the Swazis would remain intact, but the government of the whites should be left in the hands of the South African Republic which includes three sides of Swaziland. A government by the two Governments would be impossible, because the laws of the two Governments are different.

LOCH: If the government were carried on on the present lines, viz., one Commissioner to represent each of the two Governments, and one to represent the Natives who would have no vote, the government would practically rest with Her Majesty's Government, and that of the South African Republic; and a Court would be established which would administer Roman-Dutch law.

KRUGER: How can two great farmers live together in the same house?

LOCH: We start from the point that we both admit that the independence of the Swazis must be maintained. Her Majesty's Government are not prepared to hand over the administration of their affairs to the South African Republic, or to take it themselves. Therefore they propose that the system of government which has been carried on for some months should be enlarged and extended, and *that a proclamation giving effect to this proposal should be issued by the Queen of Swaziland.* Her Majesty's Government could hardly be asked to accept your Honour's suggestion that the Government of Swaziland should be handed over to the Transvaal. Affairs are progressing with great rapidity in South Africa at the present time, and I do not think Her Majesty's Government will give the assurance you ask for.

KRUGER: I am rather disappointed with what has been said on this question, as it appears that when the interests of the South African

Republic come to the front, the point in discussion immediately becomes one of great importance to Her Majesty's Government.

LOCH: You have asked that when the form of government in Swaziland may at some future period require change, it should be handed over to the Government of the South African Republic. But that is a hypothetical state of things which cannot be included in a treaty; we cannot deal with hypothetical cases in that way.

KRUGER: I cannot see any difficulty in arranging how under certain circumstances the country should be dealt with.

LOCH: At the present moment we are arranging for a government of the whites in Swaziland; if your Honour's suggestion were entertained, we should at the same time be arranging for its dissolution. The two proposals can hardly be considered together; when a man is about to make a marriage contract he does not at the same time arrange for a divorce.

KRUGER: As far as I can see the position now taken up by Her Majesty's Government is a departure from the first principles of the agreement upon which we met here. I said I would retire in one direction [i.e. the N and NW], and I thought Her Majesty's Government would retire in the other [i.e. the E]. It was on that understanding that Sir Francis de Winton came to inquire into the state of affairs in Swaziland. Now it appears that there is a complete change.

LOCH: I do not think that the question of your Honour's willingness to withdraw your claim to Matabeleland and Mashonaland ever came forward in a tangible form, because Her Majesty's Government considered that the South African Republic was *confined within its territorial limits as laid down in the convention of 1884*, and had no right to extend its borders. I fully appreciate what you say about the advantage to Her Majesty's Government of securing the goodwill of the Transvaal in Matabeleland, but at the same time no question of the extension of the South African Republic northwards ever came forward for tangible discussion at all.

KRUGER: I remember the conference with Lord Derby on this subject. Her Majesty's Government insisted that they should have the right to veto any treaty made by the Government of the South African Republic with tribes to the east and west; but on the north there was to be no restriction as to the treaty-making power of the Transvaal, and the treaty with Lobengula which I made I have been ready to give up. I had every right to make such a treaty; it is only when a treaty involves an extension of my boundary that I am bound to obtain the sanction of Her Majesty's Government.

LOCH: I should like to draw your Honour's attention to this, that

England has no power under the convention to deal with Swaziland except with the consent of the Government of the South African Republic; and I think it may be gathered from the policy which Her Majesty's Government have pursued in the past that they are not likely to desire the responsibility of dealing with Swaziland alone. I should suggest that – without making any pledges on either side – Dr Leyds, Captain Bower and Mr Schreiner might draw up a draft proposal under which the government of the whites should be carried on in Swaziland, and submit the draft for our consideration.

KRUGER: I wish first to say something further, *as I feel a little sad*. I have straightforwardly and to the best of my ability expressed my willingness to give Her Majesty's Government, as long as I live, my support in the north; however small and insignificant England may think my support, she would find it of great advantage to her. And my idea was that in recognition of my withdrawal of all claims in that direction, Her Majesty's Government would withdraw all claims in the east and support my authority there. But now it appears that my policy of giving is accepted, but I take nothing on the other side, and get no support in the east. In Umswazi's time, England had no footing in that part of South Africa, and now England is the great obstacle to my extension eastwards. I thought England would not stand in my way, and now it appears that she wants to stop me.

Not even these words melted the heart of Lord Loch and he was as firm on the issue of a railway to the sea as he had been earlier about the northern frontier. He was prepared to give Kruger a coastal port, but the railway across Amatongaland could not be built without a special arrangement with the British Government.

Kruger at once made clear that sovereignty over a railway line would not by itself interest him.

KRUGER: I wish to point out that the country through which a railway would pass is very unhealthy and marshy, and I could not undertake to make a railway unless I were given a good deal of land.

LOCH: If Her Majesty's Government give Khosi Bay to the South African Republic they would probably include certain rights round the harbour, but the line of railway cannot be given entirely to the Transvaal, as *communication between Natal and the northern portion of Amatongaland would then be cut off*. The agreement between the two Governments respecting the line of railway would be made in such a way as to satisfy the Transvaal that their rights were sufficiently secured to justify them in making the railway.

KRUGER: I am not sure that I should make the sea-port at Khosi Bay itself. For instance, there is a small lake inland near the coast, and I could make it a very good harbour by cutting a canal to connect it with the sea [this would obviously have given Kruger far more land].

LOCH: When I speak of Khosi Bay, I do not mean that the harbour must necessarily be at that particular spot. Any other place in the neighbourhood that your Honour may prefer would do as well.

KRUGER: It is of no use for me to get a bare road to the sea and nothing more.

LOCH: The road to the sea gives also the right to the land on the sea coast.

KRUGER (pointing to a map of the country): I want all this land to the north and north-east of a line drawn from the corner beacon of my country to the sea, to become part of my State, and then all difficulties will be removed.

LOCH: *Her Majesty's Government will not consent to give Amatonga-land to the South African Republic.* It is under Her Majesty's protection, and any agreement for building a railway must be made with Her Majesty's Government, who are anxious to give the South African Republic a right of way to the sea coast, *but it must pass to the north of Sambane's country, and the 27th parallel of south latitude.*

KRUGER: I should like to know about my treaties with Sambane and Umbegesa. Both these Chieftains have made application to be taken over by the Government of the South African Republic. Sambane's territory joins the southern border of the Transvaal, and a considerable number of his people live in the Transvaal and pay tribute to the Government. Sambane wished to pay tribute to me for all his people whether living in the Transvaal or not, but this I would not agree to, as being opposed to the terms of the con-vention. *A treaty was then made with Sambane, but Her Majesty's* Government did not approve of it. Now Sambane has again applied to come under the South African Republic.

LOCH: Her Majesty's Government would not agree to Sambane becoming a subject of the South African Republic; they wish the country to be kept open as a right of way to Natal. Sambane has also applied to the Imperial Government to take him over [and an official Commission had recently declared that Zamban – alias Sambane – had paid tribute to the Zulus].

KRUGER: Sir Hercules Robinson told me of this, and forwarded me a copy of Sambane's application. Sambane denied having sent the document, and subsequently asked to be taken over by the Government of the South African Republic.

LOCH: Sambane has made another application within the last few days to be taken over by Her Majesty's Government.

KRUGER: I have no hesitation in saying that if an impartial inquiry were made this document would prove to be false. Sambane has often wanted to come under the Transvaal Government, and says, "when am I to come under your Government?" I find it difficult, therefore, to believe that his application to the Imperial Government is authentic.

LOCH: The wishes expressed by Sambane, have been carefully verified, and it appears from what your Honour says that he is in the habit of making these representations to both Governments.

KRUGER: Assuming that to be the case the fact remains that he applied to me first.

LOCH: I think the last application would be the one that would carry most weight.

KRUGER: If Her Majesty's Government have made up their minds on the subject it is useless for me to endeavour to prove my case.

LOCH: I do not for a moment question what your Honour says, but I was merely telling you what Sambane has said to Her Majesty's Government. Umbegesa has also made a similar application.

KRUGER: If your Excellency has any doubt on the subject, send a Commission to inquire into the facts of the case. I have no doubt as to what the issue of such an inquiry would be.

LOCH: Her Majesty's Government have made up their minds with regard to Sambane.

KRUGER: Am I to understand then that the question will not be reconsidered, and that any representations I may make will be wasted?

LOCH: I think so; because Her Majesty's Government do not now wish to raise any questions respecting Umbegesa which they might otherwise have raised had they not made up their minds with regard to Sambane.

KRUGER: I thought I might have had some chance of utilising the Pongola river as a means of communication with the sea. This river passes through Sambane's territory; but the policy of Her Majesty's Government appears to be to keep the South African Republic away from the sea.

LOCH: Her Majesty's Government are doing all they can to assist the South African Republic in getting to the sea coast. They have raised no objection to the Netherlands line, and are now doing what they can to aid you in communicating with the coast at or near Khosi Bay. You are asking them to give up a country in which they have very great political interests, and this they will not do.

KRUGER: I do not see that the South African Republic derives much practical benefit from what your Excellency proposes. Nothing in Swaziland is given, and only a small strip of land round the harbour on the coast. I see great difficulty in building a railway under these circumstances.

LOCH: The arrangement under which you would build the railway would be entered into beforehand with Her Majesty's Government, and would be satisfactory to the South African Republic.

KRUGER: How can the arrangement be satisfactory if I do not get what I want? How could I protect my interests in the railway if I get no land besides?

LOCH: A right to build a railway of this kind would contemplate that there should be a certain amount of land on either side of the line.

KRUGER: It must be well known that the building of a railway, and its maintenance in that part of the country, would be a great undertaking.

LOCH: But these difficulties would arise under any circumstances, whether you got the right from the Native Chief or from Her Majesty's Government.

KRUGER: The sole request I make is the right to enter into arrangements with the Natives, and I have no doubt that with that right I should be able to obtain from the Queen Regent of Swaziland a concession for making a railway, and a sufficient quantity of land. Between two Governments difficulties are certain to arise. I do not ask for any land (for it is not Her Majesty's Government's to give) save in respect of the harbour; all that I ask is that I may be authorised to treat with the Natives.

LOCH: I presume you would hope to obtain from the Natives the right to the land as well as the right of building a railway; but this would cut off Natal and Zululand from the north, and a narrow strip would do so as effectually as if you acquired the whole territory.

DR LEYDS: *If we acquired the land and held it on condition that we gave a right of way across to Her Majesty's Government, would they consent to that?*

LOCH: I do not think Her Majesty's Government would consent to any portion of Amatongaland becoming part of the Transvaal State. Your Honour will probably find that all the difficulties which you are anticipating will be met by the agreement to be entered into with Her Majesty's Government.

KRUGER: If your Excellency were aware of the difficulties in the way of the construction of the railway, and of the unhealthy nature of the country, it would be apparent to you that the country *must be populated before a railway can be built, otherwise it is* not worth while building it. For Government to say that I should simply be allowed to build a railway is tantamount to a refusal.

After lunch the British made a slight concession. It would be in order for Kruger to make a treaty with Queen Zambili of the Swazis giving him proprietary rights (but not sovereign rights since both powers had guaranteed Swazi independence) over a railway to the sea provided that the line ran north of the 27th parallel, i.e., close to the Portuguese border.

But Kruger was not mollified.

He said, "I am very thankful for the consideration you have given this matter; this morning's conference gave me serious pain. But I do not see how I can get from my country to the sea if I have no sovereign rights over the intervening land. Khosi Bay itself cannot be used as a harbour; the lake I spoke of would be the harbour; but if I am only allowed the rights of an owner over the land what power of protecting my harbour would I have?"

LOCH: You would have complete rights over the land at Khosi Bay; the land there would be part of the South African Republic, and you would have sovereign rights there. It would have to be understood that Her Majesty's Government should have the right of sending troops across to the north if necessary, or to construct a line of railway.

KRUGER: There will be no difficulty about a right of way to Her Majesty's Government, but unless I have sovereign rights it will be difficult for me to protect the harbour.

How, if I cut my hand off and throw it away, can I still call it my hand? I cannot see what I should gain by obtaining access to Khosi Bay in this manner and passing a railway over country over which I have only private rights, as the expense will be very great. I might as well make a line to Delagoa Bay or Natal.

LOCH: The difference between the proposed line of railway and one to Delagoa Bay or Natal is this, that the Transvaal Government would have no sovereign rights over the ports of exit and entry as they will in respect of the railway to Khosi Bay.

KRUGER: There is one thing I should like to know about the land over which the railway is to pass. Would the Transvaal Government have the right of protecting the land, or would that right lie with Her Majesty's Government?

LOCH: I think the right of protection would be in the hands of the Government of the South African Republic. If it were attacked by Zambili's people, Her Majesty would take steps to prevent them from interfering with the property of the South African Republic, and your Honour would probably take steps on your side to defend your property.

KRUGER: Suppose a theft were to be committed at some station along the line, how would that be dealt with?

LOCH: Provision for everything of that kind will be made in the agreement to be entered into with the Government of the South African Republic.

But at this point, towards the end of the day, the Governor sprang a bombshell. "There is one point," he said, "that I should have mentioned before, and which was, I think, mentioned by Sir F. de Winton, viz., that if the Transvaal Government are given a sea-port it will be on condition that they join the customs union."

Kruger saw little objection to a customs union on his terms in return for a permanent asset such as land – particularly if the Transvaal got its full share of the customs revenue from its own port. This would be very different from a customs union imposed with a view to a confederation from which he would not be free to withdraw.

KRUGER: *I have already expressed my willingness to enter the customs union if I acquire a harbour on the sea coast. But if I only get a small piece of land on the coast* separated entirely from the country I govern, I am deprived of all power of governing the newly acquired territory, and I should like your Excellency to tell me whether you yourself think it would be worth while building a railway under such circumstances.

LOCH: If my candid opinion is asked I will give it. If I were in your Honour's place, I should jump at the arrangement. What are the terms of the concession which you hold with regard to a railway in Swaziland? *You obtained no cession of sovereignty under that, and you are offered more by Her Majesty's* Government than you were satisfied with from the Swazis.

Kruger objected that while an agreement of this kind would be satisfactory as long as Britain held Swaziland, there was always the chance that the territory might fall into other hands. That is why it would be better to make sure of its future by handing it over to the Republic.

LOCH: I do not quite understand your objection. Do you apprehend that Her Majesty's Government will take possession of the railway

at any time, or are you afraid of a possible annexation of Amatongaland depriving you of your rights in the railway?

KRUGER: There is always the possibility of a change of Ministry in
England, and though one Ministry may follow one policy today,
another Ministry may come into power tomorrow and follow
another policy; therefore, I wish to thoroughly secure my rights.

LOCH: I do not think there can possibly be any difficulty about the
line of railway as long as such matters as right of way across,
et cetera, are properly secured to Her Majesty's Government.
There is only one state of affairs that could ever lead to the acqui-
sition of the railway by England – a state of affairs which is never
likely to arise, I trust – and that would be in the event of war
between the two nations; and if such a state of affairs were to
arise the South African Republic would not derive much benefit
from the fact of having sovereign powers over the line of railway.

(In fact both the contingencies that the Governor implied were
hypothetical came to pass. Britain did annex Amatongaland and
there was a war between the two nations.)

At this point the Governor made his final offer. He could not give
away sovereignty either in Swaziland or the strip between Swaziland
and the sea, but if Kruger would commit himself to recommending
his proposals to his Executive Council and the Volksraad, he, the
Governor, would urge the British Government to let Kruger negotiate
not only with the Swazis but also with Umbegesa in the territory
beyond, for sovereign rights for the railway line, provided that Britain
should have the right to build her own railway across it and send
troops across it. "I will go so far as this, although it is beyond my
instructions, because I see that you feel strongly on the subject; and
I can only say that I will support my recommendation to the best of
my ability," Loch added.

Kruger then played his last card. "I have read your draft proposals,"
he said, "but it is impossible for me at this moment to give a definite
answer, as I must first lay the matter before my Executive Council.
If your Excellency were willing to grant me sovereign rights over the
strip of land between the South African Republic and the sea coast
over which I am to build a railway I would be prepared to go further
into the matter."

LOCH: I have told you what I will recommend to Her Majesty's
Government, but it will be impossible for me to give my recommendation unless you will promise to recommend my proposals to
your Executive Council and the Volksraad.

KRUGER: I cannot do so. I am afraid to make any promise now, as I may only weaken my case before the Executive Council by doing so.

LOCH: In that case I shall be unable to make any recommendations to Her Majesty's Government.

KRUGER: I approve of the principles of your proposal, and I am willing to recommend it to the Executive Council and the Volksraad – with perhaps a few minor amendments of certain details – on the understanding that the South African Republic should either be granted sovereign rights over the strip of country from the border of the Transvaal to Khosi Bay, *including the portion in Swaziland*, or that they should be allowed to make arrangements with the Natives themselves for acquiring sovereign rights over the country required for the railway. That I would willingly recommend to my Executive Council and the Volksraad. That is all I can say at present without weakening my power with the Executive Council; I must consult them before I can make any definite agreement.

LOCH: I am unable to agree to your Honour's proposal. I have gone to the very utmost limits I could. *With regard to Swaziland, I decline to recommend that the South African Republic should be granted sovereign rights in that country*. With regard to sovereign rights over the line of railway to Khosi Bay, that I have stated I would be prepared to recommend, but it would have to be inserted in the agreement to be entered into between the two Governments, and it would have to be understood that the agreement as drawn up and approved should be accepted by the Government of the South African Republic, even in the event of the sovereign rights asked for not being granted. Individually, I think a sovereignty of the extent and upon the conditions named could be arranged, but, unless your Honour agrees to support the agreement I have drawn up as it stands, it renders it impossible for me to proceed further with the discussion. I have endeavoured to meet your wishes in every possible way. There will be great difficulties in obtaining the approval of Parliament at home, even to the granting of sovereign rights to the South African Republic over the land at Khosi Bay. I had hoped that we should have arrived at an agreement which would have ensured to the South African Republic Khosi Bay and a line of railway to the sea, and that we should have settled the future government of Swaziland and other matters connected with the Little Free State, Umbegesa's territory, et cetera. If you come to an agreement on the lines suggested, it will strengthen my hand in obtaining for you the sovereign rights which you ask for, as it will show your anxiety to come to terms with Her Majesty's Government and work cordially with them.

KRUGER: I am placed in a very difficult situation. As President of a Republic, I have no authority to enter into any definite agreement, and if I were to do so, I should endanger my position.

LOCH: I do not ask you to enter into any definite arrangement. I only ask you to give me your assurance that you will recommend my proposals to your Executive Council and the Volksraad.

The President here asked to be allowed to confer in private with his Excellency, stating that he had no objection to Mr Rhodes and Captain Bower being present.

Messrs Schreiner and Ashburnham then retired and, after a short conference with his Excellency, the President left for Pretoria.

Select Bibliography

Allen, Vivien, *Kruger's Pretoria*, A. A. Balkema, Cape Town, 1971

Bell, E. Moberly, *Flora Shaw*, Constable, 1947

Bellairs, Lady (ed.), *The Transvaal War 1880–1881*, William Blackwood, 1883

Benson, E. F., *Queen Victoria*, Longman Green, 1935

Bigelow, Poultney, *White Man's Africa*, Harper, 1900

Blackburn, Douglas, and Caddell, Captain W. Waithman, *Secret Service in South Africa*, Cassell, 1911

Bryce, James, *Impressions of South Africa*, Macmillan, 1900

Bulpin, T. V., *Lost Trails of the Transvaal*, Books of Africa Pty, 1969

Carter, Thomas Fortescue, *A Narrative of the Boer War*, John MacQueen, London, 1900

Cartwright, A. P., *The First South African*, Purnell, 1971

Chilvers, Hedley A., *Out of the Crucible*, Cassell, 1929

Clemens, Samuel Langhorne ("Mark Twain"), *More Tramps Abroad*, Chatto & Windus, 1897

Cohen, Morton, *Rider Haggard*, Hutchinson, 1960

de Kiewiet, C. W., *A History of South Africa (Social and Economic)*, Oxford University Press, 1957

The Imperial Factor in South Africa, Frank Cass & Co., 1965

De Wet, Christiaan Rudolf, *Three Years War*, Constable, 1902

du Plessis, Gezina, *Die President en Ek (Herinneringe van Magdalena Eloff)*, Tafelberg, Cape Town, 1971

Edwards, Neville, *The Transvaal in War and Peace*, H. Virtue, London, 1900

Engelenburg, Dr F. V., *'n Onbekende Paul Kruger*, Volkstem-Drukkery, 1925

FitzPatrick, J. P., *The Transvaal from Within*, William Heinemann, 1900

Gordon, C. T., *The Growth of Boer Opposition to Kruger*, Oxford University Press, 1970

Hancock, W. K., *Smuts*, Cambridge University Press, 1962

Hardinge, Rt Hon. Sir Arthur, *Life of Henry Howard Molyneux Herbert, 4th Earl of Carnarvon*, Humphrey Milford, Oxford University Press, 1925

Hicks Beach, Lady Victoria, *Life of Sir Michael Hicks Beach*, Macmillan, 1932

Hobson, J. A., *The War in South Africa*, James Nisbet, 1900

Jackson, Stanley, *The Great Barnato*, Heinemann, 1970

Jeppe, Carl, *The Kaleidoscopic Transvaal*, Chapman & Hall, 1906

Jorissen, Dr E. J. P., *Transvaalsche Herinneringen*, De Bussy, Amsterdam, 1897

Juta, Marjorie, *The Pace of the Ox*, Constable, 1937

Kotze, Sir John Gilbert, *Memoirs and Reminiscences*, Maskew Miller, Cape Town, 1949

Kruger, D. W., *The Making of a Nation*, Macmillan, 1969
Paul Kruger, Staatsman, Tafelberg, 1972

Kruger, S. J. P., *The Memoirs of Paul Kruger*, T. Fisher Unwin, 1902

Le May, G. H., *British Supremacy in South Africa*, Clarendon Press, 1965

Leyds, Dr W. J., "Kruger Days" (as told to Kees van Hoek), in *South Africa*, London, 1939

Longford, Elizabeth, *Victoria, R.I.*, Weidenfeld & Nicolson, 1964

Mackenzie, Frederick A., *Paul Kruger, His Life Story*, James Bowden, 1899

Macnab, Roy, *Journey into Yesterday*, Howard Timmins, Cape Town, 1962

Magnus, Philip, *King Edward the Seventh*, John Murray, 1964

Marais, S. J., *The Fall of Kruger's Republic*, Clarendon Press, 1961

Marling, Colonel Sir Percival, V.C., *Rifleman and Hussar*, John Murray, 1931

Martineau, John, *The Life and Correspondence of Sir Bartle Frere*, John Murray, 1895

Masterman, Lucy (ed.), *Mary Gladstone, Diaries and Letters*, Methuen, 1930

Meintjes, Johannes, *The Commandant-General*, Tafelberg Uitgevers, 1971
General Louis Botha, Cassell, 1970

Millin, Sarah Gertrude, *General Smuts*, Faber & Faber, 1936
Rhodes, Chatto & Windus, 1933

Nathan, Manfred, *Paul Kruger, His Life and Times*, Knox Publishing Co., Durban, 1946

Palmer, Eve, *The Plains of Camdeboo*, Collins, 1966

Phillips, Mrs Lionel, *Some South African Recollections*, Longman Green, 1899

Phillips, Lionel, *Some Reminiscences*, Hutchinson, 1924

Ponsonby, Sir Frederick, *Recollections of Three Reigns*, Eyre & Spottiswoode, 1951

Ransford, Oliver, *The Battle of Majuba Hill*, John Murray, 1967

Reitz, Deneys, *Trekking On*, Faber & Faber, 1933
No Outspan, Faber & Faber, 1943

Rhoodie, Dr Denys, *Conspirators in Conflict*, Tafelberg Uitgevers, 1967

Rorke, Melina, *Her Amazing Experiences . . . Told by Herself*, George Harrap, 1939

Rosenthal, Eric, *Gold! Gold! Gold!*, Macmillan, 1970
South African Dictionary of National Biography, Frederick Warne, 1966

Schreuder, D. M., *Gladstone and Kruger*, Routledge & Kegan Paul, 1969

Scoble, John and Abercrombie, H. R., *The Rise and Fall of Krugerism*, Heinemann, 1900

Spender, Harold, *General Botha*, Constable, 1916

Symons, Julian, *Buller's Campaign*, Cresset Press, London, 1933

van der Walt, A. J. H., Wiid, J. A. and Geyer, A. L., edited by Kruger, D. W., *Geskiedenis van Suid Afrika*, Nason Beperk, 1955

Walker, Eric Anderson, *The Great Trek*, Adam & Charles Black, 1965
A History of South Africa, Longman Green, 1935
Lord de Villiers and His Times, Constable, 1925

Whitman, Sydney, *Personal Reminiscences of Prince Bismarck*, John Murray, 1902

Williams, Watkin W., *Life of General Sir Charles Warren*, Basil Blackwell, 1941

Wilmot, Hon. Alex., *The Life and Times of Sir Richard Southey*, Sampson Low Marston & Co., 1904

Wilson, David Mackay, *Behind the Scenes in the Transvaal*, Cassell, 1902

Wood, Evelyn, *From Midshipman to Field-Marshal*, Methuen, 1906
Winnowed Memories, Cassell, 1918

Worsfold, Basil, *Sir Bartle Frere*, Thornton, Butterworth, 1923

Younghusband, Captain Francis, *South Africa of Today*, Macmillan, 1898

Newspapers

Nieuwe Rotterdamsche Courant, selected issues between 1900 and 1904
The Times, selected issues between 1881 and 1904

Periodicals

Articles on Kruger in *Blackwood's Magazine, Canadian Magazine, Harper's Magazine, Harper's Weekly, Illustrated London News, Littell's Living Age, McClure's Magazine, Pall Mall Gazette, Pall Mall Magazine, Punch*
Historia, "Mijn President", Herinneringen van Dr W. J. Leyds aan President S. J. P. Kruger (edited by G. J. Schutte), September 1968

Published Documents, Booklets, etc.

de Kock, Dr W. J., *Kruger House*, National Cultural History and Open Air Museum, Pretoria, 1966
Labuschagne, R. J. and van der Merwe, J., *Mammals of the Kruger and other National Parks*, National Parks' Board of Trustees

Unpublished Official Documents

Cabinet and Colonial Office papers relating to S. J. P. Kruger, and in particular to his visits to the United Kingdom.

Unpublished Private Papers

Royal Archives, Windsor Castle

Index